Music in the Shadows

Music in the Shadows

Noir Musical Films

SHERI CHINEN BIESEN

Johns Hopkins University Press
Baltimore

2 4 6 8 9 7 5 3 1

Johns Hopkins University Press
2715 North Charles Street
Baltimore, Maryland 21218-4363
www.press.jhu.edu

Library of Congress Cataloging-in-Publication Data
Biesen, Sheri Chinen, 1962–
Music in the shadows : noir musical films / Sheri Chinen Biesen.
p. cm.
Includes bibliographical references and index.
ISBN 978-1-4214-0837-8 (hardcover : alk. paper) — ISBN 978-1-4214-
0838-5 (pbk. : alk. paper) — ISBN 978-1-4214-0839-2 (electronic) —
ISBN 1-4214-0837-6 (hardcover : alk. paper) — ISBN 1-4214-0838-4
(pbk. : alk. paper) — ISBN 1-4214-0839-2 (electronic)   1. Musical
films—United States—History and criticism.   2. Film noir—United
States—History and criticism.   3. Jazz in motion pictures.   I. Title.
PN1995.9.F54B535 2014
791.43'657—dc23   2013027717

A catalog record for this book is available from the British Library.

*For my grandmother, uncle, and family of writers, artists,
and musicians who continue to inspire my fascination
with film noir and the musical*

Contents

Illustrations

Acknowledgments

For years I have been fascinated by how film noir unexpectedly coalesces with the musical. The inception of this book began twenty-nine years ago in 1985, when I saw *Blues in the Night* and the restoration of *A Star Is Born*. I began to explore the noir musical and to research a treasure trove of primary archival materials for this project, originally a paper, which grew into graduate research at the University of Southern California School of Cinematic Arts and the University of Texas at Austin.

I am greatly indebted to many people over the course of this journey. I thank my editors and the staff at Johns Hopkins University Press for their efforts and support of this project. I appreciate the assistance of Matt McAdam, Michael Lonegro, Linda Forlifer, Mahinder Kingra, Helen Myers, Patricia Hanson, Steven Baker, Katy Meigs, Kelly Horvath, and Mary Lou Kenney. I am grateful to the archives and archival staff who assisted with the research for this project. Special thanks to Ned Comstock and the staff at the USC Cinematic Arts Library Special Collections, the USC Warner Bros. Archive, the Academy of Motion Picture Arts and Sciences Margaret Herrick Library and Center for Motion Picture Study, UCLA Young Research Arts Library Special Collections, UCLA Film and Television Archive, the Harry Ransom Humanities Research Center at the University of Texas, the New York Public Library for the Performing Arts Special Collections, the Library of Congress, the American Film Institute, the British Film Institute, Indiana University Lilly Library, the National Archives, and the Museum of Modern Art. I received support from the University of Texas at Austin, the University of Southern California, the University of California, the University of Leicester, and Rowan University to conduct research for this project. My work on this book was facilitated by a research sabbatical from Rowan University.

I would like to thank many friends, colleagues, teachers, and my students for their encouragement and support over the years, especially Thomas Schatz, Brian Neve, Brian Taves, Richard B. Jewell, Drew Casper, Thomas Doherty, Nate

Chinen, Clayton Koppes, Charles Maland, Robert Sklar, Robert Wise, Robert Relyea, Scott Curtis, Barbara Hall, Faye Thompson, Steve Hanson, Howard Prouty, Sam Gill, Noelle Carter, David Adler, Peter Lev, Kevin Hagopian, Peter Rollins, James Welsh, Felicia Campbell, Charles Ramirez Berg, Joseph Kruppa, Marsha Kinder, Michael Renov, Jon Wagner, David James, Todd Boyd, Rick Altman, Dudley Andrew, John Gizis, Mark Williams, Mary Desjardins, Leonard Leff, Dana Polan, Michael Anderegg, Cynthia Baron, Joseph Bierman, Richard Grupenhoff, Keith Brand, Nicholas Cull, Walter Metz, Diane Negra, Fred Metchick, Judith Bushnell, Martin Vego, Mary Beth Sandla, Githa Susan Srivatsa, Kelly Colla, Karah Ladd, Todd Takenaga, Tom Abbott, Mark Valente, and my family and grandparents.

Music in the Shadows

CHAPTER ONE

The Noir Musical

Crisscrossing beams of light splinter a black Los Angeles night sky. Searchlights explode at a Hollywood benefit concert. A self-destructive screen idol wreaks havoc backstage, shattering glass and assaulting performers. As terrified dancers scream in the wings, a big band belts out a jazz number in the orchestra.

Although this depiction could well have taken place in the real-life Hollywood of the twentieth century, what is described here is actually a scene from the 1954 musical film *A Star Is Born.* When the out-of-control screen idol staggers onstage (in the film), chaos ensues. Using distorted, erratic images and camera angles, the film allows the audience to experience the idol's inebriated point of view with unbalanced hand-held shots. Fans gasp and studio moguls cringe until a performing jazz singer (played by Judy Garland) dances the drunken star out of the spotlight.

A Star Is Born is a musical; however, its pervasively bleak tone and shadowy aesthetic more closely simulate the visual style of film noir. Presenting the disturbing story of Hollywood fame driving an eclipsed star to suicide, the narrative unfolds not with the lighthearted singing, dancing, and happy endings of the typical "musical," but instead cloaked behind the stark noir lens and even literally in the shadows, as suggested by a camera pan to silhouetted figures caught in struggle. This complex film strains against tidy categorization. Its darker variation on the musical is staged and shot like a musical, but in a distinctly noir vein.

Gilda, on the other hand, from 1946, is a film noir on its face, but in blending musical production numbers into its classical noir framework, it becomes another film, like *A Star Is Born,* that defies conventional definitions. In it, a distraught nightclub proprietor hears a bluesy arrangement from the stage down-stairs. He peers through venetian blinds, voyeuristically watching the show—a striptease-like number. With a spotlight illuminating her, seductive Rita Hay-worth sings and dances alluringly and then tosses her hair as a jazz ensemble plays to wild applause. Although its brooding style and storyline make *Gilda* a noir film, it is arguably most recognizable for its musical performances and is therefore in many ways also a "musical" film.

In this book I investigate the seemingly unlikely connection between the mu-sical genre and the shadowy world of 1940s and '50s film noir as well as how cinematic genres evolve in relation to cultural history. The atmospheric world of the "noir musical" was characterized by smoke, shadows, and moody strains of jazz and blues. When we compare this characterization to what we traditionally think of as a musical, we will see where "noir" and "musical" intersect. Storylines involved antiheroes—tormented performers and musicians—battling obsession and dysfunctional interpersonal relationships. They struggled equally with their art and with their ill-fated love triangles. Thus, these dark 1940s and 1950s noir musical films strayed from the norms of more typical musicals. Their plots un-covered what was happening backstage, contradicting the glamour onstage. What was supposed to stay in the shadows in unvarnished backrooms emerged into the spotlight. Extraordinary films like *Blues in the Night* (1941), *To Have and Have Not* (1944), *Gilda* (1946), *Black Angel* (1946), *The Man I Love* (1947), *The Red Shoes* (1948), *Young Man with a Horn* (1950), *A Star Is Born* (1954), *Young at Heart* (1954), and *Love Me or Leave Me* (1955) pulled back the curtain to expose the seamy un-derside of ambition, performing, and stardom.

At first glance, film noir and the musical appear to be diametrically opposed in terms of atmosphere, lighting, character motivation, and moral outlook. But earlier realistic dramas with thematic connections to music act as preludes to the noir musical. Although the classic Hollywood musical has been stereotyped as sentimental "let's all put on a show" escapist fare, films *about* musical perfor-mance, such as *Applause* (1929), *Broadway* (1929), and *Bolero* (1934), have from the very beginning handled some heavier subjects. A unifying aspect has been the use of jazz. Film noir was noted for its smoky jazz nightclubs, risqué musical performances, and duplicity also iconic of show business of the time. Just as film noir embraced jazz, a series of dark musicals invoked noir conventions. Even some of the earliest films about show business and musical performance, in which the protagonist suffers failure or heartbreak, contain the elements of stern realism that characterize later noir musical films.

World War II, the period leading up to it, and the period that came after it shaped the moving picture industry. The improbable combination of film noir and the musical evolved alongside a changing American culture as censorship, gender and ethnic roles, and technology shifted from wartime through the post-war era. Rearticulating noir style, Hollywood produced darker, socially conscious noir musicals in the 1940s and 1950s. Chapter 3 investigates the emergence of the definitive noir musical *Blues in the Night,* which influenced later films. This darker musical film linked melodic melodrama with jazz music and would inspire a strain of innovative musical drama films with troubled antiheroes, jazz musicians, smoky lounges, backstage performers, unhappy romances, and melancholy blues music in a shady milieu. Film noir paralleled on screen the violence and loosening of sexual mores that Americans were themselves witnessing or experiencing during the war years. Moreover, musical film noir became an economical alternative to big-budget musical productions during the rationing, blackouts, and other constraints imposed by World War II.

In the wake of *Blues in the Night,* darker jazz noir musical drama arose.[1] Chapter 4 examines jazz musicals such as Orson Welles' *Story of Jazz, Syncopation* (1942), and *Jammin' the Blues* (1944); darker color musicals *Lady in the Dark* (1944) and *Cover Girl* (1944); and jazz "musical" film noir, such as *This Gun for Hire* (1942), *To Have and Have Not, Phantom Lady* (1944), *Gilda, Christmas Holiday* (1944), *Black Angel, The Big Sleep* (1946), *The Man I Love, New Orleans* (1947), *Dead Reckoning* (1947), *Lured* (1947), *Casbah* (1948), and *Road House* (1948). This chapter also explores the emerging "jazz noir" trend from World War II into the early postwar era. The wartime setting certainly influenced the look and feel of the noir musical. Noir films became even darker and more shadowy, for instance, as lighting and set budgets were slashed as part of the war effort. Film noir featured a nocturnal underworld of New Orleans jazz nightspots, brothels, and speakeasies. With its psychological turmoil, violence, illicit activities of every kind, and unsavory environments, film censors deemed noir films "sordid" and disreputable. Studios responded by using abundant innuendo and cloaking risky material behind jazz numbers to appease censors. Thus, film noir's style and atmosphere evolved as a savvy aesthetic strategy, challenging and responding to censorship and wartime constraints.

Once the war ended, budgets increased and productions became correspondingly more lavish, but postwar moviemakers now faced other obstacles. Emerging technologies such as television affected the noir musical. As the film industry adopted new filmmaking technologies, dark musicals, like Hollywood itself, shifted away from black-and-white nitrate films (film noir) to widescreen color pictures in Technicolor, Eastmancolor, and widescreen CinemaScope. Chapter 5 looks at these changes and how noir musical melodrama evolved in such postwar films as *The Red Shoes, Young Man with a Horn, The Strip* (1951), *Glory Alley* (1952), *Affair in Trinidad* (1952), *The Barefoot Contessa* (1954), and *A Star Is Born.* Earlier jazz noir films became full color, a sort of "color noir," despite the seeming paradox, as classic film noir began to fade in response to censorship and techno-logical changes in the postwar period.

Along with noir, the studio system itself declined. After Hollywood's classical era, in which the industry thrived, came a less hospitable era of Cold War ten-sions, antitrust regulation, and competition from television, further threatening both the form and the industry. Robert Aldrich's *Kiss Me Deadly* (1955) and Orson Welles's *Touch of Evil* (1958) would mark the end of the classic noir period. Chap-ter 6 considers such dark musical melodramas as *Young at Heart* (1954), *Love Me or Leave Me* (1955), *Pete Kelly's Blues* (1955), *Sweet Smell of Success* (1957), *A Face in the Crowd* (1957), *Elevator to the Gallows* (1957), and the experimental *West Side Story* (1961). These noir musical films, which developed within a climate of Cold War anxiety and social turmoil, can be seen almost as the Hollywood studio sys-tem's last hurrah.

Although classical film noir is usually seen as having ended by the late 1950s, its legacy lived on in the postclassical filmmaking marked by independent and transnational coproductions after 1960. "Neo-noir" musicals of the postclassical New Hollywood era are the direct descendents of and paid homage to the earlier 1940s–50s noir musicals. Chapter 7 explores this legacy in such dark neo-noir musicals as *Paris Blues* (1961), *A Man Called Adam* (1966), *Cabaret* (1972), *New York, New York* (1977), *All That Jazz* (1979), *Pennies from Heaven* (1978–81), *The Singing Detective* (1986), *Round Midnight* (1986), and *Moulin Rouge* (2001).

THE DARK WORLD OF FILM NOIR

French critics Nino Frank and Jean-Pierre Chartier coined the term *film noir* in 1946, applauding "dark mysteries" with lifelike visual style, complex narration, harsh verisimilitude, and criminal psychology.[2] Film scholar James Naremore argues that because of noir's ad hoc creation by French critics, it is essentially a comparatively contemporary postmodern construct.

By 1955, French film scholars Raymonde Borde and Etienne Chaumeton recognized noir's "eroticization of violence," "realistic" shots, "bizarre" themes, "tough," masculine criminal women, and "nightmarish atmosphere."[3] Classic film noir is defined by certain visual conventions. Expressionistic black-and-white photography, high-contrast chiaroscuro lighting with deep shadows, oblique com-positional framing, skewed camera angles, and claustrophobic atmospheres combine to create an uneasy, troubling mood. The audience is thus aware from the outset that unpleasant events are likely to transpire. Noir films featured psychological narratives about tormented antiheroes, using such visual conventions to depict their obsessions, neuroses, and subjective point of view. The combined effect presents the fatalistic worldview that defines the noir style.[4]

Set in corrupt urban jungles, noir films took place at nighttime, among shrouded alleys, rain-slicked city streets, and boulevards of broken dreams. Characters were trapped or oppressed by their less-than-ideal circumstances. Film noir's dark themes conveyed the cultural fears, tensions, and trauma of the Great Depression, World War II, and the Cold War era in American society. Wartime conditions, Hollywood blackouts, filmmaking constraints such as war-related rationing, and censorship provided the catalysts for noir's development.

Film noir also reflected changing gender roles; although some films depicted naive "good girl" redeemers who were victimized by men, most noir films featured bold, brazen women—the femme fatale. Critics noted the juxtaposition of these dangerous women with obsessive, self-destructive male antiheroes, who projected their psychological trauma, fears, and sexual fantasies onto the femme fatale at their peril. Film historian Janey Place insightfully notes that the noir femme fatale, "comfortable in the world of cheap dives, shadowy doorways and mysterious settings," was a dangerous threat to masculinity. Some see this reversal of sexual power as reflecting broader cultural tensions and the changing gender roles of the time. With "Rosie the Riveter" symbolizing the empowered woman of the 1940s, film noir women grew multifaceted in the war years, evolving beyond the one-dimensional stereotype of lethal antagonist. The troubled romantic relationships of film noir echoed this "gender distress" of cultural relations of the wartime and postwar eras.[5] In fact, noir often featured musical women: bold, assertive, yet vulnerable "performing" seductresses who worked as cabaret singers and dancers in jazz clubs, often alongside talented, brooding jazz musicians.

Essentially, the themes of film noir do not say that everything will turn out all right (as opposed to the musical's traditional "happy ending"). Rather, they imply that the world is out to get the individual. These themes are revealed through noir's distinctive formal style. Several elements are stylistically unique to film noir. Much of its style, as well as its dark subjective psychological tone, is rooted in German Expressionism of the 1920s—attributed to the fact that many expressionistic filmmakers migrated to Hollywood from Germany and Eastern Europe during the war. Warner Bros.' art department was headed in the 1930s and 1940s by (Polish-born) East European Anton Grot, who was influenced by German Expressionism. This influence combined with a trend toward greater realism during and after the war due to wartime documentary newsreels, social realism, and the importation of Italian neorealist films (which had sad or tragic endings characteristic of the mood in postwar Europe). The result was film noir style—the use of low-key lighting to create stark contrasting images amid dark settings, as described by film critic Paul Schrader, who furthermore distinguishes it from Warner Bros.' visual style of the 1930s. The noir character is often "hidden in the realistic tableau of the city at night . . . his face is often blackened out by shadow as he speaks," unlike Warner's 1930s lighting that "accentuated" characters. "In film noir, the central character is likely to be standing in the shadow," with facial features at least partially obscured, thus "[creating] a fatalistic, hopeless mood. There is nothing the protagonist can do; the city will outlast and negate even his best efforts."[6]

MUSICALS IN A DARKER KEY

Traditional musicals, by stark contrast, typically offered escapist fare revolving around romance, a backstage story about creating a show, and an individual's journey to stardom. Their boy-meets-girl plots involved individuals performing song-and-dance numbers in lavish costumes with bright, high-key lighting, lyrical camera movements, and spectacular sets evoking nostalgic or exotic fantasy locales, all designed to create for moviegoers an uplifting show-within-a-film. The musical's union of song with dance parallels the lead couple's union as the most energetic, joyful expression of romantic love. Performers join together to put on a show, thus becoming integrated into the wider community. Music and romance fill the air as talent and beauty transform unknowns into glamorous stars, and a strong work ethic yields money, property, and success. Everything is hunky dory—the American Dream gets fulfilled. Thus, by offering an alternative reality and maybe even some hope during the economic difficulties of the Great Depression, Hollywood musicals flourished. America wanted to believe in those romantic myths of love, fortune, happiness, and success.[7]

   Film historian Jane Feuer has described conventional escapist musicals as being about "getting together and putting on a show," in venues such as Broadway, Hollywood, the Ziegfeld Follies, burlesque, nightclubs, vaudeville, Tin Pan Alley, and the circus. In exposing the production of entertainment, which draws attention to the cinematic medium and the backstage process, the musical evolved as the most self-reflexive of all genres. The typical plot of the "backstage" musicals presented "musical interludes" and "rehearsal sequences detailing the maturation of the show" interwoven with "parallel dramatic scenes detailing maturation of the off-stage love affairs." Feuer suggests the "backstage pattern" was "always central to the genre" as performances were "not restricted to onstage numbers." She observes that "multiple levels of performance and consequent multiple levels of audience combine to create a myth about musical entertainment permeating ordinary life."[8]

Yet, film scholar Rick Altman and music scholar David Neumeyer point out that a variety of different films became musicals as "technological limitations of recording and reproduction dictated that most sound films employing music in any significant way before 1932 were musicals—that is, feature-length films belonging to the romantic comedy genre but *highlighting* (not merely including) musical performances" that simulated radio shows. Altman notes that, "after the slack years of 1931–1932," the "musical began to grow in a new direction; while maintaining substantially the same" elements, the "genre increasingly related the energy of music-making to the joy of coupling, the strength of the community, and the pleasures of entertainment."[9]

WHERE NOIR AND THE MUSICAL INTERSECT

Noir musicals suggest a new way of envisioning both musicals and noir. While musicals are usually assumed to be definitively upbeat and escapist in nature, many took on a darker tone. Moreover, even presumably nonmusical serious crime films, including film noir and earlier gangster pictures, included musical jazz performances. The musical has been around as long as the sound film. In fact, as much as we think we know what we mean by Hollywood musical—that is, films that center around music and performance—there are, for example, musical Westerns,[10] and music shows up everywhere in almost every genre. The object of this book is to examine one of the more complicated, seemingly paradoxical, examples of this convergence in noir musicals. It explores this dark musical phenomenon from its beginnings through its persistence today. To a certain extent, this book is also an effort to think differently about noir.

Several critics have reexamined conventional notions of what constitutes a musical, noir, or film genre. For instance, film scholar David Bordwell notes that "stylization and realism, foreign influence and domestic genre intersect" in film noir, but because "nobody set out to make or see a film noir" unlike a "western, a comedy, or a musical," it is not truly a genre. Rather, I see film noir as a dark "period style" that influenced many different genres in the 1940s and 1950s.[11]

Altman considers this notion of genre intentionality in relation to the musical. He argues that during the early sound period, studios initially made films of various genres with music but did not intentionally create a "musical" genre. He points to the convergent nature of many genres comingling and cross-pollinating during the early cinema years. He notes the "attempts during the 1927–1930 period to build a backstage or night club" environment and iconography in a more "melodramatic" vein, with "music regularly reflecting the sorrow of death or parting."[12]

In considering how cinematic genres evolve in relation to cultural history and their interaction with other genre forms, we may also examine how more complex styles such as film noir forged an unusual coalescence with the musical in response to institutional factors in the motion picture industry, the mediation of censorship, and the wartime–postwar production environment as well as how such hybrid genre pictures were promoted by studios and received by viewers and critics at the time. These hybrid genre films deviated from the upbeat song and dance conventions of musical comedies. They portrayed a grittier undercurrent of performers struggling behind the scenes in shady entanglements as dramatic musical and dance sequences invoked topical working-class themes. By the 1940s the darker breed of jazz musicals and dramatic feature films had begun to merge.[13]

Blues in the Night from 1941 was an influential film that was immediately recognized for its hybrid nature.[14] In its wake, there was a proliferation of crime films with jazz music and blue tones. The *New York Times* noted in November 1942 that whenever Humphrey Bogart's "pianist sits there in the dark and sings 'As Time Goes By' that old, irresistible feeling consumes him in a choking, maddening wave," acknowledging the power of Dooley Wilson's nostalgic lament to drive the narrative in *Casablanca*. John Hoover goes so far as to say that *Blues in the Night* spurred a noir musical film style at Warner Bros., growing out of the studio's crime tradition.[15]

Even classic film noir such as *This Gun for Hire* and *To Have and Have Not* included musical numbers. Particularly in its early phases during World War II, film noir often added musical performances even when there were none in the original source material. Then, as film noir grew popular in the war years, musical filmmakers in the 1940s and 1950s began using noir style to treat tragic stories on the perils of stardom. Jazz, which burst into popularity in the 1920s and shifted to big band swing in the 1930s–1940s, particularly lent itself to noir treatments. The inherent conflict for jazz musicians between playing music and creating improvisational art versus "selling out" and producing commercial hit tunes, was perfect fodder for the newly emerging noir style, as we see with *Blues in the Night*. The jazz and blues music itself set the perfect dark mood to underscore the seedy backstage noir stories.

Although ostensibly about crime and the war, *This Gun for Hire* featured allur-ing blonde Veronica Lake singing in a nightclub, thus merging music with a war-time noir narrative. As film noir exploded in 1944, Bogart sparred with smolder-ing blues singer Lauren Bacall in *To Have and Have Not*, with Hoagy Carmichael singing and playing piano with a jazz band in a murky café bar. Even jazz shorts such as Warner Bros.' *Jammin' the Blues* featured musical noir style. As the war ended, Warner re-paired Bogart and Bacall in *The Big Sleep*, a film noir adaptation of Raymond Chandler's detective yarn that included a musical sequence of Bacall singing blues in a gambling club. Reimagining *Casablanca*, producers at Colum-bia wanted Bogart (but got Glenn Ford) as the antihero in *Gilda*, a fascinating amalgam of film noir and musical in which dancer Rita Hayworth, in a dramatic noir femme role, famously sings "Put the Blame on Mame" as she strips in a nightclub, then is pulled off stage and slapped by her estranged husband. These "musical noir" examples illustrate how noir comingled with musical perfor-mances following the trend set by *Blues in the Night* in the 1940s.

Noir musicals are further defined by their themes, articulating disturbing so-cial tensions and harsh realities as opposed to happy escapist fantasy. They tack-led the unglamorous or sordid topics of film noir as in *Gilda*. Noir musicals such as *Blues in the Night, Young Man with a Horn,* and *A Star is Born* experimented with themes typical of musicals, but distinctly undermined their idealism. Coun-tering the glamorized quest for stardom, they centered on the conflict between personal ambition, destructive behavior, and the remorse of protagonists who rise and then fall. Their narratives explore competing forces: an intense love of creating or performing music versus a chance encounter leading to an intimate romantic interest. Romance (love, private life) and career ("name, fame, and for-tune")[16] clash rather than flourish side by side or even synergize as in typical musicals. Noir musicals also presented an unvarnished view of professional ob-stacles and sacrifices involved in working and rehearsing to produce a show. They explore issues of gender, masculinity, and ethnic and sexual identity as well as the futility of mixing a love affair with a show business career, and—as in film noir and gangster crime films—the corrupting power of ambition. Noir musicals por-trayed a grittier show business world beneath a glittery façade. Downbeat themes of obsession, addiction, corruption, and self-destruction effectively critiqued ide-alistic musical optimism and resonated with the prewar, wartime, and postwar American experience.

CHAPTER TWO

Preludes to the Noir Musical

Even before the heyday of film noir, "preludes" to noir musicals had been produced almost from the very beginning of filmmaking. Experimental variations on silent pictures and early talkies, for example, fused gangster crime with a low-down jazz music environment. D. W. Griffith's *The Musketeers of Pig Alley* (1912) featured a backroom bar, a dance hall, and a struggling musician who is mugged by gangsters. Joseph von Sternberg's atmospheric *Underworld* from 1927 included mobsters, molls, and a dance hall speakeasy. That same year, the height of the Jazz Age and Prohibition, was significant for Hollywood, musicals, and gangsters in more ways than one. Warner Bros. musical drama *The Jazz Singer* (starring Al Jolson) ushered in the sound era. In it, Jolson's character rises to Broadway fame despite his rabbi father's objections to sacrilegious jazz music and performing on stage.[1]

Following Warner Bros.' success with *The Jazz Singer*, talkies and musicals became the motion picture rage. In 1928, Warner Bros. released the first all-dialogue talking feature, *The Lights of New York*, the first sound-era gangster film, and Jolson's *The Singing Fool*. MGM's backstage musical *Broadway Melody* won Best Picture in 1928–29. Universal adapted *Show Boat*, the pioneering 1927 dramatic musical play, as "part-talkie" (partially silent with talking-musical sequences) in 1929. MGM's King Vidor directed the Irving Berlin musical about African Americans, *Hallelujah!* (1929), which was promoted as a "smashing sex drama" that "haunts" and "thrills," a "never to be forgotten song of a people . . . [a] beautiful, tragic, sad . . . singing picture . . . of the colored race" with its "New Orleans cabarets" and "gambling hells." Ethnicity was sensationalized as illicit and taboo in gangster films set in speakeasies and live jazz venues like Harlem's Cotton Club, where Duke Ellington and Jimmy Lunceford played jazz music and barely dressed (light-skinned black) dancers performed risqué dance numbers for (white) customers.[2]

EARLY PRELUDES: *GANG WAR, MOULIN ROUGE,* AND *SADIE THOMPSON*

In Bert Glennon's *Gang War* (1928), a saxophone player falls for a taxi dancer who is entangled with a possessive bootlegger who is murdered in a gang war. *Gang War* contained suggestive songs: "Low Down," "My Suppressed Desire," "I Love Me," and "Ya Comin' Up Tonight—Huh?" Although one critic reviewing it sighed, "More gang fights. When earth's last gangster picture fades from the screen, it may . . . be a relief to more than one person,"[3] *Gang War* nevertheless demonstrated how early sound-era crime films combined musical numbers with gangster stories.

The star-is-born theme also shows up early in preludes to the noir musical. Ewald André Dupont's 1928 silent British melodrama *Moulin Rouge* cast UFA's Olga Tschechowa as the exotic star of the famed nightclub and object of desire of her daughter's self-destructive aristocratic fiancé. *Moulin Rouge*'s love triangle and risqué multiethnic jazz musical performances anticipate later dramatic musicals, such as *Applause, Dancing Lady, Salón México*, and *Moulin Rouge* remakes. Slavko Vorkapich and Robert Florey's experimental 1928 silent short, *Life and Death of 9413—A Hollywood Extra*, partially shot by cinematographer Gregg Toland (for $97 in Vorkapich's living room), explored a dark, dehumanizing side of Hollywood that influenced later downbeat films about performers, as we'll see with George Cukor's *What Price Hollywood?* (1932) and William Wellman's *A Star Is Born* (1937) (and, in turn, Cukor's subsequent 1954 remake of *A Star Is Born*, our exemplar of the noir musical form).

Another example of precursors that began to incorporate elements of the form are adaptations of W. Somerset Maugham's 1921 story "Miss Thompson." Achieving its noir musical iteration in *Miss Sadie Thompson*, starring Rita Hayworth in 1954, it was first produced in 1928 when Raoul Walsh adapted and directed silent film *Sadie Thompson* for United Artists. Starring Gloria Swanson (screen diva in Billy Wilder's 1950 noir classic *Sunset Boulevard*), the story centers on flapper fallen woman, Sadie, who carouses with GIs while stranded on a South Pacific island as a zealous missionary lusts after her and then is found dead. Lewis Milestone's *Rain*, based on the same story, came along in 1932 and also incorporated music and dancing with Joan Crawford as a jazz-dancing diva.

BROADWAY AND APPLAUSE

Universal's 1929 musical crime film *Broadway* was also an influential prelude film. Shot for a hefty $1 million, the film adapted Phillip Dunning and George Abbott's successful 1926 Broadway play about New York's hard-boiled Prohibition underworld.[4] Famed screen gangster and talented hoofer James Cagney was involved with the stage production (before Jolson got Cagney and Joan Blondell their big breaks in Hollywood).[5] Director Paul Fejos's screen adaptation of *Broadway* combined singing and dancing with murder, and black and white with elaborate two-strip Technicolor sequences (an early incarnation of Technicolor). Its spectacular stylized sets were inspired by the expressionist experimentation of Robert Wiene's *The Cabinet of Dr. Caligari* (1919) and the elaborate architectural design of Fritz Lang's *Metropolis* (1927). *Broadway* featured exquisite documentary "pre-noir" night shots of Times Square and a femme fatale in a black minidress with a plunging neckline who draws a gun and knocks off a bootlegger backstage during a musical performance. It included a salacious love triangle and abundant licentious activity at a swanky nightclub, suggestively called Paradise. Universal called it "dramatic dynamite" with a "glorious musical background" and "thrilling" "romance."[6] The *New York Times* reported that since *Broadway* opened, "there have been many, many pictures about gangsters and speakeasies and the lurking shadows that are to be found in night clubs."[7]

The backstage melodrama *Applause* (1929) marked the screen-directing debut of Russian-born opera and theatrical director Rouben Mamoulian. This scathing critique of show business featured Helen Morgan (famous *Show Boat* stage star) as the washed-up alcoholic burlesque queen Kitty Darling. Her gigolo boyfriend abuses her while lusting after her daughter (Joan Peers). *Applause* opens as Kitty gives birth after learning her husband was executed. Kitty turns down marriage proposals because she dreams of making it big on Broadway. However, her dreams of stardom become a nightmare. *Applause* is a stark glimpse of showbiz life as Kitty dies in her shadowy dressing room as neon lights flash outside while her sheltered daughter performs a striptease in her place. Critics knocked its downbeat point of view as "sordid," but its influence on later noir musicals is undeniable.[8]

With the new sound technologies available by 1930, Hollywood was producing a glut of musical films, so many, in fact, that by 1931–32 they declined in popularity. After the stock market crash of 1929, Hollywood studios not only made fewer musicals but they also actually cut musical numbers from completed films. In fact, Mamoulian's subsequent *City Streets* (1931) was not a musical, but rather a crime film adaptation of a Dashiell Hammett story that featured hot speakeasy jazz and a gangster played by Gary Cooper. Mamoulian's influential vanguard integrated musical comedy *Love Me Tonight* (1932) was far more upbeat; its nostalgic fantasy included bawdy parody, class critique that resonated in the changing socioeconomic environment, innovative sound and cinematography, and an outstanding score by Richard Rodgers and Lorenz Hart.

DANCE, FOOLS, DANCE AND WHAT PRICE HOLLYWOOD?

Another prelude film, MGM's *Dance, Fools, Dance* (1931), starred Joan Crawford as a Jazz Age society girl who is hit by the stock market crash and turns "working girl" crime reporter. She goes undercover as a moll showgirl in Clark Gable's speakeasy. Crawford's drunken brother is forced to work and kill for Gable's character, a bloodthirsty bootlegger. Swanky Gable was sixth billed as a gangster but stole the show. Jazz music, showgirls, and nightspots are depicted as reeking of "shady" criminal activity insofar as they are in direct violation of prohibition and thereby implicitly link ethnicity, overt sexuality, and bad morals to singing, dancing, and musical performance. In this film, even the "hired help" are distinct: the butlers and staff in the wealthy society mansions are white, while people of color work for gangsters, in speakeasies, in dressing rooms, or as elevator operators in sordid apartment buildings. Sex is also fraught with connotation. Crawford's editor describes her tight, extremely short showgirl disguise as that of a "cheap moll of the underworld who hangs out in nightclubs." Crawford jazzes up the "Moonlight Sonata" for tough guy Gable and then blows out his flame as he lights a cigarette. This gesture becomes iconic, later mimicked in noir classics such as *Double Indemnity* and *To Have and Have Not*.

Around the same time as Crawford works her wiles on Gable in *Dance, Fools, Dance*, Sternberg was also exploring the alluring proto-noir femme fatale musical performer in his fallen-woman melodramas starring Marlene Dietrich, including *The Blue Angel* (1930), *Morocco* (1930), *Shanghai Express* (1932), and *Blonde Venus* (1932). Fatally attractive "blonde Venus" Dietrich sings "Hot Voodoo" in a gorilla suit, blonde wig, and man's tuxedo. Louise Brooks as Lulu in G. W. Pabst's *Pandora's Box* (1929) and Brigitte Helm's nymphomaniac dancing robot stripper performing burlesque in an ethnic nightclub in *Metropolis* also lure men to their demise, as prototypical femmes fatales.

Another performer, Constance Bennett plays a waitress-turned-actress in George Cukor's star-is-born saga, *What Price Hollywood?* (1932). Anticipating both the 1937 and 1954 versions of *A Star Is Born*, *What Price Hollywood?* portrayed the "star-crossed romance" of an ingénue and an alcoholic filmmaker whose life deteriorates in the opposite trajectory to the ingénue's rise to stardom. The iconic *What Price Hollywood?* featured a central heroine and an "intense relationship" between an older man and a younger woman (like Alfred Hitchcock's later gothic melodrama-thrillers *Rebecca, Suspicion,* and *Notorious*).[9] In the 1932 film, the filmmaker antihero (Lowell Sherman) commits suicide in an impressive montage sequence filmed by Slavko Vorkapich and Lloyd Knechtel. Fame is depicted as an ordeal, with tabloids and fans viciously ripping at Bennett's clothes. She films musicals, singing in French, evoking Dietrich.

In 1933 Lowell Sherman directed *Broadway through a Keyhole*, a love triangle involving a cabaret star (who is meant to resemble real-life Ruby Keeler, best known for her work in the elaborately choreographed Busby Berkeley musicals), a gangster, and a crooner (also meant to suggest Keeler's real-life husband Al Jolson). Jolson reputedly smacked columnist Walter Winchell (ruthlessly portrayed by Burt Lancaster in *Sweet Smell of Success*, 1957) for penning the backstage story that he felt smeared his wife. Two years later, Keeler and Jolson became the actors rather than the subject of another prelude film, *Go into Your Dance* (1935, a.k.a. *Casino de Paris*). Gangsters try to plug Jolson but shoot Keeler instead in this early version of the noir musical starring Helen Morgan as the blues singer/moll.

WARNER BROS.' WORKING CLASS DANCING STREETS: BUSBY BERKELEY BACKSTAGE MUSICALS

Busby Berkeley backstage musical extravaganzas of working class dancing street life had a dark underside and are also prelude films. While kaleidoscopic fantasy numbers in *42nd Street, Gold Diggers of 1933, Footlight Parade,* and *Gold Diggers of 1935*—Ginger Rogers singing "We're in the Money," for example, and Dick Powell crooning "I'm Young and Healthy" and "By a Waterfall"—became upbeat anthems for the Great Depression, the films included disturbing social critique. Berkeley's films involve people struggling to get work and money and to produce a show. In musicals, the unity of a performing ensemble seemed to encourage Americans to stick together in a tough time, but "the whole drift of the Busby Berkeley kind of musical was towards realism," according to Stanley Donen, director of MGM Gene Kelly musicals *On the Town, Singin' in the Rain,* and *It's Always Fair Weather.* "Everything happened on the stage and you were supposed to suspend your imagination long enough to believe it was happening on the stage. You always saw where the music came from."[10]

Film historian Thomas Schatz recognizes the dark undercurrent of Berkeley musicals, and film scholar Leo Braudy notes that Berkeley's elaborate geometric patterns of ensemble crowds resemble those in Lang's *Metropolis*, another precursor film, as we have seen. Berkeley's moody dance sequences pushed the envelope of screen censorship in the early "pre-Code" years of the Production Code[11]—established in 1930 but not fully enforced until 1934—that anticipated the milieu of classic noir musicals. In *42nd Street* (1933) a streetwalker is beaten by her pimp and leaps out of a window to the street below where she is stabbed to death—all intricately choreographed to music. Joan Blondell sings the haunting "Remember My Forgotten Man" in *Gold Diggers of 1933*. This poignant song tackled serious social problems not found in escapist musical fantasies. Its anti-utopianism focused on poverty, homeless veterans, prostitution, hunger, and unemployment. In *Footlight Parade*, James Cagney croons "Shanghai Lil" blues to Ruby Keeler in a bar filled with tough sailors, and there is a backroom resembling an opium den where drugged-up, barely clad multiethnic prostitutes await their clients. Streetwalker Blondell in *Gold Diggers of 1933* leans on a lamppost, intervening when a cop rousts a bum who turns out to be a World War I veteran with a medal-of-honor pinned on his jacket. Homeless men and poor mothers with hungry babies wait in breadlines. A flashback shows men marching proudly to war and returning home maimed. A woman plunges off a balcony in a musical-dream suicide in "Lullaby of Broadway" in *Gold Diggers of 1935*.[12]

MGM'S *DANCING LADY* AND PARAMOUNT'S *BOLERO*

Robert Z. Leonard's *Dancing Lady* (1933) once more paired up Gable and Crawford in a backstager that aimed to compete with the Warner Bros.' Busby Berkeley musicals. Like *Applause* and *What Price Hollywood?*, the film featured a strained love triangle with a star-is-born theme. Crawford is a scrappy hoofer in a burlesque club who lives to dance and gets her big break from Broadway musical director Gable, who rigorously grooms her for the physically demanding lead role. Her playboy admirer Franchot Tone secretly bankrolls the show and then pays to shut it down so he can marry her and end her performing career. Tone claims that, "what is indecent in burlesque is art on Broadway," but doesn't want to be "contaminated" by "show people" and orders a champagne cocktail. This gesture also becomes iconic, repeated later by Victor and Renault in *Casablanca* (1942), Lermontov and Vicky in *The Red Shoes* (1948), and Sandra and Robert in *Lured* (1947). Tone's duplicity anticipates his more lethal love-triangle "heavy" role in the musical noir *Phantom Lady* (1944). Clearly a precursor to what's to come when musicals and film noir intersect, this movie also features abundant sexual tension, such as when ingénue Crawford and her musical mentor and chosen man Gable literally spar as they work out in the gym.

As noir musical *The Red Shoes* later shows (chapter 5), a performing career could also be a life-threatening endeavor. In Paramount's prelude film *Bolero* (1934), George Raft is the ambitious Raoul, limited by a World War I injury that weakens his heart and makes his passion for performing ballroom dance dangerous. Before the war, Raoul craves fame and rises from performing in cheap dance halls by using—and discarding—female partners. He opens a nightclub in Paris where he dances the bolero on a circular stage "criss-crossed with blinding lights and throbbing shadows."[13] His elegant partner, Helen (Carole Lombard), leaves him—and the stage—to marry another man. After the war, Raoul's ambition turns fatal. Raoul finally dances the bolero with Helen, but it kills him. In a scene of perfect dramatic irony, he dies in his dressing room as the crowd wildly applauds his performance.

Crime and low life continued to pay in film, and many movies thus themed fit the prelude category. Famed ballroom virtuoso Fred Astaire even dimmed the lights and used his cane as a machine gun to pay homage to gangster films in musical comedy *Top Hat* (1935). Bing Crosby jammed with jazz greats Louis Armstrong in *Pennies from Heaven* (1936) and Jack Teagarden in *Birth of the Blues*. Clark Gable thwarted Jeannette MacDonald's opera career, exploited her talent, and made her perform ragtime in scanty attire at his illegal Paradise gambling club on the Barbary Coast in *San Francisco* (1936). Ingrid Bergman played a beautiful piano student caught up in an ill-fated romance with a married virtuoso violinist in Gustaf Molander's Swedish film *Intermezzo*, costarring Gösta Ekman (1936, remade with Bergman and Leslie Howard in 1939). James Whale's musical film *Show Boat* (1936) costarred Helen Morgan and Paul Robeson. Producer David O. Selznick and director William Wellman exposed fame's dark side in brooding Technicolor shadows in the backstage (nonmusical) 1937 version of *A Star Is Born*. Fred MacMurray played an arrogant trumpeter who hits skid row in Mitchell Leisen's *Swing High, Swing Low* (1937). Fritz Lang's social realist *You and Me* (1938) featured singing gangsters and ex-cons. Even Walt Disney's animated musical fairy tale *Snow White and the Seven Dwarfs* (1937) included a sinister undertone and a suggestion of menace throughout that anticipates noir musicals.

MUSICAL CRIME MELODRAMA AT WARNER BROS.
AND PRELUDES ON THE CUSP OF WAR

John Garfield gained stardom as a cynical orchestra arranger in Michael Curtiz's *Four Daughters* (1938) that also featured Claude Rains and singer Priscilla Lane. A year later Busby Berkeley, already famed for his backstage musicals, directed *They Made Me a Criminal*, suggesting that crime pictures had become more popular than musical extravaganzas at Warner Bros. on the eve of World War II. Garfield played a boxer who is framed, with Rains as a detective and the Dead End Kids parodying *Footlight Parade*'s number "By a Waterfall." The *New York Times* exclaimed, "You can almost . . . hear the voice of John Garfield, accusing the Warner Brothers. But they all have to go through the same mill at Warners: Muni did it in *Scarface*; Cagney and Robinson are still doing it, and prospering at it too. So now they've made John Garfield a criminal, and since Mr. Garfield is young, resilient and no end talented, he is making the best of what, after all, is not such a bad situation . . . for a rising star."[14] Musical crime films included James Cagney as a flawed tough guy in Warner Bros.' *The Roaring Twenties* (1939), featuring returning World War I vet-gangsters, Prohibition-era jazz, Humphrey Bogart, and a singing Priscilla Lane. In *City for Conquest* (1940) New York taxi dance halls, hoodlums, East Side slums, and street bums are the background for Cagney playing a boxer who fights for his kid brother's music lessons and then goes blind, with Ann Sheridan as a dancer who leaves him for another, but comes back. Critics called it "tough and salty, right off the city's streets."[15]

In John Brahm's *Rio* (Universal, 1939), fugitive Basil Rathborne escapes from Devil's Island to kill his singer wife's lover.[16] By this time, French filmmakers were also making noir musical preludes including Marcel Carné's *Le jour se lève* (*Daybreak*) and Robert Siodmak's *Pièges* (*Personal Column*) crime films that included musical performance numbers and distinctly unglamorous backstage milieux.

Despite its critical praise, spectacular Technicolor imagery, and later success, MGM's most expensive 1939 film, musical-fantasy *The Wizard of Oz*, featuring Judy Garland's classic "Over the Rainbow," was initially unsuccessful with audiences. Although it cost $2,777,000 to make, World War II hampered overseas markets, and it lost $1,145,000 in its original release.[17] *The Wizard of Oz* begins in a stark black-and-white Kansas, and then Dorothy is swept in a cyclone to an elaborate Technicolor dream-fantasy world. In grappling with issues of isolationism and alienation as well as exposing Oz as a charlatan and the Emerald City as dystopian in comparison to "home," the film, despite its happy ending, delves into noirish territory. Its critique of the mundane rural existence of the Dustbowl presented an aesthetic anticipating the barren noir imagery of *The Grapes of Wrath*.

Also featuring Judy Garland, who captivates with her "I'm Always Chasing Rainbows," MGM's musical *Ziegfeld Girl* (1941), directed by Robert Z. Leonard provided beauty and escapism during increasingly ugly times and targeted a growing female audience. Reviewers dismissed the musical as a light glamorous escapist picture, referring to its starlets (beautiful violinist Hedy Lamarr and gorgeous star-struck Brooklyn elevator girl Lana Turner) as "décor," clearly ignoring the downbeat aspects of its plot. The film offered a backstage look at the fame, glamour, and success gained by aspiring showgirls, but also portrays Turner becoming an alcoholic egomaniac. She dumps Jimmy Stewart for a playboy, then burns out in her stage career and dies. Another film, *Second Chorus* featured Fred Astaire, who sings "I Ain't Hep to that Step, but I'll Dig It" and dances a tap-jazz-ballet mélange to Artie Shaw's swingin' big band; Johnny Mercer, with whom Garland had a longtime affair; Burgess Meredith, later star of the 1942 noir *Street of Chance*; Hermes Pan; and Paulette Goddard, playing an assertive working girl. Although the lively jazz musical was more of a comedy, Astaire's bluesy stepping to Shaw's orchestra suggests the jazz nightclub setting that would become so iconic on a darker stage in later noir musicals and jazz noir films during the war. The same year, *Second Chorus* designer Boris Leven created a shadowy illicit noir milieu in *The Shanghai Gesture* (1941).

As the war ramped up overseas, American women joined the workforce on the home front, with "Rosie the Riveter" as their unflappable, hardworking role model. Likewise, stronger female characters began appearing on screen. Combined with the emerging darker trend in films, this social change set the stage for early noir films such as Sternberg's atmospheric nonmusical *The Shanghai Gesture*, with Gene Tierney, Victor Mature, Walter Huston, Ona Munson, Marcel Dalio, Albert Basserman, and Irene Browne. Conveying an exotic underworld of vice, Sternberg's shrouded nightclub-casino-bordello suggested taboo interracial sex trade affairs, while an Anglo-Chinese diva (Tierney) is gunned down by the establishment's madam (her mother). Production Code censors rejected the film thirty-two times, and the Chinese government was outraged by its depiction of Shanghai.

Another noir crime film that year, *I Wake Up Screaming* (a.k.a. *Hot Spot*), reimagined a star-is-born plot where Carole Landis sings "The Things I Love" and is murdered. It featured musical star Betty Grable in a dramatic role with Victor Mature to the music of Alfred Newman's "Street Scene" and Harold Arlen's "Over the Rainbow," but Grable's racy boogie-woogie jazz number "Daddy" was cut from the film. Grable would soon become the most popular pinup star during the war.

THE END OF THE BEGINNING

Thomas Schatz notes that "producing movies during the war was scarcely business as usual; on the contrary, it required a massive transformation of virtually every phase of industry operations." As *Blues in the Night* was released in late 1941 into 1942, there were "deep concerns about the war overseas . . . compounded by severe problems at home due to wartime restrictions and shortages affecting every sector of the film industry," and Hollywood's "increasingly complex deal-ings with the government and the military" as the industry came to "terms with its role in the war effort."[18]

Although at the time critics generally panned what we now consider innova-tive early noir musicals like *Blues in the Night* for their downbeat themes, such movies that merged crime (melo)drama with the musical were certainly begin-ning to challenge censorship. As combat violence and war crimes and atrocities became more commonly known, propagated by graphic newsreels that were sanctioned by Washington's Office of Censorship, Hollywood's Production Code censorship was thus undermined, and musical film noir and noir musicals de-picting crime, violence, and sexual brutality managed to creep in.[19]

Moreover, patriotic crime and espionage films based on real events, such as Warner Bros.' *Confessions of a Nazi Spy* (1939), directed by Anatole Litvak, also put censors to the test. The cultural-industrial transformation brought about by the war directly contributed to a decline in PCA enforcement and the growth of film noir, allowing early noir films like *The Maltese Falcon* (1941), *Suspicion* (1941), *Citizen Kane* (1941), *This Gun for Hire*, and the experimental noir musical *Blues in the Night* to be released. Once Pearl Harbor was struck, such films acted as segués from Depression-era escapist musicals and screwball comedies into darker hard-hitting crime narratives in a disillusioned wartime America. Likewise, the new regulatory climate helped set the stage for "musical noir" as studios experi-mented with new ways of evading government scrutiny. Warner, as we saw, re-tooled its crime tradition by adding music, comedy, and social concerns in *Angels with Dirty Faces* (1938), *They Made Me a Criminal* (1939), *The Roaring Twenties*, *Brother Orchid* (1940), *City for Conquest*, *Out of the Fog* (1940), *Blues in the Night*, *Casablanca*, and *To Have and Have Not*. Early noir films were notable for their musical numbers and paved the way for noir musical hybrids to come.

CHAPTER THREE

Blues in the Night

The Noir Musical on the Brink of World War II

Director and film historian Paul Schrader commented that in "most every dramatic Hollywood film from 1941 to 1953," as Americans grew less romantic as a society and more disillusioned in the wake of the Depression, World War II, and other historical events, "lighting grew darker, characters more corrupt, themes more fatalistic, and the tone more hopeless . . . Never before had films dared to take such a harsh uncompromising look at American life."[1] Thus, as film noir emerged during World War II, a series of distinctive crime films featured jazz music and cabaret-style performances in dark, smoky nightclubs. These "film noir musicals" seem to defy classification insofar as they challenge the conventional strictures of film noir and musicals, becoming instead a hybrid form that draws from both genres.

Warner Bros.' 1941 *Blues in the Night* produced by Hal Wallis and Henry Blanke and directed by Anatole Litvak was definitive in establishing noir musicals. It opens with a "boogie-woogie" piano player jammin' with a band, jitterbugs whirling on a cramped dance floor, and neon lights flashing, "Hot Food! Hot Jazz! Hot Drinks!" In short order, the musicians start a brawl, destroy the bar, and end up in a dimly lit St. Louis jail where they hear African American prisoners wailing the blues. Inspired by that music, the group hits the road, playing, singing, and living the blues. They hitch rides on railcars traveling cross-country from St. Louis to New Orleans jazz clubs, pool halls, and cheap bars. These claustrophobic, shadowy settings suggest their entrapment behind bars in jail cells, in a dark cramped boxcar, and a psychiatric hospital. The band is lured into a dangerous underworld when they become embroiled with an unsavory crowd. They meet a fugitive who pulls a gun and robs them as they steal a ride in a boxcar. The fugitive then offers them a job. Things go downhill once they settle in a shady Jersey gambling nightspot with a backroom speakeasy run by gangsters. The band inhabits a shrouded, ramshackle garage. They make music, but barely survive the dangerous criminal milieu behind the jazz joint's duplicitous façade. Friends and lovers turn out to be back-stabbers: everyone in its noir-style yarn double-deals and betrays each other. A gangster's moll turns into a murderous femme fatale. A self-destructive jazz musician deteriorates, ends up on skid row and is sent to an insane asylum after tangling with her. She guns down her fugitive former lover and is killed by a disabled suitor who crashes his car off a cliff in a thundering rain-soaked night. *Blues in the Night* portrayed a gritty show business world where a scrappy band of jazz musicians try to play authentic blues music and score a big break after doing jail time. But they never make it to Hollywood or Broadway. They stare at the lights of the Big Apple from the Jungle, a roadhouse across the river, ride the rails, and try not to get killed by gangsters. When Richard Whorf's conflicted bandleader tries to leave the band and make it big, he ends up selling out and going crazy. After the tormented musician collapses on a piano in a bar, unable to play, a surreal nightmare montage reveals his heartbreak, subsequent psychological deterioration in a sanitarium, and loss of his blues music. *Blues in the Night* was steeped in the streetwise social realist critique of gangster films. This is the stuff of noir, set to music.

Despite the film's nocturnal setting and criminal element, music and jazz performances are at the heart of *Blues in the Night*. It captures both the spirit of film noir and the dark side of musicals. Critics noted that *Blues in the Night* was trying to do something different with the musical genre.[2] With its moody jazz/ blues soundtrack, rain-slicked city streets, dark alleys, and neon lights, it was much like film noir. In fact, music was an intrinsic facet of film noir, making it in many ways more musical than any genre other than the musical itself. Boasting impressive original music by Harold Arlen and Johnny Mercer and a famous title song that became a jazz standard, *Blues in the Night* garnered interest when it previewed in fall 1941.

ORIGINS OF *BLUES IN THE NIGHT*

Filming of *Blues in the Night* began in summer 1941, and it was originally called *Hot Nocturne* after Edwin Gilbert and Elia Kazan's play, then *New Orleans Blues*. Warner purchased *Hot Nocturne* for $12,500 in March 1941. Robert Rossen (known for *The Roaring Twenties*, *Out of the Fog*, *Strange Love of Martha Ivers*, *Body and Soul*, *Johnny O'Clock*, *The Hustler*) adapted it for the screen, but Gilbert and Kazan also contributed uncredited writing. *Blues in the Night* was Kazan's second and last screen role before he became a director and decided, "I sure as hell can direct better than Anatole Litvak."[3] *Blues in the Night* was exquisitely shot by silent-era veteran, Oscar-winning cinematographer Ernest Haller (*Captain Blood, Jezebel, Dark Victory, Gone with the Wind, Mildred Pierce, Deception, Humoresque, Rebel without a Cause*). The ensemble cast included Richard Whorf, Jack Carson, Elia Kazan, Lloyd Nolan, Betty Field, Wallace Ford, Howard DaSilva, "Dead End Kid" Billy Halop, Peter Whitney, and Priscilla Lane.

Although Warner Bros. marketed its "good girl" singer played by Priscilla Lane in promotional materials, this noir crime melodrama was anything but "wholesome." Unlike musicals revolving around a talented heterosexual couple coming together in lavish song and dance or a glamorous female singer-turned-starlet, *Blues in the Night* is an experimental variation on Warner Bros.' male action pictures centering on the criminal activity behind the scenes at jazz/blues nightclubs. However, it did emphasize camaraderie, a common Depression-era and wartime theme that worked as a metaphor to encourage Americans to pull together during tough times. Despite corruption, alienation, and a shady milieu, the musicians stick together. They've essentially gone nowhere, but they have each other.

Overall, it has a pervasively downbeat tone and led to other noir musicals that re-examined the search for fame, critically exploring backstage life. John Hoover notes that *Blues in the Night* initiated Warner Bros.' post–Busby Berkeley noir musical style that lasted from 1941 to 1957 and focused on "frustration and disorientation" in which people "no longer have any control over their lives"; suffer mental breakdowns; and sink into addiction, corruption, depression, and death because "they can no longer cope."[4]

Thus, *Blues in the Night* initiated a form and a style, but what were its own origins? Litvak, who had previously directed *City for Conquest* and *Out of the Fog*, was originally from Russia and worked in Germany's UFA studio during the 1920s. Blanke was German and had worked as assistant to director Ernst Lubitsch in 1924, and was also the son of an expressionist painter. Their dark expressionist Central European noir style melded with the Berkeley musical style and American gangster films, integrating special effects wizard Don Siegel's nightmare montages to simulate the antihero's psyche. *Blues in the Night*'s dialogue and disreputable characters also share much with gangster films. Garfield and Cagney, famous for playing gangsters, were even considered for the film. Warner Bros. even deleted a reference to Al Capone for fear of lawsuits by the notorious real-life gangster who, like the fugitive Del (Lloyd Nolan) in *Blues in the Night*, had just gotten out of jail.[5]

Challenging censorship, *Blues in the Night* was able to include plenty of scenes of degenerate corruption. In light of its many censorable inclusions such as psychosis and suicide, illicit affairs, multiple murders and other violence, and abundant criminal activity, it's indeed surprising that *Blues in the Night* was approved by censors. The film industry's moral blueprint for censorship, the Production Code, had been written in 1930. In mid-1934, Hollywood's trade association, the Motion Picture Producers and Distributors of America (MPPDA), headed by Will Hays, established the Production Code Administration (PCA), appointing Joseph Breen to enforce industry self-censorship and to negotiate with studios regarding film content that would uphold "compensating moral values" and narrative justice on screen.[6] Thus, noir fatalism was encouraged by PCA censorship, which required that bad guys go to jail or die in the end. In *Blues in the Night*, this is evident in criminal Sam's betrayal of fugitive Del and Del's murder of Sam; Del's brutality to femme Kay and Kay's murder of Del; and Kay's cruelty to Brad resulting in Brad's murder of Kay, along with his own suicide. Trumpeter Leo (Carson) is unfaithful to his wife (Lane), but their baby dies, so he pays for his flirtations with Kay. His wife is one of the most tragic characters, longing for love. Everyone pays for his or her misdeeds. And, with America's entry into the war, changes at the PCA included Breen leaving to run RKO studio from mid-1941 to 1942, creating a temporary lapse in Code censorship and allowing films like *Blues in the Night* with salacious content to be made. Because it was shot during Breen's absence from the PCA, the film was thus able to include many censorable scenes.[7]

The lapse in censorship also meant that more and more violence was becoming acceptable. The actual violence of the war, inescapable in newsreels, likewise led to an easing of censorship relating to violence in films. Noir crime films were recognized as "violent escape in tune" with the "violence of the times." "These are times of death and bloodshed and legalized murder," the *New York Times* observed. "After watching a newsreel showing the horrors of a German concentration camp . . . the war has made us psychologically and emotionally . . . calloused to death, hardened to homicide" and "capable of understanding a murderer's motives . . . getting rid of our wives or husbands and making off with the insurance money" with "no shock, no remorse, no moral repugnance. . . . If an audience can stomach newsreels of atrocities, it can take anything."[8]

BLUES IN THE NIGHT'S STYLE AND PRODUCTION

Stylistically, iconic noir conventions of expressionistic high contrast with emphasis on heavy shadows abound in *Blues in the Night*. Camera angles are also classically noir. The climactic garage murder finale is innovatively shot through staircases and wagon wheels with extremely low, skewed "Dutch" angles and, of course, abundant rain and shadow. Rationing of materials (film stock, lighting, electricity, sets) began even before Pearl Harbor. Litvak was painstaking and particular in how he shot the film, which resulted in ongoing tension between artistry and economy, reflected in studio memos regarding Litvak's financial efficiency performance. For example, studio chief Jack Warner complained to executive producer Wallis: "Litvak shot a whole day on just the one scene at the pool table . . . he took at least four unnecessary angles . . . he could have done much more work had he just made the shot panned . . . in, done one reverse shot . . . and it would have been over. That is all we will use when it is cut. I don't want to talk to Litvak personally on this picture, but . . . get hold of Blanke and Litvak . . . show why this was all unnecessary and the tremendous cost of the time alone. We can't use the film so why they keep on taking these different angles is beyond me."[9] Two days later, memos complained: "Litvak did not get his first OK'd take until 11:30 a.m. Haller complained the backing was not right, and this was fixed, but when Litvak came on . . . he said it was . . . out of perspective . . . I have told" art director "Max Parker that . . . he should never set anything up without first getting Litvak's OK. In Litvak's opinion, no one can do these jobs satisfactorily but himself, and if we go ahead he will always change it, thus causing delays." Innovative oblique angles are what film noir, and *Blues in the Night* as an early experimental noir musical, was stylistically noted for.

Despite studio complaints, Litvak and Blanke were able to create a moody atmospheric style. *Blues in the Night's* composition—chiaroscuro shadow, slices of light splintering the frame, unnerving skewed expressionistic camera shots, reflective surfaces (mirrors, rain, water) suggest the contradicting duality of noir characters and their environment; their seemingly benign appearance cloaks a malignant underside. Bad girl Kay's reflection in the mirror—as she smokes a cigarette and plots to breakup Leo's marriage, with gaudy jewelry glistening at her dressing table—conveys her corruption in a distinctly noir style. Litvak shot at oblique angles through rain-streaked windowpanes as the antihero looks for Kay in a raging storm. This scene depicts both Kay's vulnerability and her malignancy.

Ironically, Blanke had to beg the studio to keep the rain, pleading with Hal Wallis: "I just received a note . . . asking if the rain for the last sequence of the picture is necessary. Please, please don't cut this out, as I think it will enhance the climax of the picture immensely. . . . I think the expense is negligible in comparison to the effect we will get." Litvak had certainly challenged production efficiency when he shot the climactic finale. Unit production manager Chuck Hansen reported: "You will note that Litvak slipped a little yesterday . . . partly accounted for by the move from the back of the set [the garage] to the front, a reflection shot on the interior of the set, and in my opinion, Litvak overshot somewhat."[10] While these efforts at artistry were not always appreciated, the results were impressive.

The finished film was eighty-eight minutes. It was tight and fast paced. Warner Bros.' executives hoped it would play well with hip urban East Coast audiences in its many mid-Atlantic theaters. Wallis assured Blanke in October 1941 that Warner East Coast brass were pleased with the film: "We got a wire from New York, they saw *Blues in the Night*, and thought it was the most unusual picture, and thought that it would be very successful."[11] It was quite different than Wallis's earlier assessment: "The attached budget . . . speaks for itself. I don't have to tell you that a picture of this type and with this casting will have a hell of a time getting its cost back based on these figures. Therefore . . . make the picture for as little as possible . . . watch all angles with a view to economizing . . . there are plenty of opportunities to save money in the music, the shooting, etc."[12] But what type of film was he referring to? This unusual noir musical broke with typical generic convention, and Warners' budget-conscious crime tradition aided the musical's noir style.

Warner Bros., true to their economizing spirit, recycled sets as war escalated abroad and the U.S. drew closer to entering the conflict in 1941: using the turntable that housed the revolving Cumberland mountain in money-maker *Sergeant York* as a rotating cabaret set for *Blues in the Night*, and cloaked it with smoke, shadow, fog, mirrors and creative angles. This spared director Litvak from "having to maneuver his camera through the swinging doors on a long boom"[13] for interior and exterior shots of the Jungle roadhouse. Nevertheless *Blues in the Night* cost exceeded its $687,000 budget.[14] It earned $558,000 domestically and $273,000 overseas (as war reduced international markets), grossing just $831,000.[15] Wallis was correct when he anticipated that "this type" of film would have a hard time paying its way. *Blues in the Night* was a new hybrid, a noir musical.

DECONSTRUCTING MUSICAL IDEALS

Blues in the Night followed the Warner Bros. tradition of expressionistic social realist crime films developed in *I Am a Fugitive from a Chain Gang, City for Conquest,* and *Out of the Fog.* At the same time, it shattered the female ideal often depicted in escapist musicals with beautiful costumes and a soft-focus on female facial features. Although Kay wears more expensive clothing once she forces the antihero to sell out, her tacky makeup is unbecoming and overdone, revealing her harsh, ruthless character. Rossen's script describes Kay: "Her beauty is undeniable . . . not classic . . . but in a compelling, magnetic way . . . her life . . . a hard one . . . mirrored on her face in cold stares."[16] Like Ann Savage's lethal femme fatale in *Detour*, however, in the film Kay subverts ideals of aesthetic beauty. Her scrappy femme is abrasive, menacing, and manipulative, rather than "magnetically beautiful." In this sordid setting where crooks knock each other off and talk about dames and broads, she is not a glamorous woman but rather someone who is both washed-up and trying to scam a new angle. The cheap makeup visually conveys how antihero Jigger is unable to change or transform Kay into a decent humane person, despite lavishing money on her.

Blues in the Night also deconstructs other ideals. It shattered the utopian motifs of escapist musicals with their bright high-key lighting, brilliant Technicolor (as in *The Wizard of Oz*), lyrically moving camera, expansive space, glamorized settings, conventional camera angles, and joyous musical soundtrack. It countered the energy, enthusiasm, and professional success of traditional musical protagonists and subverted the musical's sense of beauty and happily-ever-after narrative resolutions. Romantic love is shown as destructive, culminating in insanity, murder, and suicide. Jigger loses his musical integrity and personal happiness for the gold-digging femme. As in *A Star Is Born* and *Citizen Kane*, he tries to make Kay the band's singing star, but rehearsals become a chaotic, disturbing montage that portends his downward spiral to madness in a psychiatric ward. His pursuit of fame, fortune, and success are destructive: he is miserable after he sells out and becomes an accompanist taking a lucrative gig with Guy Hieser's pop big band in a swanky ballroom. Clowning singers do ridiculous comedy routines as they lean on his piano and dancers tap frenetic numbers atop it as he plays corny novelty tunes. He is depicted as a puppet playing in a nightmare.

The roles that the film noir musical offered were also more akin to noir than to musical. Like other film noir, *Blues in the Night* was a gritty economical alternative to splashy color musicals. Without top name Warner stars like Garfield, Cagney, or Bette Davis, the studio promoted its jazz music, crime tradition, and "up-and-coming" Broadway talent rather than established big-name stars. Warner Bros.' ads called New York stage actor Whorf a "triple threat" and a "swell new discovery!" claiming his ability to play piano added realism to his role. Publicity referred to *Blues in the Night* as a "jazz opera" to attract upscale New York viewers.[17] As in gangster and masculine noir crime films, female characters are relegated to peripheral "love interest" roles. Warner borrowed Field from Paramount to play Kay's unsympathetic female "heavy" role. Although Lane got top billing as *Blues in the Night's* star (on the heels of her supporting role in *The Roaring Twenties*), contrary to the publicity, she had only a supporting role as a member of the musical group. Her identity is linked to marriage to another band member, the unfaithful trumpeter Leo (Carson), and (as her generic name Character suggests), she is referred to not by name but merely as "Leo's wife." *Blues in the Night* ads clamored: "She's as TORRID as a torch song!" The publicity advertised violence, misogyny, and gender distress, calling Field "a vamp and a mean one" in "black satin . . . not a nice girl. She is the consort of gangsters. She is a blues singer and a very bad one. Betrayal is in her wicked little heart. She is a sinister contrast with Priscilla Lane, who sings on key and practically never sticks a knife in anyone's back."

As in film noir and gangster pictures, men become obsessed antiheroes in this noir musical film. Ads noted how Carson loved onscreen fights, but missed sparring with Cagney, and described Nolan as "one of the toughest, most unscrupulous men on the screen . . . he has slain many men . . . he even shot some children during a gang fight" and gets "tough with a beautiful girl. Victim of Lloyd's roughhouse tactics is attractive Betty Field, who, naturally, is in love with him. That doesn't stop her, however, from pulling the trigger on Nolan after he has treated her to some rough handling." Nolan admitted, "Trying to hit Betty

Blues in the Night: "She's as TORRID as a Torch Song!" Lloyd Nolan brings Richard Whorf's band to the Jungle roadhouse. Warner Bros., 1941

without hurting her and still have the slap look realistic on the screen is the most difficult assignment I've ever tackled. . . . As a matter of fact, I think she has the perfect right to shoot this so-and-so I play in the picture."[18]

In addition to shady criminals and a tormented antihero, *Blues in the Night* also features disabled con Brad, who is stereotyped as passive, a sucker or sap, the self-described victim of femme fatale wiles. He is a gambling addict, a cynical coward, a loser in the harsh game of life. Brad is short and stocky, physically harmless, in other words, to represent his inconsequentiality. The final insult comes when the band tells Jigger he's mentally "crippled" just like Brad. After tolerating repeated cruelty, in a sadomasochistic act, Brad commits suicide-murder, sacrificing himself as well as saving the group and the antihero from the femme fatale.

NOIR SET TO MUSIC: PROMOTING JAZZ

As we have seen, *Blues in the Night* certainly incorporates many noir elements, but what of the music that sets it apart? Composed by Harold Arlen, the moody, soulful, and evocative music shared a great deal of blues elements atypical of traditional musical scores or polished big band swing music. Musical styles were changing in the early 1940s as World War II ramped up. In the jazz world, young musicians were growing restless with the strictures of big band swing. They had begun experimenting in jam sessions with small combos in clubs and after-hours venues across the country, much like the five-member band unit in *Blues in the Night*. Warner publicity said that the actors read "*Downbeat*, trade journal of the professional hep cats" to prepare for their *Blues in the Night* roles.[19]

When the Depression hit Broadway and talking-pictures arrived, talented song-writers like Arlen, Mercer, and the Gershwins had flocked to Hollywood. Arlen, known for "the wail of the blues" and writing music for Harlem's Cotton Club performed by Cab Calloway, Jimmy Lunceford, and Duke Ellington, composed the music for *The Wizard of Oz*. Arlen's compositions included "Over the Rainbow," "Stormy Weather," "I Gotta Right to Sing the Blues," "Get Happy," and the downbeat blues number, "The Man That Got Away" for Garland in *A Star Is Born* (with lyricist Ira Gershwin). Arlen collaborated with Mercer on "That Old Black Magic," "One for My Baby (and One More for the Road)," and "Come Rain or Come Shine." Mercer wrote lyrics for "Laura" and "Autumn Leaves." Usually Arlen needed the lyric before he composed melodies, but he called the song "Blues in the Night" "one of the high points of knowing in my life . . . the whole thing poured out, and I knew in my guts, without even thinking what Johnny could write for a lyric, that this was strong."[20] The blues music in *Blues in the*

Night foreshadows characters' fates such as Brad's crash, Jigger's mental break-down, and Character's loss of her child. The lyrics of "Blues in the Night" depict femme fatale duplicity: "A woman's a two-face, a worrisome thing who'll leave ya to sing the blues in the night." "Blues in the Night" enjoyed enormous popularity. Cab Calloway's band including Dizzy Gillespie recorded "Blues in the Night" on September 10, 1941, prior to the film's release. The song was later recorded by all the top women songsters: Judy Garland, Ella Fitzgerald, Doris Day, Dinah Shore, Jo Stafford, and Rosemary Clooney (each of whom made it her own by changing the lyrics to be about *male* duplicity instead of female.)

Warner Bros. advertised *Blues in the Night* as a "novel drama set to music," a "far off the beaten track of musical film formula" and a "brand new type of musi-cal film . . . a different kind of musical that's got everything," an "absorbing" "serious dramatic story with music used only to advance the plot" about a "group of youngsters who have an ideal—and little else. They believe that the music heard on the dusky waterfronts of New Orleans, in the cotton fields of Carolina, and the back streets of Memphis is the important music of America, and they want to play it. They beat their way across the country in box cars, playing where they can for what they can, hoping that someday their rhythmic blues-playing, will be recognized for what it is, the true folk music of their country." "Sweet and low-down. The soft wail of a muted trumpet. The dull pulsating rhythms of a bass drum. Music of the people. The streets. Of slamming. That's the sort of music you hear . . . something really different in the way of film musi-cals." The studio didn't know what to call it but they did distinguish it from glamorous musical spectacles: "This is not a film about a lot of beautiful girls in a nightclub, dancing on extravagant sets, to the music of an orchestra that has more swank than swing." It is realistic "music heard on the streets, in every walk of life," the "true American folk music" that "America should hear and sing." Its "small group of inspired musicians . . . get mixed-up with racketeers, race track touts, and small-time gamblers. But despite all their problems and obstacles, they accomplish one thing; the thing they want most to do. They play the songs that come from the soul of America." Warner Bros., in fact, justified the noir content of the musical as a kind of patriotism, a feeling for being American, of cultural history of its indigenous folk music tradition that certainly stemmed from the war effort.

Capitalizing on Duke Ellington's socially conscious African American stage show *Jump for Joy*, they promoted the music as, "It's *jumpin'* with Jive and Joy! . . . Recorded by the world's topnotch bands: Artie Shaw, Glenn Miller, Woody Her-man, Charlie Barnet, Eddie Duchin, Cab Calloway, and Gene Krupa. Ten recordings of hit tunes from the picture by seven outstanding bands" by "Harold (*Stormy Weather*) Arlen and Johnny (*Make with the Kisses*) Mercer." Although African American jazz/blues music is praised in *Blues in the Night*, the film's protagonist and ensemble are white musicians. Their goal is to achieve and develop the same ability as gifted black musicians playing the real blues. They're happy to just have a gig and play their music—the real blues they heard in jail that movingly captures the pain, loneliness, and hard times with which they can identify. They reject performing music they consider to be of lesser quality just to earn more money. This portrayal of jazz/blues music as an art form is distinctive from many crime films that portray jazz/blues music as seedy, shady, and evocative of Jazz Age Prohibition low life.

Growing out of the Roaring 20s Jazz Age big bands, jazz ("the blues" in *Blues in the Night*) became popular during the 1930s–1940s Swing era. Warner Bros. originally wanted Ellington but he was unavailable because he was producing *Jump for Joy*. Instead they hired Jimmy Lunceford's orchestra to play the "barn-storming band," a tight, skilled, accomplished unit, performing in a modest New Orleans club setting that inspires the film's white musician protagonists. His wonderful bluesy big band instrumental version of "Blues in the Night," cut from the film, was evocative not only of Lunceford's but also of Ellington's moody style. Lunceford's band included Gerald Wilson, who later arranged for Ellington. Lunceford's polished talented band had a grueling schedule touring on the road. Jack Warner observed that Lunceford's musicians "did not like the idea of playing in cheap clothes."[21] Jazz historian Scott DeVeaux notes challenges black jazz musicians faced in an "economic system that gave insuperable advantages to white musicians who were frankly imitators, however accomplished, of a black idiom." Remarkably, "many prominent black musicians tried to remain bandleaders when they could have enjoyed a more secure and profitable existence working as arrangers, or even star soloists, for white orchestras."[22]

Musically, one of the richest moments in the picture is when William Gillespie, trapped in a prison cage with crisscrossing bars of shadow across him and the band, sings "Blues in the Night" in a deep rich baritone. Images used in Siegel's musical montage of Gillespie singing in jail used stock newsreel footage of black workers in a cotton field that Warner Bros. acquired from Fox Movietone News. Fox advised Warner Bros. that it was "illegal to sell scenes with negroes." Warner Bros.' Lee Anthony replied: "Possibly they're getting ethical and want to be assured the negro race is properly represented by us—which they are."[23] Yet in the film African American characters are either depicted in jail or playing music in a dive rather than out in public interacting with everyone else, suggesting societal constraints.

Adding further insult, Lunceford's musical billing was initially put behind a less prominent white band by the publicity department, who believed "the white band should have preference over the colored band." Blanke, however, insisted to Warner: "I believe this is wrong and I just wanted to call your attention to this credit as I know you will decide the right thing"[24] and the change was made. The studio promoted "Jimmy Lunceford and his band, one of the nation's foremost blues orchestras . . . the popular colored maestro . . . featured with his band in a New Orleans night club." Ads proclaimed, *"Blues replacing jitterbug jive. . . .* Jitterbugs had better start to learn new dance steps if they want their feet to keep step with the latest dance music. That is the opinion of Jimmy Lunceford, bandleader, who has specialized in fast fox trots and swing for 11 years. Lunceford is gradually changing his style, for he firmly believes that the 'blues' are on their way back and will be played throughout the country in two years." In an interview Lunceford said, "The return of the blues will take a longer time than swing took to replace jazz. There are a lot of bands, such as mine, who cater almost exclusively to the younger set, who continue to demand fast music. We have to educate them gradually to the slower rhythmatic tunes." The studio's publicity noted that Lunceford believes "blues have been rejuvenated" by "jam sessions" that will continue at "impromptu meetings of musicians." He was quoted as saying, "Jam sessions are as important to musicians as board meetings are to bank presidents or as sparring partners are to fighters. Our steam rooms (gathering places for the blow and stomp men) are where we develop styles and exchange musical ideas. The accentuated second and fourth beat, or low-down blues, developed at these sessions in the wee hours of the morning when the musicians started to tire from their earlier more strenuous exertions."[25]

In musical noir, jazz and blues often signify a potentially censorable adult, after-hours environment with double entendre and illicit suggestion. Thus, what cannot be depicted gets commuted as musical numbers. And Hollywood's Advertising Code was more lenient than its Production Code censorship. The film's trailer opens with surreal nightmare montages and moody voice-over accentuating its bluesy theme song. Oblique shots show mirror reflections of jazz instruments as hands play piano and musicians jam on a packed roadhouse dancefloor. "Hear those blues in the night? That boogie woogie, brother. Music you can't write. You can't even read. You've just got to feel it. And then you ride. Just listen to that wail. Sounds like a woman's heart calling out for a man. Don't it? Hear it?"

Kay, in a trench coat, fires a gun. *"It's too exciting for words."* The band plays. "So they had to set it to music!" Promising noir gender distress, self-destructive love-hate relationships, and love triangles, Whorf's "strange adventures follow the haunting call of the Blues." Lane warns the band about fatal attraction, "Can't you understand it? You can be in love with someone and know that it's wrong, that it's poison, and not be able to do anything about it." She confronts Kay "I'd slap you right in the mouth." Del fires a gun as Kay screams. *"Drama! What a torchy story! It's rockin' with rhythm! 6 terrific tunes by Harold Arlen and Johnny Mercer, with Jimmy Lunceford and his band sockin' 'em solid!"* Warner touted the film's originality: *"'Blues in the Night' different? Why, it's out of this world!"* It was atypical for a musical.

Lyricist Johnny Mercer admitted, "A musical is an incredibly complicated piece of machinery. You can have all the elements, the right songs, the right book, the right cast, the right director, the right costume designer—and the lighting man can screw it up."[26] It is clear in *Blues in the Night* how critical lighting was to establishing the right mood. The shadowy lighting melded with the blue tenor of the music to create the distinctive atmosphere for *Blues in the Night*. Mercer's lyrics include themes of pain and loneliness, such as title track "Blues in the Night," poignantly sung by William Gillespie in the shrouded corner of a jail cell: "My momma done tol' me. . . ." Character sings the hopeful "This Time the Dream's on Me" with sorrow as her husband is absent from the band, out carousing with Kay, undercutting the song's lyrics. The script describes Character singing the lyrics "to express the hurt in her heart."[27]

Lane, who sang in Fred Waring's band before she came to Hollywood, provided authenticity to the bluesy musical aspect of the film: "Orchestra leaders, who have been ready for the change for months, will soon definitely swing their customers into a blue revival. What's the difference between blues, jazz and swing? Swing rhythm, eight to the bar and out of this world, is running down like a cheap clock that was wound too tight. The next thing in popular music will be the moan of the blues. The jitterbugs are on their last legs. *Blues in the Night* is on the up-beat with the new trend." Publicity quoted expert Lane: "The only difference between the old blues, the kind that started from the lonely voices of cottonfield workers in the South, and modern blues is that the original blues started as folk-music—and today blues exist both as a style of playing music and as a form of music itself. . . . As for jazz, that's simply a device that can be applied to any kind of music. Just a noisier aspect of the blues. . . . We lost so much of the real music during the swing and jazz eras. Jazz is just variations on a theme. . . .

Top-billed Priscilla Lane sings the *Blues in the Night*. Warner Bros., 1941

But in the blues, you have that minor key, a kind of sweetness and sadness, and that's your blue note."[28]

Warner promoted *Blues in the Night* as the vanguard of a new musical trend. But swing continued to retain popularity in live concert performances in a booming wartime economy, especially as record companies released stockpiled jazz recordings made before a musicians' union strike on recorded music that began in 1942 and lasted through 1944. Scott DeVeaux suggests "increased defense spending put money in the pockets of potential customers, giving a badly needed boost to the entertainment industry. The artificial stimulation of a wartime economy temporarily disguised the structural problems in the music industry and postponed the inevitable collapse of the Swing Era until shortly after the troops returned home in 1945."[29] By January 1942 *Music and Rhythm* magazine proclaimed, "The Blues Are Dead!"[30] Yet, Warner's noir musical anticipated several trends. Its downbeat minor key resonated with a wartime climate of rationing, labor shortages, travel restrictions, the draft, inflated salaries, and "frenetic 'live-for-today' atmosphere" related to separations and loss of life and injury of combatants. This created a "new environment" for "musicians fortunate enough to remain behind on the home front. The war years were a time of barely controlled chaos, ripe with opportunities for those not averse to risk."[31] Big bands eventually were replaced by experimental minor-key blue strains of bebop, smaller jazz combos, vocalists (like Frank Sinatra), and rhythm-and-blues. Lane acknowledged: "There's a lot of woe in the world . . . we got the right to sing the blues."[32]

THE "MUSICAL THAT IS REALLY DIFFERENT"
IS RELEASED TO THE WORLD

When *Blues in the Night* previewed on October 29, 1941, the *Motion Picture Herald* called it a "musical that is really different" that "combine[s] musical blues with dramatic action."[33] *Variety* noted the "musical drama" was a "favorable departure" from the "usual film musical formula."[34] The *Hollywood Reporter* recognized its "strange and interesting combination" of "hot music" and "straight melodrama" with "pounding, forceful" performances in a "web of romantic intrigue," a "tense, exciting screenplay." It called it the "most accurate insight into musicians lives" on screen, "none of the heartaches are softened" and commented that the story's "sordidness" with "revolting" characters may "mitigate against its box office success." (Breen considered film noir "sordid" and censorable.) Yet reviewers noted it "abounds in swing music . . . jitterbugs will go for the attraction in a big way."[35]

The *Los Angeles Times'* Philip Scheuer called *Blues in the Night* "high-powered," a "fast-action . . . tuneful . . . musical melodrama" that "gets in the groove and stays there," with "hot tunes . . . cleverly dubbed." He noted Arlen and Mercer's "blues classic" played by Lunceford's "crack band." It "doesn't pretend to be a documentary of American music," just the "story of five natural jivers, their friends and their enemies, as they swing round the country" amid "violence, unbridled passion and sudden death . . . customary concomitants of the barrel-house boys." In other words, it was the stuff noir was made of. He acknowledged its masculine ethos with "only two femmes," with Field a "menace" as the ruthless racketeer-moll. Scheuer praised the "exceptionally vivid" montages and Litvak's brisk direction "tempo" that "leaves no room for dawdlers, on screen or off. One may be grateful that neither he nor his scenarist, Robert Rossen, has dragged the band into Carnegie Hall for the usual symphonic finale!"[36]

When *Blues in the Night* opened on the East Coast on December 12, 1941, just days after Pearl Harbor, however, the *New York Times* complained: "Harold Arlen and Johnny Mercer . . . have produced a melodious sound track. . . . That's just about all the film has to offer." Litvak has "directed the musical sequences . . . in showmanly fashion, employing montage shots most effectively to maintain fast tempi. But when he gets into the story of the ups and downs of his vagabond musical quintet [he] loses control . . . with the melodramatic material."[37] The *Wall Street*

Journal reviewed it saying that "while the poorer points are more noticeable than the good," it's "well directed, fast paced and has some fine musical numbers." Its story concerns "five young swing enthusiasts" who "conceive a real blues band" while "staying overnight in a mid-western jail. With the aid [of] desperate criminal benefactors," they land a "booking in a Jersey hot spot," but the musical's "melodramatic . . . situation . . . could only happen in a Hollywood script." It screened with a live jazz stage show featuring *Gone With the Wind* Oscar-winner Hattie McDaniel singing with Count Basie's orchestra.[38]

The *Washington Post* lauded its music while panning its downbeat story: "In *Blues in the Night* the Brothers Warner combine two of their studio's strongest points—melodrama and le jazz hot. Le jazz hot wins hands down." The film gains "vitality" from Lunceford and Arlen and Mercer's "musical interludes" rather than its "hackneyed story" of a band traveling in a boxcar "ambitious to spread" the blues. Racketeer Nolan, "key to their success and ultimate disaster . . . lands them a job at a spot under his own benevolent protection, The Jungle." The reviewer noted the "emotional turmoil," the existence of an "unborn baby," and "as nasty a female character, played by Betty Field, this tired old year has brought forth." Praising the originality of the dark musical it concluded: "It would be too bad to condemn *Blues in the Night* for being a musical with a grim, foreboding story rather than the tinsel stuff one gets used to from the usual run of musical films. Cheers for *Blues* on that account, for it's a try in the right direction."[39]

AMERICA GOES TO WAR

Blues in the Night's bizarre amalgam that defied audience expectations in terms of genre, narrative, and stars contributed to its lack of success but so did its timing in light of what was happening on the world stage. As one might expect, eliminating glamour and romance in a musical was less than successful. Unlike popular Busby Berkeley, Fred Astaire-Ginger Rogers, or color Betty Grable musicals, it did not provide escapist musical fantasy/comedy or a glamorous star-studded utopian alternative to reality that could counter social tensions. This atypical musical lacked a big star, especially a beautiful central female musical performer like Grable, Rogers, Hayworth, Garland (thus, Warner's top billing of blonde Lane). It also lacked a major male star like Bogart, Cagney, or Garfield to draw viewers to a masculine noir gangster/crime film. Bogart's *Maltese Falcon* and Cary Grant's *Suspicion* were huge 1941 hits. The war, however, shifted male crime/gangster stars to combat films. *Blues in the Night*'s downbeat mood, fiery explosive car crash with loss of human life, and the plight of vagabond jazz musicians may have seemed insignificant as America mobilized for war. The fact that

Lane and Whorf are "just friends" and not a romantic couple also hurt the unusual musical film.

Filmgoers in 1941 and 1942 who were looking for uplifting entertainment and musical comedy were disappointed. (Imagine if Dorothy never left the Dustbowl or made it to Technicolor Oz, and *The Wizard of Oz* remained a gritty, shrouded, black-and-white *Grapes of Wrath*-like exploration of struggle in Kansas with Garland singing the blues.) Unlike earlier Depression-era backstage musicals in which an artist's determination and hard work led to success, *Blues in the Night* (and subsequent noir musicals) subverted myths about show business opportunity and the American dream.[40] Yet, as in preparation for war, the band in *Blues* embraces camaraderie, reminding each other, "We're a unit." They remain together despite hardship with music as the binding agent: "You're never alone if you stay in the groove."

Pearl Harbor brought the international crisis home, instilling apprehension that the West Coast might be attacked. Los Angeles was officially considered a "theater of war."[41] Warner Bros. was one of the first studios to mobilize for the war effort. Given Hollywood's proximity to the Pacific coast theater and the Warner studio's topical streetwise sensibility, publicity and exhibition enthusiasm diminished for this suddenly less-than-topical film. *Blues in the Night* had been created at a time when Warner Bros. felt freer to experiment (within its tightly managed studio), as we saw earlier. The result was this definitive noir musical. However, just six months after its release, with the war on our soil, industry censorship and Washington's Office of War Information's (OWI) regulation would have prevented *Blues in the Night* from being produced. As the OWI's Bureau of Motion Pictures (BMP) and Office of Censorship infused propaganda into films, these war agencies banned gangster pictures in favor of combat films. This shift in wartime male action pictures and Hollywood's regulatory climate would surely have precluded or curtailed *Blues in the Night*'s production. Ironically, the Office of Censorship later allowed atrocities and violence to be depicted in propaganda newsreels, which violated the movie industry's PCA limits on criminal violence and political content. Although the OWI and Office of Censorship regulated screen depictions of combat and home-front gangster violence in order to support the war effort, they contradicted the Code and eventually enabled greater noir violence during the war.[42]

BLUES IN THE NIGHT'S LEGACY

For a film that did not achieve huge box-office success, *Blues in the Night* was surprisingly influential both in music- and filmmaking. Dark jazz musicals repeatedly reference it: femme fatale Lauren Bacall mentions *Blues in the Night* to tormented jazz trumpeter Kirk Douglas in *Young Man with a Horn* (1950), and Louis Armstrong plays "Blues in the Night" with a New Orleans jazz combo in *Glory Alley* (1952). Just prior to his definitive noir *Double Indemnity* (1944), Billy Wilder in *The Major and the Minor* (1942) featured *Blues in the Night*'s theme song as a cadet dances singing its lyric "A Woman's a Two Face" to Ginger Rogers. Bacall works "Her Mama Done Told Her" into a jazz number in *The Big Sleep* (1946). Calloway performed in Minoco's 1942 *Blues in the Night* "soundie" musical short, a filmed precursor to music videos. Garfield, who turned down the lead role in *Blues in the Night*, parodied its acclaimed theme song in *Thank Your Lucky Stars* (1943). "Blues in the Night" is sung in *She's Back on Broadway* (1953) and played in Dennis Potter's *The Singing Detective* (1986). *Blues in the Night*'s melancholy title song and the original soundtrack enjoyed enormous success. "Blues in the Night" was nominated for an Academy Award for Best Original Song and topped music charts along with other songs from the movie, including hits by Woody Herman, Jimmy Lunceford, Cab Calloway, Artie Shaw, Dinah Shore, and Rosemary Clooney.[43] Lunceford's bluesy instrumental recording, omitted from the film, was a smash on radio. Versions of "Blues in the Night" recorded before the 1942–44 strike soared in popularity during the war (like Sinatra's prestrike recordings that made him a huge star.) If Lunceford's version or any of the hit radio versions of "Blues in the Night" had been in the film itself—or William Gillespie's moving vocal in the picture was released as a record for radio—it might have increased *Blues in the Night*'s popularity, which had been renamed to match Arlen's song title. A nightclub plays "Blues in the Night" in *All Through the Night* (1942).

Moreover, moody jazz melodrama and noir musicals imitating its downbeat spirit emerged during and after the war. *Orchestra Wives* (1942) portrayed difficulties on the road with Glenn Miller, and *The Hard Way* (1943) shows Ida Lupino and Jack Carson committing suicide as Joan Leslie rises miserably to Broadway fame.

Decades after its release, critics championed *Blues in the Night*. "Made back in 1941," *New York Times*' Howard Thompson wrote in 1966, *Blues in the Night* "probably remains the most full-bodied movie of jazz players," although it was a "drama of a barn-storming band" that "detoured into violence and sex." Praising its outstanding music, he wrote, "What nailed the film down for posterity was Harold Arlen's magnificent title ballad, superbly chanted" by baritone Gillespie "through jail bars." He noted a trend toward jazz musical crime films in the wake of *Blues in the Night*: "The next year . . . at the Warner studio, there emerged still another tune destined to become a classic, along with the picture, *Casablanca*.

Today it is almost impossible to hear 'As Time Goes By' without recalling Dooley Wilson and his smooth piano-chanting. The song fitted perfectly into the very action of the film," as did his "quietly effective performance" portraying a musician "pal of Humphrey Bogart."[44]

Blues in the Night opened with the United States on the precipice of war. Though it was not financially successful, it established the trend of using jazz in dramatic musicals with criminal themes in a noir manner. Sometimes called "melodrama"—literally, drama with music—the jazz noir dramatic musical film merged film noir style with jazz numbers in 1940s musical dramas. Like *Blues in the Night*, these films forged an unusual generic amalgam and reflected sociological changes related to the United States' entry into the war, such as an increased allowance for violence, greater latitude in screen content including more explicit sexual content, shifting representations of gender and ethnicity, new cinematic styles from the influx of influential refugee film talent, and technical filmmaking adaptations required by the economic constraints of the war effort.

CHAPTER FOUR

Smoky Melodies

Jazz Noir Musical Drama

As with the definitive noir musical, *Blues in the Night,* World War II contributed to the deep shadowy look in wartime 1940s film noir and musical noir by placing certain economic and other constraints on filmmaking. Blackouts; more restrictions on location shooting; and the rationing of film, lighting, electricity, and set materials all combined to force filmmakers to get more resourceful. Sets were recycled or cleverly disguised in shadow, fog, and rain. Cigarette smoke, mirrors, and skewed camera angles also helped change the look of an already-used set. As Robert Sklar explains, the claustrophobic mood of psychological noir thrillers derives from "material limitations of wartime filmmaking: restrictions on travel virtually eliminated location shooting where interior sets could serve, and stringent budgets . . . cut down on lighting." Yet the "gloom and constriction were not merely an accommodation to forced economies; their film-makers intended them that way."[1]

Besides restrictions in lighting, wartime filmmaking constraints discouraged huge sets, lavish costumes, crowds of extras, and big production numbers, which contributed to the development of film noir style and altered the ambiance of musicals. Modest black-and-white film noir with popular jazz numbers served to provide a cheaper alternative to expensive color musicals while showcasing sexy female pinup stars coveted by military personnel, as in *This Gun for Hire, To Have and Have Not, Phantom Lady, Christmas Holiday, The Big Sleep,* and *Gilda.*

Even color musicals were darker themed, such as Mitchell Leisen's *Lady in the Dark* (1944) and Charles Vidor's *Cover Girl* (1944), which fused brilliant Technicolor spectacle with a clash between romance and career at a time when Rosie the

Riveter was encouraging American women to go to work. Growing out of the war, noir musical melodramas showcased the dilemma of holding down a job that would come to interfere with romance. Like film noir, many musicals became more psychological, portraying a tormented antihero's (or heroine's) point-of-view, conflicted dreams, sexual fantasies, disturbed conscience, or repressed inner psyche. Musical film noir and a more cynical musical style led to some unlikely cinematic experimentation. Color musicals like *The Wizard of Oz, Lady in the Dark, Cover Girl, Meet Me in St. Louis* (1944), *The Pirate* (1948), and *The Red Shoes* (1948) featured an extravagant use of color and aesthetic—three-strip Technicolor, elaborate costumes, glamorous women, bright lighting, and visual design rarely seen during (or in the immediate aftermath of) the war to convey psychological dream states. Both *Lady in the Dark* and *Cover Girl* featured beautiful red-headed female singing and dancing stars with fabulous legs (à la famed World War II icon Betty Grable) cast as strong, independent women coming into conflict with the men in their lives over their careers.

Bigger changes than aesthetics were also afoot, however, and this chapter explores how noir musicals coalesced during and just after the war as gender, masculinity, and ethnicity shifted in the wake of the conflict. Roles for women evolved to reflect the social psyche of the time. Ethnic minority depictions also underwent change. By 1943, the federal government actively encouraged cinematic depictions of gender and ethnicity to aid the war effort. Hollywood responded both with "all-black" musicals, adapting Harold Arlen's *Cabin in the Sky* (the first film directed by Vincente Minnelli) and *Stormy Weather* with Lena Horne, and integrated multiethnic screen images in an effort to promote solidarity among Americans.[2] Lena Horne was the first black performer signed to a long-term contract by a major studio.[3]

Behind it all was jazz. We will see how jazz music was inextricably tied to these new themes and roles both onscreen and off.

JAZZ MUSICALS

Blues in the Night's atmospheric noir style established the trend for later musical film noir and dark noir musicals that fused jazz performances with melodrama. As the war drew to a close, critics noted the popularity of psychological crime pictures and the public's penchant for realistic graphic depictions of violence and a brooding, dark visual style (characteristic of film noir) growing out of the war. They took note of *Blues in the Night*'s verisimilitude, which Warner Bros. promoted as "a real story about real people!" Hollywood jumped on the noir bandwagon as the shadowy, stylish noir films seemed to appeal to the new war-hardened audiences. *Blues in the Night* was also influential in terms of *depicting* jazz in musical film noir—that is, celebrating jazz artistically as an improvisational musical art form (despite its humble working-class origins) rooted in African American culture and experience. This aspect recurs in noir musicals throughout the 1940s.

Orson Welles, for example, loved jazz. In noir styled *Citizen Kane* (though not a musical), a jazz trio croons "It Can't Be Love" in a melodramatic moment after Welles forces his wife to become an opera singer. Welles pursued his love for jazz in *The Story of Jazz*, a project he planned on the history of jazz at RKO while *Blues in the Night* was in production at Warner Bros. Based on the life of Louis Armstrong and the evolution of jazz, Welles brought Ellington in as a consultant and put him under contract to provide music for the film.[4] Billie Holiday auditioned for a role in the film but was apparently never signed. Screenwriter Elliot Paul worked with Welles on it. Even avant-garde animator Oskar Fischinger, who had worked on Disney's *Fantasia* (1940), was brought in. Casting for Welles' jazz project began in fall 1941. RKO shot test footage in color of jazz combos and considered shooting the project in Technicolor. However, World War II constraints made the expensive three-strip Technicolor process unaffordable and, with rationing of film stock and other production materials, perhaps impossible.

On October 26, 1941, jazz critic Leonard Feather reported that Welles' *Story of Jazz* film, "a general survey of swing music," was based "largely on the stories of Louis Armstrong and his musical mentor, the late Joe 'King' Oliver." Armstrong was identified as a "hot jazz wizard" whose twenty-five-year career marked the "birth of a younger generation" who "know the same music under a different name, as 'swing,'" thus identifying jazz with popular swing music as in *Blues in the Night*, but adding an historical dimension. Although in the "present densely populated sphere of popular music, Louis Armstrong's name is merely one of an ever-increasing number of attractions which to the man in the street may have no more importance than that of Glenn Miller, Artie Shaw, Cab Calloway, or Erskine Hawkins . . . the story of jazz runs strangely parallel with that of Armstrong himself born in New Orleans at the turn of the century, moving later to Chicago and finally making its spiritual home in New York and taking Europe by storm." Feather emphasized, "Armstrong is a creator of unparalleled originality, whose spontaneous inventions laid the foundations for the swing of 1941." His work "still bears the touch of genius which made him the irreplaceable hero of the very musicians who have received more votes than Louis in the swing magazine polls." Praising Welles, he said: "It will be a treat to see Louis in a part worthy of him, directed by a man with a sincere understanding of the subject."[5]

In late October, as Welles began filming dark gothic melodrama *The Magnificent Ambersons,* his *Story of Jazz* project was put on hold. As the war took precedence and at the request of RKO stockholder Nelson Rockefeller and U.S. Office Coordinator of Inter-American Affairs (OCIAA) chief John Hay Whitney, Welles was sent to South America to aid the war effort through the Good Neighbor policy with a production in Brazil, *It's All True,* in which he planned to include a segment called *The Story of Samba.* Soon after, a regime change at RKO meant big changes for Welles: the studio fired him and drastically cut his *Ambersons* film. *It's All True* remained uncompleted; his jazz film project was effectively dead.

Welles continued to champion jazz music and, in 1944, hosted the *Orson Welles Almanac* radio shows that showcased the Mercury All Star Jazz Combo. He bragged: "The men we've gathered in the studio to play jazz" are "among the finest instrumentalists on Earth. They are the great men of jazz." Describing jam sessions, Welles offered a brief history of jazz that he was not able to put forward in his tabled film: "The whole thing started in that good time, wide-open, all night Carnival City, which was New Orleans before the last war. Jazz then swam the riverboats and carried this new kind of music up to Chicago. From there it spread—all over the world and influenced all popular music and the greater part of what's called serious music. . . . Jazz is art for art's sake. . . . It's music musicians play for themselves, for their own satisfaction, the way they like it."[6] We can only imagine what kind of jazz musical film with noir inflections Welles might have created with Louis Armstrong, Duke Ellington, and Billie Holiday. It would likely have been extraordinary.

The Musician's Strike of 1942

After *Blues in the Night,* a musician's strike banned recordings from 1942–44. The strike affected jazz recordings and soundtracks. In July 1942, record companies, anticipating the strike that ultimately began on August 1, began to stockpile records. Recording companies began to switch to recording vocals in lieu of band numbers. The strike lasted through November 1944.[7] Noir musical performances presented jazz music on film without having to cut a record, which was prohibited by the strike. A leaner wartime economy eventually popularized vocalists over instrumental records and smaller jazz combos over big bands. Individual vocalists and small combos took the place of orchestras and big production numbers. Vocalists like Frank Sinatra and the Andrews Sisters became popular, and singers/musicians dubbed jazz behind-the-scenes. As the strike ended, famed jazz musicians performed a sultry noir-styled jam session in *Jammin' the Blues,* thus visually rendering its complex sounds as a musical noir art form, and Bacall sang with a vocal group in *The Big Sleep*. As a musical documentary short, *Jammin' the Blues* eloquently elevated jazz and noir style, rather than using shadows and music merely as a narrative device to subvert PCA censorship as in narrative noir crime feature films.

Syncopation

Several experimental musical films about jazz emerged in Hollywood during this time. The synopsis for *The Story of Jazz* project bears a striking resemblance to RKO's subsequent jazz musical drama *Syncopation* (1942), directed by William Dieterle (who later directed noir *Dark City*, 1950), and to *Birth of the Blues* (1941), the Bing Crosby film dedicated to the "musical pioneers of Memphis and New Orleans" who "favored the hot over the sweet—those early jazz men who took American music out of the rut and put it 'in the groove.' "[8] *Birth of the Blues* had faced censorship objections for its prostitution, murders, African American jazz dancing, and interracial mingling. Like *Blues in the Night*, *Syncopation* featured hip young jazz musicians passionate about their blues and backroom nightspots, tracing jazz from New Orleans roots to Chicago and on to New York.

However, unlike the self-destructive male antihero of *Blues in the Night* or its salacious temptress, *Syncopation*, in the new World War II work world of "Rosie the Riveters," featured Bonita Granville as a strong musical female protagonist. Originally titled *The Band Played On*, *Syncopation* was filmed from October 13 to December 5, 1941, just as *Blues in the Night* hit theaters. *Syncopation*'s finale was shot at Fox Movietone Studios in New York on February 23, 1942, in a jam session with Charlie Barnet, Benny Goodman, Harry James, Jack Jenny, Gene Krupa, Alvino Rey, and Joe Venuti. Ellington cornetist Rex Stewart plays a character modeled on Joe "King" Oliver in the film. Released May 22, 1942, *Syncopation* included jazz numbers "St. Louis Blues," "Jazz Me Blues," "You Made Me Love You," and "Sugarfoot Stomp." It cost $567,000 to make and overall lost $87,000 for RKO.[9] Just as jazz noir musical *Blues in the Night* was criticized for defying upbeat musical expectations, critics likewise panned *Syncopation* as "a lot of shoddy, stylized pretense . . . [that] dragged in a great many turgid montage sequences to suggest the sweep and surge of jazz music" and "youngsters in random, un-even moods." It was called a "studied attempt to build something picturesque and glowing around a trumpet's mournful wail." Critics noted that a "bang-up film about early jazz music is yet to be made."[10] As with the tremendous success of *Blues in the Night*'s songs, however, *Syncopation*'s jazz music was praised.

Jammin' the Blues

Jazz featured prominently in short musical performance films, which predated music videos. Such "musical shorts" include *Black and Tan* (1929, with Ellington), *Rhapsody in Black and Blue* (1932, with Armstrong), *Symphony in Black* (1935, including Ellington's "Reminiscing in Tempo"), *C Jam Blues* (1942, with Ellington), *Blues in the Night* (1942, with Calloway), *Hong Kong Blues* (1943, with Carmichael), and *Jammin' the Blues* (1944). In 1944, award-winning photographer Gjon Mili created art cinema in his incomparable jazz short produced for Warner Bros.' *Melody Masters* series. *Jammin' the Blues* was based on his *Life* magazine photo-essay on jazz musicians. Mili had never directed a motion picture before and used noir cinematographer Robert Burks, who later shot Alfred Hitchcock's *Rear Window* (1954), *Vertigo* (1958), and *North by Northwest* (1959). The technical director was Norman Granz, who was producing the first Jazz at the Philharmonic series in Los Angeles. *Jammin' the Blues* was a stylish documentary look at an actual jam session with a legendary array of musicians: Lester Young (just drafted) on tenor sax, Red Callender on bass, Harry Edison on trumpet, Marlow Morris on piano, Joe Jones on drums, Sidney Catlett on drums, John Simmons on bass, Barney Kessel on guitar, and Illinois Jacquet on tenor sax. It uniquely captured jazz improvisation with its noir-style chiaroscuro photography. The film opens with a fluid shot of Young's hat moving away to reveal musicians in shadow and silhouette sitting down to create incredible jazz. As Young begins to play, atmospheric low-key lighting, wafting tendrils of cigarette smoke, silhouetted dancers, and shrouded interiors simulate a musical noir after-hours club. Marie Bryant sings a nuanced bluesy Depression-era number "On the Sunny Side of the Street" in the dark, ironically suggesting a sunnier outdoor setting than the blackouts so familiar during World War II. She then pairs up with dancer Archie Savage to do the jitterbug in artfully stylized silhouette.

Guitarist Kessel, the only white performer, was seated in the shadows of this apparently all-black jazz film. His hands were stained with berry juice to shade his skin for close-ups. During the filming, Bette Davis and Humphrey Bogart reportedly dropped by the set to observe what was rumored to be something impressive artistically and musically hip happening at Warner Bros. (A musician recalled Bogart remarking to him shortly after the end of the fabled musicians strike, "Are you getting paid good money for this? If you aren't, you should strike!") The avant-garde artistic short *Jammin' the Blues* was screened for war workers in November 1944 at the same time as Billy Wilder's noir *Double Indemnity* and the musical noir *To Have and Have Not* premiered.

Lester Young plays the sax in an atmospheric "jazz noir"–styled jam session in *Jammin'* *the Blues*. Warner Bros., 1944

While the jazz short did not get the same attention that a feature film would in industry trade papers, *Motion Picture Herald* praised *Jammin' the Blues* for Mili's innovative style, which "recorded skillfully" the "atmosphere" of a "jam session" by a "number of photographic devices" that are "ingeniously conceived and executed." It continued, "The technique makes use of some of the subtler tricks of lighting effects and the silhouetted movements of the dancers against a white drop are thoroughly effective. Many of the shots give the impression of stills, some achieve unusual depth, breaking into sudden animation, and the third dimension, while not attained, is approached closely. . . . Mili and Norman Granz, technical director, have succeeded in an admirable piece of experimentation with the possibilities of the camera."[11] The *Los Angeles Times* lamented "great moments that could have been preserved" if Hollywood made more films like *Jammin' the Blues*, the "first art film ever devoted to jazz."[12] Six years later, Granz and Mili reprised *Jammin' the Blues* in the visually brighter unreleased short *Improvisation* with Charlie Parker, Coleman Hawkins, Young, Ella Fitzgerald, Edison,

Ray Brown, Hank Jones, and Buddy Rich, this time in a racially integrated jazz combo.

NOIR MUSICALS AND JAZZ FILM NOIR WITH MUSICAL NUMBERS: CHANGING THEMES

The distinctive milieu of *Blues in the Night* influenced not only jazz musicals such as *Syncopation* and *Jammin' the Blues*, but also lived on in the iconic smoky night-club atmosphere of later "jazz film noir" featuring musical performance numbers, as in *To Have and Have Not, Phantom Lady, Gilda, Black Angel, The Man I Love, New Orleans,* and *Road House,* and even contributed to a brooding vein of color musicals with dark undertones, as in *Lady in the Dark* and *Cover Girl.* The war's violence helped ease film censorship, and its changing socioeconomic conditions, with women working and men serving abroad, led to the desire for different narratives, including those that expanded roles for women. A growing number of femme fatale screen divas during World War II paralleled the increasing autonomy of women working in factories to support the military as well as filling other manpower shortages including writers, editors, and producers. Female talent included *Big Sleep* writer Leigh Brackett, *Mildred Pierce* writer Catherine Turney, and writer-producers, such as *Phantom Lady*'s Joan Harrison (who coscripted Alfred Hitchcock's *Rebecca* and *Suspicion*) and *Gilda*'s Virginia Van Upp, who wrote *Cover Girl* then rose to studio production executive. The depiction of strong, bold women in wartime films, including musicals and noir pictures, represented this cultural shift in traditional gender roles over the course of the war.

The postwar period would lead to even more changes. Women characters evolved from Rosie the Riveter tough broads and executives joining the wartime workforce to shady ladies, pinups, and femmes fatales. But, after the war ended and war veterans returned from abroad, women were expected to curb their independence, retire to the household and become once again the sweet, loving helpmate.

Jazz becomes the soundtrack for the actions of many independent women in noir films. Performing jazz numbers, moreover, seems to suggest that the performer is sexualized and often also dangerous. *Dead Reckoning*'s smoky-voiced blonde femme Lizbeth Scott sings "Either It's Love or It Isn't" and dances romantically with Bogart, then tries to knock him off in the "slug 'em-love 'em and leave 'em" noir picture that "makes with the music." Ida Lupino's hard-boiled jazz chanteuse belts the blues in *The Man I Love* and *Road House. This Gun for Hire*'s voluptuous blonde beauty Veronica Lake, known for her "peek-a-boo" hairstyle covering part of her face, alternately concealing and revealing it, is a complex,

Musical femme Lizbeth Scott sings and dances with Humphrey Bogart before trying to gun him down in *Dead Reckoning*. Columbia, 1947

multifaceted female who is simultaneously a compassionate girlfriend, night-club performer, and undercover secret agent. Bacall sings in a bar in *To Have and Have Not* and in gambler Eddie Mars' casino in *The Big Sleep*. Ella Raines' working detective masquerades as a "hep kitten" hanging out with jazz musicians in a backroom jam session in *Phantom Lady*. Deanna Durbin plays a dancehall jazz singer/prostitute in *Christmas Holiday*. Hayworth's *Gilda* sings, dances, and exudes sex in smoky bars. *Detour*'s piano player antihero is enthralled with an ambitious blonde singer who seeks stardom in Hollywood, leaving the dive where they played as he becomes entangled with a femme fatale.

Sex and Ethnicity in Musical Noir
The war brought changes that undermined censorship and complicated such issues as violence, sex, and ethnicity. Music stood in for what could not be clearly stated. Wartime brought new stronger images of working women and commodified them as pinups.[13] Its economic restrictions brought necessary new

aesthetic styles that were leaner and darker. It brought in new talent as Jewish filmmakers and others fled the Nazis. While many classical musicals and melodramas featured jazz performance numbers, jazz was also an intrinsic part of film noir. Filmmakers used singing and dancing in a shrouded smoky jazz or blues nightclub setting to stand in for a whole array of otherwise censorable sex (including prostitution, adultery, and interracial affairs), gambling, drug use, and illegal activity that were prohibited by Hollywood's Production Code. Film noir's iconic milieu of smoke, shadow, sultry femme songstresses, and musicians performing jazz in dark nightspots presented a mysterious, alluring world—suggesting sex, danger, and illicit deeds in an exciting, hard-boiled or exotic setting. Its atmospheric ambiance played havoc with the Code. Some films were set overseas to evade wartime censorship of gangsters or a criminal home front, as in *Casablanca, To Have and Have Not*, and *Gilda*. Yet ironically, greater misogynistic violence was permitted as a result of the war. PCA censors haggled over suggestive music and dancing in noir films, scrutinized songs, and set limits on how much flesh costumes could reveal. Noir's after-hours setting was evocative. In *The Big Sleep* Bogart finds Bacall singing jazz in a hoodlum's speakeasy and slaps drugged-up, disheveled Carmen (Martha Vickers) sitting "higher than a kite" in a tight, sexy satin dress posing for a late-night photo—in a house with exotic décor, a hidden camera, and a "dead man laying at [her] feet."

Ethnic depictions took some new directions as enemies were made, allies were courted, and émigrés aided the war effort. Washington's Good Neighbor policy made an ally of Latin America to support morale. Wartime noir films, screened for Allies and troops in Europe and the Pacific, often included ethnic spaces with Latin American, European, or Asian-Pacific settings, characters, and iconography, and featured African-American jazz or ethnic clubs to appeal to minorities and boost overseas morale. In the aftermath of the war, some of the changes stuck and others did an about-face as women were expected to return home; men were suffering trauma; and émigrés, minorities, and others were suspected of communist sympathies and banned from filmmaking.[14] New technology and bigger budgets brought a change in visual and musical possibilities as well.

Noir musicals from 1942 through the end of the 1940s exemplified these themes. *Lady in the Dark, Cover Girl, To Have and Have Not, Phantom Lady, Lured, Christmas Holiday, Gilda, Black Angel, The Man I Love, New Orleans, Casbah*, and *Road House* are each very much movies of their time.

Lady in the Dark

Paramount's extravagant color musical *Lady in the Dark*, directed by Mitchell Leisen, illustrates the darkening psychological mood, shift in gender roles, and romantic distress of the period. Shot from December 1942 to March 1943, it was initially stockpiled like many wartime films noir because it didn't focus on the war, and was finally released in February 1944. Wartime working woman Ginger Rogers plays high-powered fashion magazine editor, Liza, in masculine suits. She lives out her Freudian sexual fantasies and childhood psychic trauma in fantastic musical numbers composed by Kurt Weill with lyrics penned by Ira Gershwin. In her professional career, Liza is not pursuing a musical art form, or even showbiz fame and stardom, as in so many other noir musical movies that were about the Hollywood backstage. Instead, she is already established securely in her career and is trying to sort out how her romantic life collides with it. She undergoes psychoanalysis to try to come to terms with the mistreatment she suffered as a child by an egomaniacal mother. Rogers' psychologically tormented heroine is presented as almost masculine in her devotion to her career but discovers her sexuality through her musical dreams and ultimately finds love.

Lady in the Dark premiered in New York on George Washington's birthday, and patriotic colors figured prominently in publicity photos. In true pinup style, Rogers wears a gown with a plunge neckline and a glittering copper-scarlet split skirt lined in mink, revealing the dancing star's spectacular legs with red high-heeled ankle-strap pumps.[15] The film received rave reviews that praised its "dream worlds" and psychic "analysis" that are "magnificently embodied." "Not every movie delight possesses the substance to make you return home and ponder your own submerged childhood."

The *New York Daily News* exclaimed: "This Technicolor musical film . . . is the most lavish and gorgeous color film made by Paramount Pictures since the war began." Given tremendous wartime rationing of materials and film stock, the *New York Post* recognized *Lady in the Dark*'s opulent appeal, asserting that it "dazzles": "Here is a picture in which an original approach vies with intrinsic beauty for your attention." The *New York Sun* called *Lady in the Dark* a "grand show" with "psychoanalysis simplified dramatically," a "lavish display of gowns and costumes (including that mink dinner suit)." The *Post* observed, "We will not see its like again during the war while materials and money are limited. Nor will more varied entertainments be frequent after the war either." The *Los Angeles Examiner* noted that *Lady in the Dark* was exceptional in "mingling Freud and Walt Disney":

"The spectacle, the color, the unusual theme add up to being the real stars of *Lady in the Dark*."[16] Another noir musical stylishly followed suit.

Cover Girl

Born Károly Vidor in Budapest, Jewish émigré Charles Vidor directed *Cover Girl*, a star-is-born Technicolor musical with dark undertones. Virginia Van Upp, who scripted Fritz Lang's 1938 gangster film *You and Me* (with songs by Kurt Weill) and produced Vidor's musical noir *Gilda*, wrote the script, which also explored expanding gender roles and psychological distress at a fashion magazine like *Lady in the Dark*, which came out about the same time. In depicting a successful working woman with pinup appeal, it was aimed at both a female domestic audience and overseas servicemen.

The narrative focuses on the talented dancer Rusty (Rita Hayworth), who performs in boyfriend Danny's (Gene Kelly) Brooklyn jazz club, is discovered, and becomes a famous magazine cover girl and eventually a Ziegfeld Follies star. Her man is threatened by her career success and becomes insanely jealous. Like *Ziegfeld Girl*, *Blues in the Night*, and *Lady in the Dark*, *Cover Girl* reveals success colliding with private life. On loan from MGM, Hollywood newcomer Kelly, known as antihero *Pal Joey* onstage, gained recognition for the "Alter Ego" dance number he choreographed (with Stanley Donen) in which his tormented antihero shatters his mirror-image reflection in a window on a deserted street after Rusty leaves his club for fame on Broadway. Kelly "decides to let his light of love pursue stardom on Broadway," then "argues and dances with his animate conscience on a Brooklyn sidewalk." The *New York World-Telegram* praised the "trick and slick photography" of Kelly "dancing with himself . . . in and around a night club, as it ever does in musicals of this kind."

Critics noted the color film was reminiscent of prewar films, yet there was a noir dark side to the distress about womens' wartime careers. The *New York Daily News* observed, "Columbia's elaborate, Technicolor" musical production of *Cover Girl*, comparing Hayworth to Rogers and Grable. Color musicals showcase their red hair in a way that black and white never could. "Rita Hayworth takes to Technicolor like a bathing beauty sticks to dry land and her gorgeous auburn hair gives her a perfect right to be called Rusty." Critics also compared the noirish romance to *Lady in the Dark*, which opened a month earlier. *Cover Girl*'s "essential loyalties" "strain opulently" between "uncompromising alternatives of whether the best-looking redhead in the world (Rita Hayworth) should let herself be photographed for a magazine cover or remain just a bloom growing in Brooklyn, at

Gene Kelly suffers distress and confronts his alter ego when dancer-girlfriend Rita
Hayworth gains *Cover Girl* fame. Columbia, 1944

Danny McGuire's cabaret. As Danny (Gene Kelly) laments after Rita has taken
the first step over the bridge in the direction of fame."[17]

    Cover Girl was filmed at Columbia from July to November 1943 and released
in late March 1944. Ads showed Hayworth's gown blowing up to reveal her legs
as she embraced Kelly above a flaming scarlet title (with sunburst yellow and sea
green background). Taglines heralded: *"The most brilliant musical of our time!"*
and *"The most memorable musical of 1944!"*[18] *New York Herald Tribune* raved that

Cover Girl "boasts some extremely catchy song numbers" filmed in "superb Technicolor," the "stage loses" and "the movies win so far as Kelly is concerned." *Cover Girl* was nominated for Best Color Art Direction, Cinematography, and Song ("Long Ago and Far Away") at the Academy Awards. It won Best Score.

In September 1943, a real-life Hollywood conflict between love and career arose as Orson Welles whisked beautiful Rita Hayworth off the Columbia lot and married her. The talented young couple mirrored the fictional couple in *Cover Girl.* By October—as Hayworth filmed in Hollywood—Welles, was desolate when he had to give a Free World speech in New York. "I knew it would be lonely—but this is even lonelier than I let myself fear," he wrote to his wife. "I'm too blue for anything." Evoking a noir movie set, he writes, "This is going to be my last saloon 'till you get here. 3:30 (a.m.) (coffee kicking in) The late traffic yawns in the echoing streets below. The wind whistles. The rain drips. . . . Look I can't even write! Sweet one—I can't live without—you!"[19] (Hayworth cherished Welles' love letters long after their marriage ended less than four years later, keeping them in her traveling makeup case.)

As wartime shifted to postwar, cultural tensions and romantic conflicts were articulated in noir musicals. Musical noir got darker by the war's end as Hayworth surpassed Grable in popularity after she moved from the color musical *Cover Girl* to the black-and-white musical film noir *Gilda* in 1946. The brooding tenor of noir musical films grew out of an evolving noir climate. Once film noir exploded in 1944, from 1944 to 1948 a series of black-and-white musical noir dramas emerged that incorporated elements of the musical into jazz film noir with musical performances.

To Have and Have Not

Producer/director Howard Hawks (and his former-model wife Slim) discovered *Harper's Bazaar* cover girl Betty Bacall (born Betty Joan Perske) and turned her into sexy star Lauren "The Look" Bacall, the husky-voiced jazz-singing siren in the 1944 musical film noir *To Have and Have Not.* Like David O. Selznick, Hawks developed and refined new feminine star talent, then sold his actresses' contracts to various Hollywood studios for profit. Hawks sold Ella Raines to Universal for the jazz noir film *Phantom Lady,* for instance. Likewise, he cast Bacall in the musical noir *To Have and Have Not* and sold her to Warner Bros. after its success. Hawks modeled Bacall's image on musical diva Marlene Dietrich, collaborating with writer Jules Furthman, who worked on Dietrich's *Morocco* (1930), *Blonde Venus* (1932), and *Shanghai Express* (1932).

To Have and Have Not featured ample noir elements. It was based on Ernest

Hemingway's story about hard-bitten fishing captain Harry Morgan who lives with prostitute Marie and smuggles contraband between Cuba and Key West. Multiple censorship agencies influenced the film production, however, and the screenplay diverged significantly from the book. PCA censors objected to its prostitution, ethnic slurs, adultery, smuggling, rum-running, gangsters, and Cuban revolutionaries. Washington's U.S. Office Coordinator of Inter-American Affairs (OCIAA) was concerned about the story's Cuba setting regarding Cuban-American relations, so screenwriter William Faulkner changed it to Martinique (after the fall of France to the Nazis in 1940) to satisfy the Good Neighbor policy.[20] Since gangsters, immigrants, revolutionaries, and "unsavory" characters were not approved, villains became French Nazi supporters. Like in *Casablanca*, Bogart is a hard-boiled loner-turned-reluctant patriot who aids the Resistance. Bogart's Harry (a.k.a. Steve) and Bacall's Slim are not married. Rather than working as a prostitute, she sings the blues and dances alluringly while Hoagy Carmichael plays piano in a jazz bar.

Bacall's bold debut in *To Have and Have Not* sizzled with sex appeal as she sang with Carmichael and a jazz band opposite Bogart. Just as performing song and dance numbers represented romantic courtship in escapist musicals, in musical noir, racy jazz performances by sultry performing women are suggestive of sex and other taboos. As Bacall shimmies up to Bogart in her sexy costume, she tells him as he leaves to meet another woman, "Give her my love." Bogart replies: "I'd give her my own if she had that on!" Channeling her sex appeal, Bacall delivered this now famous innuendo-laden line to her costar Bogart: "You know how to whistle, don't you, Steve? You just put your lips together and blow." She tells Carmichael: "Don't make it sappy," as he plays a blues number, "I don't feel that way." He replies: "You don't look that way."

While the PCA often censored, or "whitewashed" screen ethnicity, multiethnic interracial depictions were able to comingle in musical sequences. Bacall sings the blues and does her own vocals with Carmichael on piano and a jazz combo in "Am I Blue" and "How Little We Know" (written by Carmichael and Mercer). A jazz band plays Carmichael-Mercer's "The Rhumba Jumps." Carmichael's "Hong Kong Blues" describes a "very unfortunate colored man" who gets "arrested down in old Hong Kong" with "twenty years privilege taken away from him when he kicked old Buddha's gong." The PCA sanitized: "Won't somebody believe I've a yen to see that Bay again. Every time I try to leave, Sweet opium won't let me fly away." Carmichael sings an overseas soldier's lament: "I need someone to love me, I need somebody to carry me home to San Francisco, and bury my body there."

Bogart with his kind of woman! Lauren Bacall with Hoagy Carmichael in *To Have and Have Not*: "Don't make it sappy." Warner Bros., 1944

To Have and Have Not is a musical noir that subverts the ideals of glamour and fame in classical musicals. Although she makes a big splash with Bogart, Carmichael, and the masculine crowd at the club, "Slim" Marie is not rich or famous or successful; rather she is so strapped for cash that she is trapped on the island . . . avoiding giving sexual favors for a living, or so she implies to Bogart in having "just enough to say 'no' if I feel like it." As she cases the joint to find a sucker to dance with, light her cigarette, and rob, Bogart (robbed broke by Nazi thugs) asks: "Picked him out yet?" Bacall: "You don't mind do you?" Bogart: "You're thirsty, go ahead. If I get tired of waiting, I'll be back at that hotel."

Critics called Bacall an "arresting personality," "slumberous of eye and softly reedy, she acts in the quiet way of catnip and sings a song from deep down in her throat." *Variety* noted her onscreen combustion: "She can slink, brother, and no fooling!" Bogart eloped with Bacall while filming *The Big Sleep*. Like a real-life noir star-is-born story, Hawks was not amused when Bogart married his discovery and star property.

Ads for jazz noir films such as *To Have and Have Not* featured a "color noir" aesthetic in black, white, and red. Posters for *To Have and Have Not* advertised (in bright scarlet), "Bogart . . . with his kind of woman in a powerful adaptation of Ernest Hemingway's most daring man-woman story!" above Bogart and Bacall in a hot embrace (with *The Look's* red lips). Ads also promoted how its "mood" "harmonized" "smoldering sex" and "violent intrigue" in a "smoke hazed cabaret" "reminiscent" of *Casablanca*.[21]

Phantom Lady *and* Lured

Émigré filmmakers were significant in bringing with them from Europe a noir wartime vision. In Germany, UFA-alumnus Robert Siodmak worked for *The Cabinet of Dr. Caligari* producer Erich Pommer and collaborated with brother Curt and roommate Billy Wilder on *Menschen am Sonntag* (*People on Sunday*, 1929). With the rise of the Nazis, the Jewish Siodmak moved first to France and then Hollywood, returning to Europe after the war. Siodmak directed French noir musical prelude *Pièges* (1939, a.k.a. *Personal Column*). *Pièges* influenced his noir musical *Phantom Lady*, as both have many similar plot and character elements as well as jazz bands.[22] African American "female Louis Armstrong" Valaida Snow sings "My Sweetheart" and plays trumpet in it. But noirs *Phantom Lady, Gilda, Black Angel*, and *Lured* were darker.

Siodmak's *Pièges* was stylishly adapted by German émigré director Douglas Sirk as the noir mystery *Lured* (1947, *Personal Column* in the UK). *Lured's* story of a taxidancer-detective who snares a serial killer was a melodramatic variation on gothic thrillers. With an expressionistic black-and-white mise-en-scène of dim streetlamps, glistening cobblestones, and fog-shrouded alleys, it evoked George Cukor's 1944 *Gaslight*. Like Erich von Stroheim's eccentric fashion designer in *Pièges*, dark campy humor infuses Lucille Ball, George Sanders, and Boris Karloff's performances. Bluesy strains of jazz ("You Stole My Peace of Mind") waft from a café.

Siodmak intensified the milieu of *Pièges* in *Phantom Lady*, an atmospheric jazz noir collaboration with British émigré producer Joan Harrison. Amid shadow and rain-soaked streets, undercover "hep kitten" Kansas (Ella Raines) mingles with "hep cat" drummer Cliff (Elisha Cook Jr.) to solve a murder and clear her boss. Jazz symbolically presents sexual or illicit content in many jazz noir films to challenge the Code. PCA censors implied that jazz musicians were a morally loose, dangerous crowd, and Breen warned that they might be seen as "dope addicts." He banned drugs, complained about *Phantom Lady's* excessive drinking, sex, suggestive dancing, and divorce and required PCA approval of all songs, costumes, and the "jive sequence," but an orgiastic drum solo conveyed ample sexual innuendo.[23] Raines in a tight black satin dress, fishnet stockings, and sti-

Drummer Elisha Cook Jr. plays a suggestive jazz-cellar jam session in *Phantom Lady*. Universal, 1944

lettos comes on to Cook in a surreal jazz montage. She is shot from below to show her face, breasts, and legs in an angle denoting sexual power and independence. *Phantom Lady*'s jam session functions as a gateway to a corrupt urban underworld of lies, pay-offs, betrayal, and murder. Publicity for *Phantom Lady* featured Raines being roughed up by jazz drummer Cook.[24] Cook is strangled by wealthy psychotic killer Franchot Tone who, like his playboy in *Dancing Lady*, is clearly not a fan of jazz or "show people." *Phantom Lady* also targeted a Latin American audience as Carmen Miranda's sister, Brazilian singing star Aurora, performs musical numbers in it.

Christmas Holiday

Siodmak's *Christmas Holiday* (1944), produced by Felix Jackson, was based on W. Somerset Maugham's 1939 novel, which the PCA rejected for filming as a "story of gross sexual irregularities." It was adapted in 1943 by Herman Mankiewicz (who collaborated with Welles on *Citizen Kane*). Maugham's novel centered on an

Reporter-pimp Richard Whorf, fugitive-murderer Gene Kelly, singer-prostitute Deanna Durbin cast against "type" in *Christmas Holiday*. Universal, 1944

English college student on Christmas holiday in Paris who meets Russian émigré Sonya, who prostitutes herself for her insane lover. In 1943, the Nazis were occupying Paris, so Mankiewicz eliminated the original story's sex and politics from his screenplay. He set the story in wartime America, where Lieutenant Charles Mason (Dean Harens) departs on Christmas Eve leave for San Francisco to get married. Mason's fiancé marries another guy, and a storm diverts his plane to New Orleans. Devastated, Charles befriends alcoholic reporter Simon Fenimore (*Blues in the Night*'s Richard Whorf) who takes him to a dive brothel run by Valerie De Merode (*The Roaring Twenties*' Gladys George). He meets hostess/jazz singer Jackie Lamont (Deanna Durbin) a.k.a. Abigail, who is married to convicted murderer Robert Manette (Gene Kelly). Challenging the Code censorship, musical stars Durbin and Kelly are both cast against "type" as a singing prostitute and sociopathic criminal in fine noir style.

The PCA haggled over "excessive drinking" by reporter Simon and "hostesses," who are clearly prostitutes in Mankiewicz's screenplay. Deviating from her perky upbeat operetta persona, Durbin sings a downbeat bluesy jazz rendition of Frank Loesser's torch song, "Spring Will Be a Little Late This Year" and Irving Berlin's "Always." In conforming to—yet pushing boundaries to subvert—PCA regulatory strictures, *Christmas Holiday*'s jazz club/dance hall clearly suggested a brothel and Durbin a prostitute. Her attendance at mass and repentance of sins, however, appeased the PCA. Shot from late November 1943 through early March 1944, *Christmas Holiday* went into production on the heels of Charles Vidor's collaboration with Van Upp on the noir musical *Cover Girl*, Siodmak's collaboration with

Harrison on jazz noir *Phantom Lady*, and Wilder's collaboration with author Raymond Chandler on influential noir *Double Indemnity*. Musical noir *Christmas Holiday* was Oscar nominated for best music score by Hans J. Salter. Released in late June 1944, by July it grossed over $2 million, more than any other Durbin picture.[25]

Gilda

Musical films noir *Lured*, *Phantom Lady*, *Christmas Holiday*, *Mildred Pierce*, and *Gilda* employ jazz performance with the gender conventions of "roman noir" gothic melodrama—such as Hitchcock's *Rebecca*, *Suspicion*, *Spellbound*, and *Notorious*—that depict "working" redeemers who are strong, independent, and proactive yet exploited or marginalized by men. Like *Lady in the Dark* and *Cover Girl*, *Gilda* embodies psychosexual fantasy nightmares that project *Blues in the Night's* masculine trauma into female-centered noir melodramas. *Gilda* combined several trends that were coalescing at war's end.

Gilda reteamed Hayworth with the writer (now producer Virginia Van Upp) and director (Charles Vidor) of *Cover Girl*. In a darker reimagining of *Cover Girl*, *Gilda's* infamous musical striptease and romantic fireworks coincided with Hayworth's glamorous rise to "love goddess" pinup stardom and off-screen marriage to Welles. In the film, Gilda marries possessive criminal Ballin (George Macready) who owns a gambling casino. She taunts and tantalizes ex-lover Johnny (Glenn Ford, resembling a young Welles) who manages her husband's illegal business affairs (and enjoys male bonding camaraderie with him). She eventually marries Johnny after the kingpin fakes suicide to avoid murder, espionage, and antitrust charges. Reimagining a *Casablanca* love triangle, Van Upp wanted Bogart as Gilda's lover. Bogart declined the role, but Ford had recently returned from four years of military service. *Gilda* echoed the distress of war romances and separation. Like *Casablanca's* antihero, Johnny finds his lover married to another man in his absence and lives in an office above a casino bar. Johnny's relationship with Ballin is disrupted by a woman displacing them while Latin American detectives pursue his mysterious employer. Like *Lady in the Dark*, *The Big Sleep*, *Lured*, *The Red Shoes*, and *The Big Combo*, *Gilda* found creative ways to suggest homosexuality despite PCA censorship, as in Ballin's private jokes with Johnny about his phallic "little friend" swordstick. When learning Ballin has suddenly eloped, Johnny resentfully complains, "I thought we agreed that women and gambling don't mix." Sexual tension in *Gilda's* love triangles suggests men reluctantly leaving combat buddies overseas to return home to their wives/lovers.

Censors rejected *Gilda* as a wartime American gangster film in 1944; the story

Musical femme Rita Hayworth dances, sings the blues, tosses her hair, peels off her gloves, and performs "Put the Blame on Mame" striptease in *Gilda*. Columbia, 1946

was eventually set in Buenos Aires. Like *To Have and Have Not* and *Phantom Lady*, *Gilda* sought to appeal to a Latin American audience. Breen objected to its "sex suggestiveness" and adulterous affairs lacking compensating moral values. Hayworth's musical numbers "Put the Blame on Mame" and "Amado Mio" were scrutinized by the PCA.[26] Hayworth's racy striptease, like *Phantom Lady*'s jazz session, pushed the envelope in trying to outwit censors. Gilda's singing, dancing, and demeanor connote sex, openly and outrageously articulated. She engages in foreplay, proclaiming: "I'm a dancer." She fluidly moves across the dance floor in a tight embrace with her ex-lover. Gilda tells Johnny: "No one can dance like you . . . it's like being a part of you . . . I can help you get in practice." While Breen was concerned with the lyrics in "Amado Mio" (like drinking/drugs in *Phantom Lady*'s "jive sequence"), salacious innuendo was instead conveyed in the way Hayworth *performed* "Put the Blame on Mame," pulsating her hips, bending, throwing up her hands, then wildly tossing her hair and peeling off her gloves. Hayworth smoldered like smoky-voiced Bacall in *To Have and Have Not*. Van Upp targeted servicemen, returning home in 1946, who voted Rita top pinup star in 1945. In *Gilda*'s glove-peeling blues number, she encourages men to rip off her clothes and unzip her gown, then is unceremoniously yanked off-stage smacked around by misogynistic beau Johnny and humiliated in front of her fans. As in *Phantom Lady*, the fact that Gilda is "performing," that is, pretending to be a loose woman in a suggestive musical club setting while not really being a prostitute, allowed the film to work around the censors—it was "all an act," as Detective Obregon (Joseph Calleia) explains in the film.

Gilda exposed societal tensions and changing sexual roles at the end of the war with scathing cynicism and sadism highlighting dissentions about love, career, pleasure, and violence in misogynistic gender relations as combat-hardened veterans returned home. As heightened brutality in increasingly graphic combat newsreels enabled the censors to accept more screen violence, film noir was able to portray misogynistic violence directed against alluring femme fatale heroines in *Gilda*, *Phantom Lady*, *To Have and Have Not*, *The Big Sleep*, and *Scarlet Street*. Musical noir films amplified the conflict between love/private life and career/public life as screen misogyny endeavored to contain "unsavory" female sexuality and womens' independence in love or career. Though not stated in words, Johnny's slap silences his wife Gilda from publicly declaring that she's a prostitute. Like *To Have and Have Not* and *The Big Sleep*, *Gilda* created a jazz noir ambiance of sexual innuendo.

Gilda premiered in March 1946, immortalizing Hayworth as a sex goddess, inspiring atomic scientists at Bikini Atoll to name their atomic bomb "Gilda." *Gilda* tapped into nuclear trauma as tremendous cultural anxiety about nuclear destruction and fears of the atomic bomb arose in the aftermath of the war and Hiroshima. Ads heralded her star-is-born fame: "*Rita Hayworth a success story . . . who made something of an atomic impression on all the GI's.*"

Publicity for *Gilda* emphasized provocative sexual relations. In black, white, and red posters the star is backlit with her hair aflame. She wears a skintight strapless satin gown and drags a mink on the floor while holding a smoldering cigarette. Taglines blared: "There *never* was a woman like *Gilda!*" Ads proclaimed:

"There NEVER was a woman like *Gilda!*" Columbia, 1946

"*Gilda* used men the way other women use makeup!" They also showed her on the floor pleading: "Please let me go. I can't stand it any more," as Johnny looms above her. *Gilda* projects returning GIs' paranoia about infidelity as jealous lover Johnny is filled with hate when Gilda feigns "sordid" relations with other men. Ads promoted Johnny getting revenge by imprisoning her at home and denying her sexual fulfillment until she escapes and becomes a cafe singer. Performing music liberates her until Johnny slaps her. Like combat sparring, in addition to hyping erotic sexuality, publicity androgynously suggested "glamour girl" Rita don masculine boxing gloves and learn the "art of fisticuffs" because of "indignities" "suffered" getting "slapped around" in "stinging blows to the face lustily administered" by Ford, promoting sexual violence.[27] Women were beaten back into the home. Like the performing heroines in *Cover Girl* and *To Have and Have Not,* Gilda curtails her career of singing, dancing, and guitar strumming and tames her "unruly" sexual independence and reunites with Johnny. Like a returning vet fantasy, Johnny flies off to the U.S. with his sexy love goddess wife—once it's clear she's not a prostitute.

Hayworth's Latina ethnicity (she was born Margarita Cansino) was ironically "whitewashed" in the Latin American setting of *Gilda.* Studios dyed her naturally dark brunette hair a fairer red (like Grable and Rogers). Hayworth's image became less and less Hispanic. After *Gilda,* director-costar-former husband Welles radically transformed her image by making her a platinum blonde with an extremely short androgynous style for *The Lady from Shanghai,* in which she sings and speaks fluent Chinese (switching between Mandarin and Cantonese).

Paradoxically, Van Upp's increased power, involvement, and authority as a female studio executive from 1945 to 1947 contributed to Hayworth's strong transgressive diva persona and mirrored her own and Hayworth's career dilemmas. Van Upp rose to studio executive in charge of production at Columbia (under Harry Cohn) as the industry faced a wartime labor shortage. Wartime noir films targeted independent home-front women, many working masculine jobs in booming defense industries, and servicemen overseas. As veterans (many suffering posttraumatic stress from combat) returned seeking civilian employment, women lost their jobs. As Hayworth's marriage to Welles deteriorated while she was playing estranged married femme *Gilda,* she moved in with Van Upp, who gave up producing at Columbia when her spouse returned from the war—before getting a divorce.[28]

Black Angel

Black Angel was British émigré director/coproducer Roy William Neill's last film before his death just months after its August 1946 release. It was based on Cornell Woolrich's 1943 novel. The PCA initially rejected the story for its adultery, prostitution, violence, nudity, and the graphic depiction of an epileptic seizure. *Black Angel* was a fascinating amalgam of many musical noir crime film elements. The film wastes no time killing off its working femme fatale singer in the very beginning: she's murdered as her record "Heartbreak" plays. Like *Blues in the Night's* self-destructive musician, the dead singer's washed-up composer husband Martin (Dan Duryea) suffers from psychological instability. Elaborate nightmare montages suggest that he suffers from postwar trauma. He ends up in an asylum as do characters in *Blues in the Night* and *A Star Is Born.* Martin hits the

Like Ford when Hayworth clings to his feet in *Gilda*, musician "*DURYEA!* . . . that fascinating tough-guy of *Scarlet Street!*" towers over singer June Vincent, as Peter Lorre pulls a gun. Duryea hits the bottle in alcoholic torment in *Black Angel*. Universal, 1946

bottle in anguish like Bogart in *Casablanca*. As in Raymond Chandler's original story for *The Blue Dahlia*, Duryea's antihero turns out to be a psychopath who killed his wife without realizing it.

Publicity also mimicked previous ad campaigns. Recalling Hayworth clinging to Ford's feet in *Gilda*, Universal promoted *Black Angel* with musician Duryea towering over singer June Vincent as nightclub gangster Peter Lorre pulls a gun. Radio spots publicized *Black Angel* as a "story of strange crime with a stranger love" involving "hard facts about a hard guy," promoting Duryea as a "piano play-ing honky tonk man" "no lady ever forgot" with bluesy "Heartbreak" music and a tough girl clamoring, "This is comin' to you from Skid Row where the tempera-ture's sultry and the ladies are torrid . . . you're listenin' to 'Heartbreak.' " Duryea was called "that guy who's murder with a blonde or a piano . . . strictly a *Lost Weekend* guy with dames in his eyes and tunes in his fingers but he can throw stardust in a lady's eyes so she don't know what's cookin' . . . even if it's a little thing like murder!" Vincent was a "torch singer on the trail of a killer," Lorre the "gangster who'll surprise you!" with the "character that plays its part in every mystery thriller . . . the black angel of death!" Targeting battled-hardened men returning from overseas and hard-bitten women: "If it's thrills you want Mr. see *Black Angel*, if it's romance you're looking for lady get a load of Dan Duryea, that fascinatin' tough guy of *Woman in the Window* and *Scarlet Street*." Another ad opened with the sound of a foghorn and piano playing "Heartbreak." A tough girl purrs, "Yellow fog, deadfalls, clip joints, and honky tonks. This is the kind of street that people don't talk about much." Like *Blues in the Night*, it promoted atmospheric blues music. "That's him sister, playing that number again. The song that means trouble for some dame! . . . They call him psychopathic. You know that word. It means trouble for women." It called *Black Angel* "daring in romance [and] taut with suspense" that "fascinates" women and "thrills" men, a "sensational" version of Woolrich's "torrid" bestseller.[29]

The Man I Love

Warner crime movie veteran Raoul Walsh's *The Man I Love* (1947) centered on a jazz singer. It starred Ida Lupino, soon to become one of Hollywood's rare women directors, as independent bluesy songstress Petey who croons, "Someday he'll come along . . ." waiting for her man to return. She sings George and Ira Gershwin's melancholy "The Man I Love" and Jerome Kern and Oscar Hammerstein's "Why Was I Born?" in a musical noir atmosphere evocative of *Jammin' the Blues*. The film was scripted by *Mildred Pierce*'s Catherine Turney and adapted by Jo Pagano and Turney from Maritta Wolff's novel *Night Shift*. Like a lone gunman in a western, androgynously named Petey is an outsider who comes to town and moves on in the end in *The Man I Love*. Like many noir films at the end of the war, including *The Big Sleep*, *Mildred Pierce*, and *The Lady from Shanghai*, *The Man I Love* was "stockpiled": filmed in mid-1945, it was not released until 1947.

Although atmospheric noir musical drama *The Man I Love* is more a melodrama than a crime film, it features criminal elements in a shadowy noir visual style with fog-shrouded settings that recall blacked-out wartime cities. It opens at the 39 Club on New York's 52nd Street, with flashing neon lights and the sounds of live jazz—all filmed on Warner's Hollywood soundstage. Drunken revelers, hearing a late-night jam session, try to get in after hours but are turned away. They shout that jazz musicians are "maniacs" and "crazy people." Lupino's scrappy Petey smacks guys around (in her sexy singing-costume gown) to prevent a shooting. As the musical melodrama progresses, she morphs from a strong working woman singing the blues in a jazz club to a nurturing role in domestic spaces while pursuing piano man San (*Mildred Pierce*'s Bruce Bennett). The film included recognizable Warner noir players: *Big Sleep* gangster Eddie Mars (John Ridgely) as the traumatized vet, Carmen (Martha Vickers) as a good girl babysitter, and *To Have and Have Not*'s Dolores Moran as a negligent wife and mother who runs around drunk in fur coats, carousing with men while abandoning her two babies to the babysitter across the hall. When her husband makes excuses for his philandering wife by saying, "I work the night shift—I can't take her anywhere," Petey replies, "Well, honey, all I can say is you better change to the day shift." (His wife dies in an accident—moral retribution for being a bad mother—allowing babysitter Vickers to pair up with him.)

Disillusioned love triangles abound in this noir-inspired blues melodrama. Lupino's sultry chanteuse carries a torch for a tormented jazz musician who's got it bad for another woman, his ex-wife, who destroyed his passion for music. While Lupino's blues singer and the jazz pianist she desires both perform music, the passionate pursuit of jazz as a musical art form, or even for fame on Broadway is deemphasized. San admits, "I ran down like a clock. It was just as though I'd been wound up too tight and the spring broke." Yet, the film's most passionate conversation is their discussion of jazz and the blues on a foggy night at the boardwalk when they discuss possibilities for their future. San warns, "I'd make you sing the blues, honey." Petey replies, "I'll take that chance." San mutters, "Isn't life difficult enough without mixing it up with memories?" Lupino sings and plays the blues as music therapy for her troubled man. As in wartime romances, San decides to return to his merchant ship, vowing to return someday. Petey leaves California for New York to resume performing, holding down the home front until her sailor returns.

The Man I Love is a noir musical that captured the cultural climate as Hollywood shifted from wartime to postwar. Warner Bros. purchased the novel *Night Shift* in October 1942 and planned to cast Humphrey Bogart and Ann Sheridan. When Bogart's fame exploded with the success of *Casablanca*, Jack Carson was selected to replace him. The PCA objected to the film's "low moral tone" of "adultery and illicit sex." It was shot from July to September 1945, shortly after President Roosevelt's death and during the atomic bombing of Hiroshima and Nagasaki and the end of the war. During the filming, Lupino collapsed from exhaustion, exacerbated by heat, fatigue, and her tight costumes. Like other black-and-white films, *The Man I Love* was economical compared to lavishly budgeted Technicolor musicals. Although it ran $100,000 over budget and was nineteen days behind schedule, it cost a relatively modest $860,000. Cross-promoting the atmospheric music feature, Charlie Barnet's band performed live jazz with the film. Warner Bros. advertised it in color noir style, with muted tones of steel blue and domi-

Hardboiled blues singer Ida Lupino awaits her tormented jazz piano man in *The Man I Love*. Warner Bros., 1947

nant red. Above the bold scarlet title were images of Lupino embracing Robert Alda against a bright splash of red, with Lupino in a sultry pose sitting atop a piano in a tight dress and heels, holding a cigarette. It was a female-centered variation on *Blues in the Night* publicity with a tagline that clamored: *"There ought to be a law against knowing the things I found out about men!"*[30] Lupino's character appealed to women ready to welcome their men home from the war. Lacking any big-name male lead, *The Man I Love* exemplifies Hollywood's shortage of big-name male stars not yet back from the war in mid-1945.

Variety called *The Man I Love* a "brittle sex romance."[31] Others critiqued its "depressing" tone that went against escapist musical expectations. "No one denies that the Warners have got a right to sing the blues or that actress Ida Lupino has a right to feel low-down, if they think that makes for entertainment of the lachrymose customers. More than one film has subsisted on a generous combustion of torch." Lupino, however, was praised for her "amazing directness," "wisdom," and knowing "how to handle everything—except [the] baffling gentleman who refuses to respond to her love." While returning veteran Ridgely recovers from his postwar breakdown, moody jazz musician Bennett remained "truculent and dour," and "sleek" Alda was "persistent" as a "skirt-chasing night-club man." *The Man I Love*'s downbeat melodrama was criticized for its tormented romance, "erratic" love triangles, "melancholy airs," and "emphasis upon heartbreak." Even its classic songs—"The Man I Love," "Why Was I Born?" and "Body and Soul"—were deemed unnecessarily melancholy. *The Man I Love*'s "slow incineration" of "moods" was called "silly," "depressing," "dull," and "routine."[32] It appears that the downbeat tenor of musical melodrama was less popular two years after the film's summer 1945 production. As with noir musical *Blues in the Night*, fusing downbeat noir melodrama with a musical was seen as counterintuitive. Yet, *The Man I Love* earned $1,547,000 domestically and $491,000 overseas, totaling $2,038,000.[33]

By 1945, with the end of the war and rationing, both film noir and musicals were changing. As film noir surged drawing on the harsh violence of the war, musicals were now being panned for not being gritty enough.[34] Yet, as wartime shortages and filming constraints subsided by 1946, Welles shot the brooding noir film *The Stranger*—set in a small town—on a bright Hollywood back lot. Studios planned ahead for "spectacular" postwar color films, hoping to bring back prewar colossal sets and luxurious costumes.[35] Joseph Lewis, known for low-budget noirs *Gun Crazy* and *The Big Combo*, directed musical sequences for the lavish $2,800,000 Technicolor 1946 musical biopic *The Jolson Story*, featuring Jolson performing as himself in a cameo.[36] In the dramatic conflict between career and personal life, Jolson's wife (based on Ruby Keeler) leaves him to obsessively perform to adoring crowds in the film's downbeat finale.

Female images tended to change from cosmopolitan and promiscuous to domestic, while masculine noir protagonists moved from criminals to crime-fighting investigators. Gene Tierney had played mysterious working girl in the black-and-white 1944 noir *Laura* and murderous femme fatale in the 1946 color noir melodrama *Leave Her to Heaven*. Like so many women after the conflict, however, Tierney settles into onscreen domesticity: she is a widow who has an affair with a ghost (Rex Harrison) in *The Ghost and Mrs. Muir* and a tormented housewife in *Whirlpool*.

THE "MODERN" SOUNDS OF BEBOP: JAZZ EVOLVES

Like film noir and the "modern" sounds of *Blues in the Night*, strains of bebop in the jazz music world were percolating during the war. Saxophonist Charlie Parker improvised over Ray Noble's "Cherokee" one night "and bop was born." Although the musicians' union ban precluded recordings of Parker and Dizzy Gillespie's early wartime bebop experiments at Minton's Playhouse, jazz critic Nate Chinen notes that by early 1944, bebop made its "first incursion onto swing-centered 52nd Street, between 5th and 6th Avenues: a Gillespie-spearheaded engagement" at the Onyx Club.[37]

As noir production peaked in 1946, the burgeoning sounds of bebop were captured in Gillespie's *Jivin' in Be-Bop*. Much lighter than *Jammin' the Blues* which was shot during the shadowy blackouts of the war, jazz variety revue *Jivin' in Be-Bop*, directed by Leonard Anderson and Spencer Williams, showcased Gillespie's bebop orchestra. Its African American producer William D. Alexander made OWI propaganda films and *All-American News* reels during the war for African American GIs, then started independent Alexander Productions aimed at an African American audience. A zoot-suit-clad Gillespie performed incredible trumpet solos and led his band with bassist Ray Brown, vibraphonist Milt Jackson, pianist John Lewis, singer Helen Humes, Kenny "Pancho" Hagood, an array of tap-modern-jazz-jitterbug dancers, and Freddie Carter. Racy color noir publicity in black, white, and bright scarlet promoted Gillespie and the derrières of the "Hubba Hubba Girls." Like the suggestive musical numbers in jazz noir, *Jivin' in Be-Bop* featured abundant sexual innuendo in dance routines and blues vocals to bebop tunes "Ornithology," "A Night in Tunisia," "Oop Bop Sh'Bam," "He Beeped When He Should Have Bopped," and "Salt Peanuts" that would challenge the PCA. But modest B pictures, short films, and independent productions were less scrutinized than hefty-budget A features at major studios. Subsequently, Alexander made shorts *Burlesque in Harlem, Rhythm in a Riff* (with singer Billy Eckstine), and *Souls of Sin* and founded the Associated Film Producers of Negro Motion Pictures before moving to London and making films on emerging independent African nations.[38]

Gillespie described bebop as "the most serious music ever made in America, and a lot of people have died for it." Saxophonist Dexter Gordon observed, "Bebop

is such a light name for such a demanding music." At the war's end, like a brilliant self-destructive jazz noir antihero, bebop maestro Charlie Parker had a nervous breakdown and was committed to Camarillo State Mental Hospital for six
months, struggling with heroin addiction. Jack Kerouac in his influential postwar
classic *On the Road* wrote: "At this time, 1947, bop was going like mad all over
America."[39] By 1947 another film explored the origins of jazz and the blues in
New Orleans.

New Orleans

In 1946, while Welles was occupied with noir films *The Stranger* and *The Lady
from Shanghai*, Elliot Paul went to independent producer Jules Levey with Welles's
Story of Jazz project. Louis Armstrong and Billie Holiday were hired for *New Orleans*, with director Arthur Lubin and musical director Nat Finston. Paul shared
story credit with writer-associate producer Herbert Biberman and screenplay
credit with Dick Irving Hyland. Evoking an atmospheric jazz noir milieu like
Blues in the Night and *Syncopation*, the *New Orleans* "story of jazz" was a black-
and-white musical melodrama. The story revolved around a romantic entanglement: classical vocalist Miralee Smith (Dorothy Patrick) falls for tall, dark, and
handsome gangster/gambler Nick Duquesne (Arturo de Cordova), who hails
from the wrong side of the tracks. The singer's family doesn't want her hanging
out at Duquesne's hip jazz club in the disreputable Storyville red light district of
New Orleans, but the music is too enticing. Jazz singer Billie Holiday belts the
blues with a hot jazz band composed of Armstrong, Kid Ory, Red Callender, and
Woody Herman, who play "West End Blues," "Sugarfoot Stomp," "Basin Street
Blues," and "Buddy Bolden Blues."

Like *Blues in the Night* and *Syncopation*, *New Orleans* concerns jazz artistry and
authenticity. It begins with a jam session by Armstrong's combo in Storyville and
integrates a star-is-born narrative ending with its blonde female singer, now a
famous classical singer, paying tribute to jazz in New York's Carnegie Hall. The
final symphonic jazz performance presents jazz as high musical art, despite
its humble Basin Street beginnings. However, the style has changed from Armstrong's lively jazz combo to more Gershwin-like orchestral sounds.

New Orleans was shot from September to November 1946 and released in
April 1947. Publicity played up the film's jazz music and its sexual content. Taglines exclaimed, "*Torchy! Scorchy!*" (reminiscent of *Blues in the Night*) in bright
scarlet with navy blue musical notes and "It's the Lowdown on Sinful Old Basin
Street!"[40] By May 1947, the *Motion Picture Herald* recommended that film exhibi-
tors emphasize the jazz music over anything else to publicize *New Orleans*, which

due to "over-enthusiasm for authenticity of setting," included sequences showing the "seamy side of life."[41]

Noting its "story of jazz" cultural history and musicology, Biberman promoted *New Orleans* as a genre film, calling it a "gambler-singer romance" with a "blue-conscious gambler" and "sympathetic young opera singer," tracing early New Orleans beginnings of jazz and moving to Chicago. Like *Blues in the Night, New Orleans* recognized jazz and the blues as indigenous American folk music. Admitting its music was more compelling than its romantic melodrama, Biberman praised *New Orleans* for its history of jazz and "exciting musical line-up."[42] While promoting jazz, *New Orleans'* classical music subplot (panned by critics) fused music styles. Like *Blues in the Night* and *Syncopation*, jazz is shown as a rebellious, liberating endeavor by youth.[43]

Had *New Orleans* been a documentary-style noir musical in the spirit of *Jammin' the Blues* and directed by Welles (with an Ellington jazz score and a story based on Armstrong's life as originally conceived) it would no doubt have been a more fascinating film. Philip K. Scheuer of the *Los Angeles Times* acknowledged, "If jazz—hot jazz—is the only true American folk music (as many authorities believe) then Hollywood ain't done right by her. We haven't come up with a really definitive history of a movement." *Syncopation* was criticized as "solemn," yet jazz itself was described as "basically joyous." The documentary nature of earlier films, the "splendid isolated sequences of authentic jazz" in *Jammin' the Blues* and "glorified biographies of composers and band men, sagas of Tin Pan Alley" were praised. But the "real, low-down inside" of jazz is "still to be told." Scheuer commended *New Orleans'* "Real Story of How American Folk Music Developed" as an "Elusive Saga of Jazz."[44] Although Biberman explained, "We're not archae-ologists. We're trying to be accurate and still turn out an entertaining picture."[45] *Variety* called *New Orleans* "one of the pleasantest musicals of the season." *New York Times* critics lauded the "frequent tooting of Louis Armstrong on his horn," but the film's "wretchedly routine" romance was panned: "any modern bobby-soxer" would be "naturally" drawn "toward hot music" and slip off to midnight jam sessions. "Love and jazz run a rough course," but they panned the melodrama as predictable where the "inevitable grand passion occurs."[46]

Kid Ory's Creole Jazz Band performed in social realist *Crossfire*, directed by Edward Dmytryk and produced by Adrian Scott. *Crossfire* was RKO's biggest 1947 hit. It was highly regarded for its stance against bigotry, anti-Semitism, and (origi-nally homophobic) hate crimes and recognized by *Ebony* magazine for "improv-ing interracial understanding."[47] As *New Orleans* and *Crossfire* were released in 1947, the new Cold War claimed many noir filmmakers as casualties. Dmytryk,

Scott, Biberman, and Albert Maltz (*This Gun for Hire, Naked City, Cloak and Dagger*) were among a group of writers, directors, producers, and actors known as the Hollywood Ten, who were labeled "unfriendly" witnesses before the House Committee on Un-American Activities (HUAC) and blacklisted. Formed in 1938, HUAC focused on purging Communist and left-wing filmmakers from the film industry. In October 1947 Dmytryk, Scott, Biberman, Maltz, and others were charged with contempt and given prison sentences. *New Orleans* was the last Hollywood film Biberman produced. He did not make another picture until his acclaimed independent social realist film *Salt of the Earth* (1954).

Casbah

Italian neorealism and French poetic realism were influential to film noir. Many European émigrés fleeing fascism were noir writers, directors, and other creative talents dedicated to social realism and experimental expressionist aesthetics. When these persecuted talents fled to the United States, they tended to support the American Popular Front against fascism. Cultural historian Michael Sherry notes that Wilder, Kazan, Ellington, Cukor, Leonard Bernstein, and others formed a "new generation of plebeian artists and intellectuals . . . rooted in the Popular Front politics of the 1930s and linked to the rise of mass culture."[48]

The Popular Front actively combated the Nazi menace through film, not always in the social realist vein. American propaganda also included musicals that projected camaraderie, optimism, and escapism to bolster public morale. Americana and nostalgia for a rural lifestyle were promoted—as in MGM's *Meet Me in St. Louis* (1944, with Minnelli's "American Gothic" aesthetic) and even *The Wizard of Oz*. All-American pinup girl Betty Grable, known for her beautiful blonde hair, peach skin, and fabulous legs was Hollywood's highest-paid female star and an iconic image of World War II. Despite extensive rationing and blackouts, Grable's contract at Fox guaranteed Technicolor for her musicals.

After the conflict, absent the common enemy of Fascism, the cultural terrain shifted to growing Cold War atomic fears, xenophobia, and the Red Scare of the McCarthy era. Many of the émigré noir filmmakers who had been part of the Popular Front were blacklisted. Others were pressured to inform on their colleagues to continue their careers. As a result of these trends, film noir evolved into visually lighter social realism and eventually declined altogether.

Son of Jewish immigrants but American-born John Berry worked with Welles' Mercury Theatre (acting in its famous production of *Julius Caesar*) and directed the noir musical *Casbah* in 1948 and the noir film *Tension* in 1949. He was blacklisted after directing the 1950 documentary *The Hollywood Ten*. Berry's *Casbah* was an atmospheric noir musical version of the 1937 French crime film *Pépé le Moko*. *Casbah* starred Tony Martin as gangster fugitive Pépé, a role made famous by Jean Gabin and reprised by Charles Boyer in 1938 in *Algiers*, in which sultry Hedy Lamarr entices him to "come to the Casbah," a tantalizing line famous with World War II veterans. *Casbah*'s most iconic performance is by Peter Lorre as a hardboiled detective given to sardonic barbs. Cigarette smoke wafting around his chair keep this ambiguous figure in shadow. It features *Criss Cross*'s Yvonne De Carlo as Pépé's lover, alluring Marta Toren as the woman Pépé desires (and dies for), and songs by *Blues in the Night* and *A Star Is Born* composer Arlen.

Casbah was shot from October to December 1947 and metaphorically critiqued the Red Scare. Its narrative featured deceitful double-dealing, informing, and betrayal. Friends-turned-informers lurked in the dark, shrouded corners, tunnels, alleys, and passageways of the Casbah. As in noir, ambiguous criminals and hard-boiled detectives in this exotic, *Casablanca*-like atmosphere comingle in complex relations. But duplicitous "inspector" (Lorre) and "commissioner" (Thomas Gomez) set a spiderlike trap when Pépé tries to leave the underworld to pursue the object of his desire. Instead of sending her off with her beau (à la *Casablanca*), he is gunned down by police as her plane takes off (and she is oblivious). Much of *Casbah* was shot in documentary style at low angles. North African dance sequences anticipated stylized Afro-Cuban/Latin jazz dance sequences in *Salón México* (1949), *Lady without Passport* (1950), and *West Side Story* (1961). Arlen's "For Every Man There's a Woman," sung by Martin (and De Carlo), was nominated for an Oscar. The film was produced by independent Marston Pictures (a joint venture between Martin and producer Nat Goldstone) and Universal-International. The next year, Berry's noir *Tension* featured a rousing Andre Previn jazz score and starred Martin's wife, musical star Cyd Charisse, the moll dancing with Kelly in *Singin' in the Rain* and Astaire in *The Band Wagon*.[49]

Road House

The postwar era's growing Cold War tension was reflected in musical noir *Road House* (1948). It featured a love triangle set against a backdrop of crime with a blues-singing Ida Lupino. Originally titled *Dark Love*, about two male friends (one married, the other having an affair with his wife) who run a bowling alley/bait-and-tackle shop, the PCA censored the story's adulterous extramarital affair. In the film Lupino is a jaded unmarried Chicago singer who comes to their backwoods town and belts the blues in a roadhouse (like *Blues in the Night's* jazz band in Jersey). She is desired by friends Richard Widmark and Cornel Wilde, inciting a jealous rivalry and severing their friendship. A stylish musical noir set in the rural outdoors in daylight, *Road House* was directed by Warner Bros.' veteran Jean Negulesco (who directed *Humoresque* and contributed to the screenplay) in his first film for 20th Century-Fox. Revealing Lupino's influence as an increasingly powerful woman in Hollywood, the rising female star (and eventual director) initiated and commissioned the writing of the project based on an original story and script by Margaret Gruen and Oscar Saul.

In September 1947, Fox bought the screen rights from Lupino for $130,000, which included $100,000 for Lupino to star in the film. Shot from March 22 to May 11, 1948 with shadowy cinematography by Joseph LaShelle, *Road House* was produced and adapted by Edward Chodorov and released in November 1948. Its songs included "One for My Baby" by Arlen and Mercer, as well as Lionel Newman's "Again" and "The Right Kind." Like Hayworth in Welles' *The Lady from Shanghai*, *Road House* transformed former-brunette Ida Lupino into a platinum blonde with short, cropped hair. (In *The Man I Love*, Lupino's screen nephew says, "You didn't have that color hair the last time I saw you.") Black-and-white publicity featured stark black noir shots; color noir promotion splashed red against muted tones . . . with Widmark strangling his buddy.

Despite Lupino's top billing, *Road House* is more masculine than many wartime musical noir films. Noteworthy in postwar noir films is the narrative shift from male camaraderie during the war to male antagonists who betray friends in the Cold War era of informing and xenophobia. Women are channeled back into the home into more nurturing relationships with returning veterans. *Road House* revolves around tormented, psychologically unstable men and has a subjective point-of-view. As in *The Man I Love*, *Road House* begins with Lupino singing the blues, but it quickly shifts from musical performance to a more masculine terrain. Critics called Lupino "expertly brittle," able to "do more without a voice than anyone." "Her graveltoned voice lacks range but has the more essential quality of style, along the lines of a femme Hoagy Carmichael." Widmark was "excellent" as "cinematically anti-social" "prize tough guy" with chilling laughter in "danger of being typed" as "screen's prime psychotic." Wilde is "sedate but muscularly attractive."[50] Noir's wartime femme fatale is replaced by Widmark's homme fatale in *Road House*.

JAZZ NOIR MUSICAL DRAMAS COME TOGETHER

After the definitive noir musical *Blues in the Night*, jazz noir musical melodrama began to emerge with darker undertones than previous musical fare. As musicals and dramas merged during and just after the war years, elements found in noir dramas and dark jazz musicals coalesced to create noir musicals. Musical film

noir combined with dark musical melodrama (that fused criminal and jazz cabaret elements) into jazz noir musical dramas. Musical film noir, including many
early noir films, featured moody jazz performance in an unsavory underworld
or cabaret setting. The noir style combined bars, nightclubs, and—usually jazz—
musical performers.

Critics recognized *Blues in the Night*, linking it to *Casablanca* and a trend of
crime films laced with jazz music.[51] Noir films codified jazz musical performance
and recognized tormented antiheros as self-destructive genius-musicians as in
Blues in the Night. Like *Blues in the Night*, even *Casablanca* resembles noir musicals as Bogart's tortured Rick hits-the-bottle drunkenly pleading with friend Sam
to play "As Time Goes By" in the dark deserted nightclub, then descends into
turbulent flashback memories of his torrid Paris affair. Musical performing is
considered so threatening in *Casablanca* that the Nazis close Rick's Café to silence
the band and the crowd from singing the "Marseillaise" or subversive jazz songs.

Even the few Technicolor musicals were darker and more psychological, deal-
ing with the underside of showbiz. This more hard-boiled terrain resonated with
the wartime mood. In the grittier "realistic" crime films and downbeat backstage
melodramas, jazz numbers replicated live stage music or radio shows. Filming an
atmospheric wartime film in black-and-white with low lighting, simple sets and
costumes, and relatively simple musical numbers reduced costs and used fewer
scarce materials. Given the harsh realities of war, musical film noir was less romantic about love and less reticent about sex. There were also new attitudes toward ethnicity resulting from the war with its shifting gender roles, masculinity,
European émigrés, Allies, and mix of GIs thrown together on a necessary basis
of equality and camaraderie.

Such jazz noir as *Phantom Lady*, *To Have and Have Not*, *Christmas Holiday*, *The
Big Sleep*, *Gilda*, *The Man I Love*, *Black Angel*, *New Orleans*, *Casbah*, and *Road
House* included musical performances focusing on illicit love triangles in a shady
criminal milieu. Films tended to reference each other. Bacall, Hayworth, and Lupino were not the only blues-singing noir women. Others included Marie Bryant,
who performed in *Jammin' the Blues* and Ellington's *Jump for Joy* and in a gangster's club in Nicholas Ray's *They Live by Night* (produced in 1947, released 1949).
Moll-showgirl Jean Hagen croons Cole Porter's "Easy to Love" until her hoodlum lover strangles her in Anthony Mann's *Side Street* (1949). Femme fatale Ava
Gardner sings jazz in Robert Siodmak's *The Killers* (1946) and Robert Z. Leonard's
The Bribe (1949). Detective Ricardo Montalban investigates the murder of Jan
Sterling's B-girl performer in John Sturges's *Mystery Street* (produced in 1949,
released in 1950).[52]

Many postwar films noir highlighted the violence of the war, disturbing real-life misogynistic relations, and dealt with the difficulty soldiers had "readjusting" to "civilian life" and the "profound social trauma that can result when that goes awry." Often, this difficulty manifested in domestic abuse. Unsolved crimes like the 1947 Black Dahlia murder inspired—and drew on—noir films. Cultural critic Seth Schiesel observes that by 1947, Los Angeles was "awash in young men who got used to killing every day in the war, then returned and were expected to take orders from their wives. Not all of them could."[53]

The war was over, but its effects were still being felt by society and reflected back to them on the Hollywood screen.

CHAPTER FIVE

Le Rouge et le Noir

From The Red Shoes *to* A Star Is Born

Cinematic trends such as dramatic realism, documentary style, melodrama, and the star-is-born motif influenced film noir and musicals after the war, contributing to darker postwar noir musicals. In the absence of wartime production constraints, economical musical film noir gave way to grander big-budget postwar color musical films with downbeat narratives and noir-styled production design. For example, Michael Powell and Emeric Pressburger's (known collectively as The Archers) *The Red Shoes* was a musical melodrama that featured a female protagonist's struggle in brooding Technicolor. George Cukor's definitive noir musical *A Star Is Born* was a comeback film for former-MGM star Judy Garland that took advantage of new technology.

Meanwhile, black-and-white film noir was also changing, adopting a new look and style in response to postwar industrial and cultural challenges, shifting gender roles and themes, and adapting to changing filmmaking conditions and new emergent technologies.

As men returned from war, black-and-white film noir evolved in the late 1940s and early 1950s to incorporate a lighter, grayer documentary-style visual aesthetic (like television anthology dramas and police procedurals) increasingly targeting a masculine audience. While black-and-white noir crime films became more masculine and shifted away from hard-boiled "Rosie the Riveter" femme fatales, dark "color noir" musical melodramas resonated with postwar women.

The evolution of noir musicals provides a fascinating microcosm of the changes simultaneously taking place in Hollywood over the postwar era. The industry faced antitrust regulation, and the studio system was breaking up. There was declining film viewership and stiff competition from television. There was a changing American cultural and economic climate and innovative European art cinema to reckon with. The Red Scare blacklisted creative talent and content. Looking back at this paranoid time, musical director Stanley Donen pondered, "How do you tell a story which has a human feeling? Because you don't dare have too many human feelings, they'll be thought of as 'Communistic.'"[1] As the industry moved from standard-screen black-and-white films, noir creative talent moved to other genres including musicals, where they brought their darker, realistic dramatic tendencies to color and stereophonic sound films. Many darker musicals presented a distinctive "color noir" aesthetic, emulating shadowy noir style with color film, as Hollywood's response to television. Studios also employed this color noir aesthetic in ads and promotions even for black-and-white noir pictures. *The Red Shoes, Young Man with a Horn, The Strip, Glory Alley, Affair in Trinidad, The Barefoot Contessa,* and *A Star Is Born* explored a brooding noir musical world. Jumping on the bandwagon, even film noir veteran John Huston (director of *The Maltese Falcon*) made a color noir musical—*Moulin Rouge.*

Talented émigrés, women, and jazz musicians had influenced film noir during the wartime labor shortage. Just as blackouts and rationing of film stock (including color film) and lighting contributed to the development of a shadowy black-and-white film noir aesthetic in wartime, the postwar competition with television helped move motion pictures in the direction of colorful spectacle. By 1950, industry executives discouraged production of hard-hitting noir pictures tackling social problems. By the late 1940s and 1950s, popular escapist color musicals, comedies, melodramas, historical period epics, science fiction, Westerns, fantasy, and presold Broadway adaptations were preferred.

Just as early sound films (even gangster pictures) included musical numbers, in the postwar move to color widescreen spectacles with stereophonic sound, noir aesthetic adapted to new technology. The impact of television from 1946 to 1962 was tremendous on Hollywood business practices, technology, censorial structures, genres, styles, and stars. After peaking in 1946, American filmgoing declined. Television (especially color television after 1953) provided a free and convenient alternative form of leisure entertainment that could be consumed by viewers in the privacy of their own homes. The U.S. population shifted away from urban centers—where many had flocked for work during the war and where first-run theaters were located—to outlying suburban communities. Television and the Broadway stage experienced a postwar golden age that threatened the film industry.

Moreover, the Supreme Court's antitrust Paramount Decision of May 3, 1948, was a day of reckoning for Hollywood and ultimately brought about the collapse of the classical studio system. It required the "vertically integrated" Big Five major studios—Paramount, MGM, 20th Century-Fox, Warner Bros., and RKO, which owned all three (film production, distribution, and exhibition) branches of the motion picture business—to divest and sell off their theater chains by 1959 or earlier. While this decision signaled a major blow, divestiture was ultimately viewed favorably by studios whose large holdings of exhibition properties had become an economic liability with the significant decline in viewership due to television. To compete with television, for a brief period between 1948 and 1952, they practiced alternative exhibition measures such as broadcasting major televised cultural and sports events in theaters. In dire need of revenue, studios produced television programs and, as the studio system collapsed, they reduced large numbers of contract employees, sold off expensive real estate holdings, and increasingly turned to independent productions.[2]

As production costs rose after the war, many studios and independent filmmakers shot "runaway" films on location overseas to capitalize on the 20 to 50 percent reduction in production costs outside Hollywood and to present exotic locales to American audiences. Hollywood also responded to competition from television by producing fewer but bigger films, with more stars in glorious color and widescreen formats (sometimes in 3-D from 1952 to 1953) with multitrack stereophonic sound. These "road shows" such as *Oklahoma!* and *Ben Hur* simulated elite theatrical events, touring the country. Technophilia was the rage in postwar American consumer society. In an effort to compete with the tremendous popularity of television, Hollywood attempted to cash in on this trend toward technophilia with the infusion of new technologies into film production and exhibition.

Thus, the film industry developed sophisticated measures to distinguish itself as a bigger, more spectacular, more elite leisure activity using new technologies. *This Is Cinerama* introduced Cinerama's extravagant three-camera/projection system in 1952, followed by its competitor Cinemiracle. *The Robe* premiered 20th Century-Fox's CinemaScope anamorphic widescreen system in 1953—a process ultimately improved on by MGM's Panavision, which evolved into standard widescreen Panavision 35. Paramount's *White Christmas* featured VistaVision, a wideframe system exposing an eight-perforation image twice as wide as a standard screen. Technirama added Technicolor to an anamorphic process, which expanded the width of the screen image. *Giant* showcased widescreen. Todd-AO and Super Cinerama introduced 70mm processes. Even "Smell-O-Vision" was tried. Unfortunately, the novelty of new technologies waned by 1957, and the industry slumped. Film noir and musicals had declined by the late 1950s. Musicals, expensive to produce, labor intensive, and heavily reliant on contract talent, had benefited from the studio system's vast resources.[3]

Responding further to the inroads of television, Hollywood increased sex, violence, profanity, and formerly forbidden subjects that were not allowed on television. The dominant style during this transition period was realism, including documentaries, film noir, and imported Italian neorealist films. This topicality was seen in noir musical dramas like *The Red Shoes, Young Man with a Horn, The Strip, Glory Alley, A Star Is Born, Young at Heart,* and *Love Me or Leave Me* and melodramas (drama with music, especially domestic and male melodramas) like *The Bad and the Beautiful, From Here to Eternity, A Streetcar Named Desire,* and *On the Waterfront.*

Darker, "revisionist" Westerns became popular and also depicted "real" themes that resonated with the postwar American male. Howard Hawks moved from making film noir to the noir Western *Red River* with volatile John Wayne and Montgomery Clift. Arthur Penn's debut *Left Handed Gun* starred Paul Newman as a violent antihero. Newman is a tormented antiheroic musician with Sidney Poitier in the jazz melodrama *Paris Blues.* Melodrama, including musical melodrama, exposed emotional fractures in the postwar American family that contrasted with the more "wholesome" representations on television during this time.[4] Thus, as Hollywood competed with television, the unvarnished realism of documentary newsreels, the stage, noir, and imported neorealist films influenced color musical dramatic spectacles.[5]

The trend in Hollywood to adapt stage productions for film also allowed for the inclusion of explicit subjects such as sex, violence, and profanity or vulgarity insofar as such subjects were both "realistic" and occurred in the originals. As such content could not be shown on television, films drew audiences away from smaller screens at home and into theaters to view these taboo subjects that could be considered high art when derived from Broadway. As postwar foreign markets reopened, imported international art cinema pushed boundaries. *The Bicycle Thief, The Red Shoes,* and *The Miracle* included heightened realism, challenging and undermining PCA censorship. As the studio system unraveled, the Paramount Decision also undermined the industry's self-regulation by the PCA, and the 1952 Supreme Court *Miracle* decision gave films greater free speech protections, which eventually led to an easing of censorship.[6] Censor Joseph Breen retired in 1954, and the Code was liberalized in 1956.[7] Female "sexpots" such as Jane Russell, Jayne Mansfield, Marilyn Monroe, and Dorothy Malone began to emerge. Even Doris Day expanded on her wholesome, girl-next-door image to play a more realistic, sexually charged role in MGM's dramatic noir musical biopic, *Love Me or Leave Me*.[8]

The power, volatility, and realism of noir musical and melodrama performances offered an alternative to television—Anton Walbrook's tormented antihero in *The Red Shoes*, Kirk Douglas in *Young Man with a Horn* and *The Bad and the Beautiful*, James Mason in *A Star Is Born* and *The Story of Three Loves* (modeled on Walbrook in *The Red Shoes*), Frank Sinatra in *Young at Heart* and *From Here to Eternity*, James Cagney and Doris Day in *Love Me or Leave Me* were notable for their intensity and verisimilitude. Method acting transformed screen characterizations. Marlon Brando gained fame for his Oscar-winning method acting in Kazan's *On the Waterfront* and *A Streetcar Named Desire* as well as in the gangster musical *Guys and Dolls*, for instance. Paul Newman as an insecure psychotic in *Left Handed Gun* and a moody jazz musician in *Paris Blues* and James Dean in *Rebel without a Cause* and *Giant* also used this method. Like the tormented antiheroes in film noir, realist noir musical melodramas *The Red Shoes*, *Young Man with a Horn*, *A Star Is Born*, *Love Me or Leave Me*, and *Paris Blues* focused on strong independent individuals struggling with inner demons.[9]

Hollywood had to respond to the challenges of television on one hand and influential European art cinema on the other. These included Italian neorealist films such as Roberto Rossellini's *Open City* and Vittorio DeSica's *The Bicycle Thief*, British thrillers such as Carol Reed's *The Third Man*, and color noir musical melodramas such as *The Red Shoes* with its stylized Technicolor realism exquisitely shot on location in Europe. In this chapter, we will see how *The Red Shoes* inspired a dark revisionist musical trend that crystallized with the quintessential noir musical *A Star Is Born*.

THE RED SHOES AND COLOR MUSICAL NOIR

The Red Shoes conveyed the clash between a romantic relationship and a performing career in an interesting and influential variation on the Hollywood backstage musicals made in the years before and during the war. Instead of a blues singer in a jazz club as in *Blues in the Night*, *The Red Shoes* was set in the world of ballet and classical music in three-strip Technicolor yet with an atmospheric noir style. It told the tragic story of a love triangle of ballet impresario Boris Lermontov (Anton Walbrook), gifted dancer Victoria Page (Moira Shearer), and composer Julian Craster (Marius Goring). Vicky lives to dance. She rises to fame aided by passionate, possessive mentor Lermontov. He represses his love for her and resents it when she falls in love and marries Julian—who, in turn, resents her love of dance once she is his wife. Vicky struggles to pursue both her art and her

Walbrook's impresario Lermontov broods, cigarette smoke swirls in silhouette shadows in *The Red Shoes*. Eagle-Lion, 1948

romantic love. Thus, *The Red Shoes* encapsulates the postwar dilemma faced by working women asked to sacrifice their careers to resume domestic life with their (often tormented) men.

As *Blues in the Night*'s antihero performs jazz, Vicky's talented heroine in *The Red Shoes* pursues classical ballet. While musicians play great jazz/blues in jam sessions at modest clubs (*Blues in the Night*'s shady Jungle roadhouse, *New Orleans*' unsavory Storyville), *The Red Shoes* takes place in the more elite world of premier ballet companies. Vicky tries to gain the opportunity to perform with Lermontov's first-rank troupe. This requires a serious commitment free from romantic entanglements or marriage. Her mentor insists that she repress romantic emotions if she is to be successful.

The Red Shoes' moody color mise-en-scène evokes film noir. Shrouded in shadow, inhaling a smoldering cigarette with tendrils of smoke, brilliant impresario Lermontov is backlit in silhouette through an open window. He recites Hans Andersen's "The Red Shoes" to Julian, foreshadowing the film's bitter conclusion: "Time rushes by. Love rushes by. Life rushes by. But the red shoes dance on." When Julian asks, "What happens in the end?" Lermontov replies, "Oh, in the end she dies." When his star leaves to marry Julian, Lermontov explodes in smoke and shadow, smashing a mirror. The couple are cloaked in blackness suggesting their doomed affair as they ride along the Mediterranean. After Boris fires Julian, they sit in darkness at a Villefranche café as melancholy jazz plays. A claustrophobic train cabin mirrors Vicky's cramped confinement in her marriage. Boris entices Vicky to return to dance the incomparable *Red Shoes* ballet that made her a star, which he had Julian compose for her.

An undercurrent of noir psychosis permeates *The Red Shoes* as both brilliant artistic men manipulate Vicky. Julian is talented (like Vicky) and arrogant (like Boris) but exposes a surprising darker side. Brooding, obsessed, he confronts Vicky backstage. Music blares a piercing warning. He appears ominous, scowling in a black shiny raincoat (with menacing makeup). Threatened, jealous of her artistic pursuit, he demands that she not go on, forcing her to choose between dancing and their marriage. Lermontov, meanwhile, is obsessed with his protégé. He seems to be an antagonist, yet he emerges as a complex figure. Walbrook's nuanced performance is mesmerizing. A dramatic reversal takes place in this confrontation. Lermontov, though a manipulative tyrant, seems to actually love Vicky; he recognizes her talent, understands her love of dance, and wants her to realize her dreams as an artist. Her seemingly mild-mannered spouse, however, has turned into a crazed, resentful control-freak who wants to marginalize her talent and deny her ambition.[10]

The duality of these artistic performing characters and their volatile love triangle is reflected in her dressing room mirror. Vicky is torn between love and career aspirations. Her distorted tear-streaked stage makeup undercuts the beauty of her white costume, red shoes, and flaming hair. Lermontov announces, "Nobody can have two lives, and your life is dancing! Would you be satisfied with anything less than the best? If you would, you would never be a great artist—perhaps you never will." He challenges Julian, "Would you make her a great dancer? Never. Why do you think I have waited day after day since you snatched her away from me? For a chance to win her back!" Calling her "infatuation" with Julian "adolescent nonsense," Boris gives Vicky an ultimatum: "If you go with him now, I will never take you back. Never!" Disgusted that she'd abandon her talent and passion, Lermontov articulates Vicky's dilemma that resonated with so many women after the war: "All right. Go then. Go with him. Be a faithful housewife with a crowd of screaming children and finish with dancing forever!" Vicky says she loves Julian, who knows she loves dance more. She chooses dance—to Boris' relief. Julian walks

In a jealous rage, Walbrook shatters a mirror when Moira Shearer leaves to marry in *The Red Shoes*. Eagle-Lion, 1948

out. His riveting operatic *Red Shoes* score captures Vicky's tumult. Suddenly her red shoes flee down spiraling stairwells, plunging her off a balcony into an oncoming train as its horn blares and black smoke plumes fill the sky. Vicky's accident, highly suggestive of suicide, prevents her from reuniting with either man, subverting the iconic coming together of a romantic musical couple. The red shoes propel her to death, not to dance.

The Red Shoes' "sordid" realism and tragic denouement echoed the existential fatalism of both film noir and the documentaries that had soared in popularity by the end of the war. The final scene embodies the spirit of noir musicals with a "shattered body of the ballerina lying on the railroad track, and her Red Shoes, red with blood." Director Powell explained, "The whole point of the scene was the conflict between romance and realism, between theater and life. But I suspect that what they really wanted was a happy ending. Our public knew better—growing up in countries that had been racked by war—the real reason why *The Red Shoes* was such a success was that we had all been told for ten years to go out and die for freedom and democracy . . . and now the war was over, *The Red Shoes* told us to go out and die for art." He added, " 'Oh mon dieu! C'est terrible!'. . . Nearly all the British critics, having failed to understand the rest of the picture, picked up on this final scene as typical of the bad taste of The Archers, and particularly of Michael Powell. 'Why all this blood,' they asked, 'why all this sordid realism in a romantic and beautiful fairytale?' "[11] The film's tragic clash captured the essential conflict expressed in postwar noir musicals and melodramas—many of them shot in color.

Production, Design, and Promotion of The Red Shoes

As the other half of The Archers, Pressburger originally wrote *The Red Shoes* as a project for Alexander Korda in 1937 for Korda's future wife Merle Oberon. Powell and Pressburger bought the screen rights several years later in 1946 and emphasized its music, ballet performances, and backstage aspects, wanting to cast an actual ballet dancer rather than a nondancing actress in the lead. Powell told Pressburger, "I'll do it if a dancer plays the part and if we re-create an original ballet of *The Red Shoes* instead of talking about it." The Archers created an elaborate 17-minute *Red Shoes* ballet as a show-within-a-film, creating their own ballet company of choreographer Robert Helpmann and fifty-three dancers, including Leonide Massine, Ludmilla Tcherina, and twenty-year-old Moira Shearer, the Sadler's Wells ballet dancer who declined the role for a year and had never acted in a film. Thus, in real life, stars were "born," as ballet dancers turned to the screen. After Shearer's successful debut in *The Red Shoes*, ballet dancers Leslie Caron, Cyd Charisse, and Audrey Hepburn became huge Hollywood stars, and Shearer reprised her *Red Shoes* role in MGM's *The Story of Three Loves*.[12]

The Red Shoes included stunning panoramic three-strip Technicolor sequences shot on location in Monte Carlo and Villefranche by Jack Cardiff. Cardiff's magnificent cinematography influenced later color noir musicals. Powell praised Technicolor musicals *The Wizard of Oz* and *Cover Girl* as outstanding influential American films notable for their use of color and music.[13] *The Red Shoes* creates a noirish atmosphere with black, white, muted tones, midnight blue, and bright scarlet red. Powell and Pressburger use expressionistic set design, chiaroscuro lighting, makeup, and costumes to reflect Vicky's turbulent psyche with surreal shots of hallucinations, raging surf and ocean waves crashing on shore as she performs the stylized ballet of a dancer's red shoes driving her to death (foreshadowing her own demise). Dancers perform against a stunning backdrop with brooding Germanic designs by art director Hein Heckroth.

In August 1947, Breen insisted bare thighs of ("can-can") dancers, embraces, and "damn" be omitted from the film, but he relented a year later. Produced and filmed in London, Paris, and the South of France in summer through early fall 1947, *The Red Shoes* opened in Britain in the summer of 1948 and was released in the United States beginning in late October 1948 in New York. Its trailer show-cased brilliant color travelogue images, music, and the star. Ads promoted *The Red Shoes* as: "A Dancing, Singing, Swinging Love Tale!" with such taglines as, "Dance she did, and dance she must—between her two loves." Black, white, and red color noir posters featured a leggy ballerina with flaming hair, red shoes, and a skimpy black strapless leotard caught between two scowling men in long black coats. Shearer complained about the film and its advertising in a 1949 interview: "Making [*The Red Shoes*] was a mistake; and pictures on the [publicity] hoardings made me look like Jane Russell in black tights."[14] She evidently didn't appreciate the visual comparison to wartime pinups.

Reception of The Red Shoes

Critics commended the film's innovative choreography and cinematography as "beautifully danced" by Moira Shearer and Massine and "photographed with imagination: you see its settings, the stage and glimpses beyond the footlights through the dancer's mind." Reviews praised its spectacle, design, and photography. *Picture Show* hoped that the "inevitable tragedy of the ending may be averted."[15] After its August 1948 London release, *Picturegoer* proclaimed: "Shearer is not only a brilliant dancer but a beautiful girl, a Greer Garson of the dance," adding that "this uncommonly beautiful film is one that you certainly should not miss. . . . The Archers, always enterprising, once again have broken new ground. . . . All the cosmopolitan, colourful intensity, confusion, concentration, temperament, and creative fervour are there. You see a new ballet take shape out of chaos, and as you do so you learn something of the spirit of the people whose life is ballet." *Picturegoer* describes it as a "tale of a girl whose affections are torn between her work as a dancer and her love of the young composer who writes the ballet for her. The ballet itself, which you see in its entirety, parallels this personal story in bringing imaginatively and spaciously to the screen the fable of the dancer who wears the red shoes that drive her to dance to her death."[16] The British Film Institute exclaimed that Shearer brought a "fragile loveliness" and "freshness wholly lacking" in "stars of today" to a "most appealing" performance and praised her dancing and the "whole corps-de-ballet" as "superb." *Monthly Film Bulletin* called it a "fantasy," noting its star-is-born narrative.[17]

While critics praised Shearer, its dancing, and Brian Easdale's stunning music score as "powerful," "effective," and "brilliantly recorded," as with other noir musicals that defied escapist expectations, *The Red Shoes'* melodramatic story, down-beat ending, and Walbrook's intense performance as the demanding taskmaster were sometimes panned. *Picturegoer* commented mostly favorably: "In sensitively used Technicolor, marred only by some daubs of blood in the closing scenes, it provides a feast of beauty and some fine acting."[18] But *Monthly Film Bulletin* complained: "The Technicolor is not too 'glorious,' but one feels at times in the *Red Shoes* ballet that a sharper and less kaleidoscopic tone would have been more effective."[19]

The Red Shoes' American reception was a marvel in itself—especially given British distributor J. Arthur Rank's skepticism of, and lack of confidence in, its box-office appeal in England or abroad, denying it a London premiere. As The Archers finished *The Red Shoes* they ended their relationship with Rank and signed a deal with rival Korda. The film's backers were so skeptical of its market-ability that they forced Powell and Pressburger to sacrifice part of their cash ad-vance for a bigger portion of its gross receipts. Powell commented, "Twenty years later, when *The Red Shoes* was one of the top-grossing box-office films of all time and was included in *Variety's* Golden Fifty, we were glad to have made the sacri-fice." Shearer recalled, "It was received with great excitement. I discovered only recently that Rank and John Davis tried to stop the film halfway through, having seen the rushes. They thought it was going to be a total disaster at the box office and it had cost a fortune already, so they decided to close it down one Saturday. Luckily, Alexander Korda stepped in with the necessary backing and shooting continued on the Monday. Then it became a huge box-office success."[20] Kenneth Turan of the *Los Angeles Times* praised its success (running two years in New York and receiving five Oscar nominations) as "unusual for the time," a "work of art that passionately celebrated creativity and the artistic impulse."[21]

The Red Shoes' success is even more remarkable given its release during a postwar era of declining revenue domestically and overseas. Both British and American markets faced eroding box-office returns and competition with each other over film distribution and import/export revenue, even as independent international coproductions proliferated by the late 1940s and 1950s. *The Red Shoes'* distributor Rank was severely hit by this rapidly deteriorating economic climate. Speaking to his shareholders in October 1948, just before *The Red Shoes* was released in the United States, Rank "quietly told them that bank loans and overdrafts stood exactly at £13,589,858. Within a matter of months, the Rank Organisation was £2,700,000 'in the red.'" Alan Wood described "the inside story of Mr. Rank" in *Everybody's Weekly* on February 23, 1952: "Here, indeed, was the tragic fall from the great plans—made only a few years before—for a grand conquest of world markets by an ever-increasing flow of British films. What had happened? Sixteen million pounds in debt." Given this strained economic reality, "there were many other things that he knew nothing about when he entered the film industry. But, he had promised, 'I can provide the money.'" In the case of *The Red Shoes*, Wood asserted, Rank "kept to that promise with a vengeance. . . . The story of *The Red Shoes* is particularly instructive to anyone who thinks there are easy answers to the perennial problems of film finance. The first budget estimate was about £380,000. In the end, *The Red Shoes* cost over £500,000. It was a story of miscalculation and overspending to horrify any business man; to be quite candid, it horrified Rank. Moreover, *The Red Shoes* won no particular success at the box office in England; certainly it came nowhere remotely in sight of recovering its cost." Yet, by 1952 *The Red Shoes* had grossed roughly $5 million and earned the distinction of being the most successful British film ever released in the United States. In fact, *The Red Shoes* was the only import (number 22) on *Variety*'s 78 All Time Top Grosses in the United States list (each earning at least $4 million), alongside *Gone with the Wind* and *The Best Years of Our Lives*. Ironically, Wood explains, "Not only in America, but in Japan and many other countries, *The Red Shoes* was to prove Rank's biggest money-spinner by far."[22]

The Red Shoes' U.S. reception was a striking contrast to Rank's fears. It was a smash hit. The film was premiered in a prestigious 250-seat stage theater, the Bijou, with advance (more expensive) tickets, reserved seats, an intermission, and program just like in a live theater. Kate Cameron of the *New York Daily News* exclaimed: "A new cinema star was born last night at the Bijou Theatre, where beautiful, red-haired Moira Shearer danced her way to fame."[23] Alton Cook of the *New York World Telegram* proclaimed: "For once, the sumptuous resources of a large musical movie budget are treated with taste, discretion and imagination."[24] Released gradually in selective theaters, *The Red Shoes* built up public interest and momentum in its staggered road show, gaining increasing popularity through word of mouth, simulating a touring company, and eventually going into a wider release. Eagle-Lion's press book noted how much *The Red Shoes* made in each city through the early 1950s and how folks could now see the film at regular ticket prices. There were innumerable ballet cross-promotion tie-ins as well. Taglines called it a "singing" film to promote it as a musical, despite its being a dance melodrama. They also played up the noir love triangle, behind-the-scenes backstage realism, and the fantasy spectacle.[25]

When *The Red Shoes* opened in Los Angeles in December 1948, film critic Philip Scheuer wrote: "The most ambitious—and probably the most dazzlingly successful—use of traditional-type ballet in any motion picture to date occurs in

The Red Shoes, a production of the Archers . . . a couple of conscientious movie makers in England who paint with color as Josef von Sternberg once painted in black and white." Powell explained Hollywood's influence on *The Red Shoes*: "American films with music that I have liked best were *The Wizard of Oz* and *Cover Girl*. They used color as color should be used . . . they were terrific."[26] *The Red Shoes* reimagined a deadly side to Garland's ruby slippers as Dorothy looks over the rainbow in *The Wizard of Oz*. Mozelle Britton Dinehart of *Hollywood Nite Life* called *The Red Shoes* "definite Academy Award material," "one of the finest pictures of all time," "magnificent" in its color presentation with "superb" photography and a "marvelous understanding of character and everyday realities," praising its Technicolor location filming and Mediterranean "scenery" as a "thing of beauty."[27] *The Red Shoes* downbeat musical even drew war-hardened veterans to a ballet movie: veteran Fred Metchick recalled how he and his war buddies rushed out to see *The Red Shoes* and were fascinated by the unvarnished quality to the musical and Walbrook's riveting impresario. The leggy and scantily attired redhead in the posters was an added lure.[28]

MGM'S FREED UNIT: ON THE HEELS OF *THE RED SHOES*

Not surprisingly, over at Hollywood's MGM studio, famed musical producer Arthur Freed aimed to surpass *The Red Shoes* in elaborate musicals such as *The Pirate* (1948), *Words and Music* (1948), *On the Town* (1949), *An American in Paris* (1951), *Singin' in the Rain* (1952), and *The Band Wagon* (1953). Freed's lavish musical *The Pirate* was released the same year as *The Red Shoes* and targeted a female audience with its beautiful spectacle and rich Technicolor. It starred Gene Kelly and Judy Garland and was directed by Vincente Minnelli. Moody and experimental for an escapist Technicolor MGM musical, it featured color noir visual design, black magic, hypnosis, a sexy adult Garland who was married to Minnelli and had just given birth to daughter Liza, and a scantily clad Kelly dancing wildly around a campfire as the object of desire in Garland's racy fantasy. As in wartime film noir, the stylized, brooding mise-en-scène was created on enclosed sound stages and studio back lots rather than the outdoor locations of *The Red Shoes*. Critics noted that Kelly performed "some of the fanciest gymnastic dancing of his career," scaling balconies and swinging through the air with the "authority and grace exhibited by the late Douglas Fairbanks . . . brilliantly photographed in flaming shades of red and punctuated with yellow bursts of flashing gun powder . . . the pinnacle of spectacle." Yet *The Pirate* flopped; it was an astounding $2,290,000 loss for MGM.[29] Life mirrored the art of noir musicals

Prostitute Vera-Ellen dances to her demise in "Slaughter on Tenth Avenue," *Words and Music*. MGM, 1948

when, at the end of filming, Garland suffered a nervous breakdown and was sent to a sanitarium.

Another MGM Freed musical, the biopic *Words and Music* (originally *The Lives of Rodgers and Hart*) was filmed from April through July 1948 and opened in December 1948. It had a faux documentary-style introduction (by actor Tom Drake as Richard Rodgers) and ended with Gene Kelly (as himself) delivering a eulogy for Lorenz Hart. Kelly's extraordinary jazz ballet choreographed to Rodgers's "Slaughter on Tenth Avenue" anticipated the remarkable dance sequences in *On the Town, An American in Paris, Singin' in the Rain,* and *The Band Wagon.* "Slaughter on Tenth Avenue" featured the sultry, violent athleticism of Kelly with dancer Vera-Ellen. In an atmospheric color noir-styled sequence (evoking Berkeley's "Shanghai Lil") filmed with a wide-angle lens, Vera-Ellen gets shot in a speakeasy by sparring gangsters and tumbles head-first down a flight of stairs. *Dancing Times* exclaimed, "Suddenly, the whole picture is made worthwhile. The *Slaughter on Tenth Avenue* ballet comes on. It brings so much vitality into the film that it makes up for all the duller patches. *Slaughter on Tenth Avenue* is a brilliant ballet. I rank it as second only to the *Red Shoes* ballet."[30] As in many musical biopics, Hart's homosexuality was changed to a heterosexual romantic entanglement gone bad to avoid censorship. *Words and Music* depicts Hart as an antihero (Mickey

Rooney) struggling with alcoholism, depression, and poor health.[31] *Words and Music* depicts Hart's death in atmospheric noir style; he staggers from his hospital bed in pouring rain on opening night, collapsing on the wet sidewalk outside the theater below the store window ironically advertising his platform shoes.[32] Unlike *The Red Shoes*, *Words and Music*'s star-studded revue-biopic cost a hefty $3,048,000 to make and resulted in a $371,000 loss for MGM.[33]

Directors Gene Kelly and Stanley Donen's Oscar-winning *On the Town* (1949), on the other hand, was an impressive success for MGM and the Freed unit, costing $2,100,000 and making over $4,440,000. Like *The Red Shoes*, it boasted Technicolor photography combining dance sequences, night shots, and spectacular location filming in New York City. Kelly's moody black, white, and red choreographed fantasy of Leonard Bernstein's "A Day in New York" ballet with Carol Haney adapted Jerome Robbins' 1944 ballet *Fancy Free*. The film opens and closes with Kelly, Frank Sinatra, and Jules Munshin dancing/singing Bernstein's rousing "New York, New York" on waterfront docks, Manhattan streets, and skyscrapers. Freed wrote to *On the Town* directors Gene Kelly and Stanley Donen: "Dear Gene & Stanley: I just ran the cut numbers of *On the Town* and they were the greatest and most inspiring works I have seen since I have been making movie pictures. Pressburger and Powell can't shine your shoes—red, white or blue. Much love from your proud producer. Arthur"[34]

In keeping with MGM's "Ars Gratia Artis" ("Art for Art's Sake") motto, Kelly's atmospheric jazz ballets for Freed's dance musicals at MGM helped elevate color noir to an art form, as *The Red Shoes* had done. Kelly acknowledged the influence of *The Red Shoes* on his ballet sequences in later films like the moody jazz ballet finale in Minnelli's Academy Award-winning *An American in Paris*, shot by noir veteran John Alton with Leslie Caron and Oscar Levant, and featuring Gershwin's music. Minnelli praised *The Red Shoes* for its serious drama and realism. In 1952, as he was directing the hard-hitting nonmusical backstage Hollywood melodrama *The Bad and the Beautiful*, he said, "People look down on musicals, but they have to have just as much quality as good comedy or drama. You must take them seriously while making them. The possibilities are immense in a musical film, they're only beginning. Your *Red Shoes*, for instance, the whole story and drama were wonderful. It was believable, it has great flavor and authenticity." He described the most difficult aspect in making a film musical as "the conception and setting the style, especially when you combine reality and fantasy. The reality must be a little unearthly and the fantasy a little earthy so that they will blend with no shock. . . . It's bad if the story goes along and then the music breaks in, they have to blend."[35] Such realism influenced postwar Hollywood musicals.

FROM BLACK-AND-WHITE NOIR TO COLOR NOIR

Many noir musicals shot in black and white (*Blues in the Night, Young Man with a Horn, The Strip, Glory Alley*), like film noir, were male centered, whereas color noir musicals (*The Red Shoes, A Star Is Born, Young at Heart, Love Me or Leave Me*) were more often about women's dilemmas. Film noir after the war was changing in terms of visual style, gender roles, theme, and emphasis on musical performance. Unlike wartime film noir, increasingly macho late 1940s and 1950s noir pictures were less likely to revolve around musical women such as Hayworth's *Gilda* or Bacall's Slim, who had appealed to home-front women and GIs overseas while bringing economical musical entertainment to crime films. Late 1940s–1950s film noir included fewer musical numbers than *Blues in the Night* or noir films produced during and just after the conflict. Instead, Hollywood turned to darker realistic noir-styled musical dramas, including color noir musicals, biopics, and musical melodramas.

In 1950, five years after sultry Rita Hayworth tantalized troops as top pinup, GIs voted flaxen-haired girl-next-door Doris Day their number one favorite. Day gained fame and popularity singing "Sentimental Journey" as an anthem for World War II servicemen returning home, then starred in postwar noir musicals *My Dream Is Yours* (1949), *Young Man with a Horn* (1950), *Young at Heart* (1954), and *Love Me or Leave Me* (1955). Day sang with Les Brown's big band, married (and divorced) a sax player, and endured many hardships in her personal life that resembled noir musical plots.[36] Dramatic Warner Bros. musicals *My Dream Is Yours* and *Young Man with a Horn* directed by noir veteran Michael Curtiz rearticulated *Blues in the Night*'s jazz noir in variations on the star-is-born narrative. Day plays singers rising to fame while her self-destructive male romantic partners spiral into failure (drunken egomaniacal singer Lee Bowman in *My Dream Is Yours* and alcoholic jazz trumpeter Kirk Douglas in *Young Man with a Horn*.)

My Dream Is Yours depicts postwar realities: Day is a singer and working mom (with a young son), a war widow. A charismatic antihero and a noir visual style would have made it more of a noir musical, but even without such noir musical conventions, it was still darker than traditional musical comedy. Despite Curtiz's expensive Technicolor location filming to "reflect the atmosphere of the fabulous sun flooded town" of Hollywood (as *The Red Shoes* captured the French Riviera), critics called the film formulaic, a "hackneyed reworking of the how-tough-it-is-to-get-a-break-in-show-business." They complained about the downbeat storyline where "disappointment meets his every effort"[37] until the predictable ending. Yet they praised the inclusion of the incongruous cartoon fantasy about the Easter

Bunny. Fans also enjoyed Lionel Hampton's orchestra performing live jazz at the theater.

Fusing Noir with Jazz Musical Melodrama:
Young Man with a Horn

While the female-centered color musical *My Dream Is Yours* focused on Doris Day, Curtiz's next project for Warner Bros., *Young Man with a Horn,* was grittier, featuring a powerful antiheroic leading man. It teamed Curtiz with producer Jerry Wald (*Mildred Pierce*) and writer Carl Foreman (*Champion, The Men, High Noon*) and had music by Ray Heindorf and Harry James. *Young Man with a Horn* was a black-and-white musical noir melodrama revolving around male star Kirk Douglas.

Reimagining jazz noir *Blues in the Night, Young Man with a Horn* was much darker in theme and visual style than *My Dream Is Yours,* though not as dark as *Blues in the Night.* Based on real people and actual events, the film's noir realism allowed alcoholism and other "sordid" topics to go uncensored. Based on Dorothy Baker's 1938 novel (itself inspired by the tragic life of jazz musician Bix Beiderbecke, who died at the age of twenty-eight from pneumonia and alcoholism), *Young Man with a Horn* was the story of talented but self-destructive jazz trumpeter, Rick Martin (Douglas).[38] Rick is a passionate, misunderstood musical genius who wants to push his art beyond formulaic strictures of big band swing to the greater complexity and experimentation of bebop.

To Have and Have Not's Hoagy Carmichael plays the band's piano-player Smoke, who narrates the story. Like *Blues in the Night, Young Man with a Horn* features a psychologically unstable musician antihero (Douglas) in a love triangle with two women. Beautiful Jo Jordan (Day) is a perky blonde singer with a jazz band. (Day's Jo is androgynously named like Lupino's Petey in *The Man I Love* and Lane's Character in *Blues in the Night.*) Rick encounters obstacles in pursuing his jazz music career and achieving success, most notably from his fatal attraction to cold and calculating Amy North (Lauren Bacall)—a femme fatale who actually mentions *Blues in the Night.* She is rich, spoiled, and irresponsible. She destroys Martin's priceless jazz records to play mind games with Martin. As in *Blues in the Night,* a sexual encounter nearly destroys a tormented jazzman. Corrupted by fame, egomania, and obsession Martin eventually collapses, unable to play (like Whorf's antihero in *Blues in the Night*) in a striking noir photographic sequence. He ends up redeemed by his romance with Jo who helps him revive his passion for jazz and women.

Instead of the studio-bound chiaroscuro of *Blues in the Night* and wartime noir, *Young Man with a Horn* featured a lighter, less shadowy visual style shot on location in Los Angeles with backgrounds filmed in New York.[39] *Young Man with a Horn* presents a positive rendering of jazz as in *Blues in the Night.* Juano Hernandez movingly portrays African American jazz trumpeter Art Hazzard, who introduces Rick to music and becomes his mentor, is heartbroken by him, then tragically dies in a sudden accident.

Douglas gave a riveting performance as Rick Martin. While Warner Bros. considered it a vehicle for Douglas, it was actually a multistar draw at the box office with music by Day, Carmichael, and James (who dubbed trumpet solos for Douglas).[40]

Publicity for *Young Man with a Horn* featured sunny blonde Day below top stars Douglas and Bacall, who was portrayed more sexually in a flaming red dress. *Young Man with a Horn* capitalized on Bacall's sultry appeal as enticing diva opposite Bogart (and Carmichael) in musical noirs *To Have and Have Not* and *The Big Sleep.* Against a red backdrop suggesting passion, danger and violence, taglines above Bacall roughly embracing Douglas with her hands gripping his hair clamored: *"Put down your trumpet, Jazzman—I'm in the mood for love!"*[41]

Warner Bros.' trailer promoted the film much like *Blues in the Night* with Douglas as the musician, Bacall with "The Look," and singing blonde Day. "Music: The kind you can't write. The kind you just gotta feel. He played it. Listen: Its haunting beat is telling the whole story of his fight to rise above the past, of his climb from Dixieland jive joints to Broadway's starlit roofs, of the strange adventure that brought him into the lives of two different and exciting women, two dangerous and demanding loves."

In February 1950, *Variety* exclaimed, "For the jazz devotee this is nearly two hours of top trumpet notes. For the regular filmgoer, it is good drama," praising Douglas's "single-minded concentration on a horn," his "eventual downfall" sending him to "alcoholic skidrow," Foreman's "topnotch" adaptation, and Curtiz' direction that "misses no bets in walloping over all the drama and heart-tugs." Douglas "falls for" Bacall, the "marriage that results falls apart, he hits the bottle and winds up a drunk, only to be saved by the wholesome affection that band canary Doris Day has had for him over the years."[42] Critics commended its "slick pictorial smoothness," "exciting" jazz score, Douglas' intense antihero as a "very definite asset as the unhappy young horn player," Day's "sparkling vocalist," and Carmichael's "piano-thumping jazz man" who "recounts" Martin's "tortured life" as "nonpareil of the trumpet." But the *New York Times* noted the "unseen star of the picture is Harry James . . . who supplies the tingling music which flows wildly, searchingly and forlornly" from his "beloved horn." The "soundtrack is more than a complementary force. It is the very soul of the picture." Bacall was called

Bacall: "Put down your trumpet, Jazzman—I'm in the mood for love!" *Young Man with a Horn.* Warner Bros., 1950

a "confused, mentally sick wife," in a "heavy, disagreeable part that would tax the ability of a more accomplished actress."

Thus, critics lauded *Young Man with a Horn*'s jazz music and Douglas and Day's performances, but panned its "stale" melodrama (like they had with *Blues in the Night* and *The Red Shoes*).[43] Nonetheless, *Young Man with a Horn*, which cost $1,310,000 to make, was successful and earned $2,322,000.[44]

By 1950, the psychic instability in noir musical melodrama, such as Douglas's self-destructive jazz musician and Bacall's psychotic femme fatale in *Young Man with a Horn*, mirrored the psychological trauma and paranoia in film noir. In Rudolph Maté's *D.O.A.*, a Bogart-like Edmond O'Brien is poisoned in a nightclub with a luminous substance that suggested radiation poisoning, capitalizing on the fears of the postwar atomic age. All the while, a band blares hot jazz for "jive crazy" beat culture fans. Bogart battles psychological demons in Nicholas Ray's *In a Lonely Place* (1950). Sterling Hayden is a psychotic criminal in Huston's *The Asphalt Jungle* (1950). Gloria Swanson goes crazy after losing her career as a silent film star and murders screenwriter-lover William Holden in Wilder's *Sunset Boulevard*.

BEGINNING OF THE END: FILM NOIR FADES IN A CHANGING HOLLYWOOD

Sunset Boulevard, filmed from April to June 1949, in fact, was the last major feature shot on nitrate film. At the same time, MGM mogul Louis B. Mayer called Wilder a "foreigner" at *Sunset Boulevard*'s 1950 premiere and slammed his negative portrayal of the film industry. Darryl Zanuck of 20th Century-Fox wrote that *"Sunset Boulevard* was a masterpiece until it was released throughout the country and failed to do business. It is not so big a masterpiece today." He cautioned against producing "downbeat," "sordid," "underworld" films with "violence," "low backgrounds," "unsympathetic," "psychopathic" antiheroes or "extreme brutality." He warned his directors and producers, the "public has been saturated with pictures of violence" and "films with underworld or low backgrounds," calling them a "very high risk."[45] It seemed to mark the demise of film noir. Many veteran noir filmmakers moved to other genres and brought noir style to new generic forms.

Film noir's demise paralleled that of Hollywood's Golden Age. In 1950, Hollywood switched from high-contrast nitrate black-and-white film stock with jet blacks and stark whites (better quality images but with fire/explosion risk) to nonflammable acetate safety stock (cellulose triacetate), creating a lighter, grayer style.[46] Studios grappled with antitrust decisions, competition from television, foreign and runaway films, and escalating costs. The Cold War's Red Scare and "blacklists" created a social climate of uneasiness. Gritty noir films and social realist pictures were scorned in favor of entertainment that might ease the pervasive anxiety among Americans.

Noir filmmakers were affected by this evolving climate. Many became a casualty of the Red Scare. *Murder, My Sweet/Crossfire's* Edward Dmytryk and Adrian Scott, *This Gun for Hire/Naked City's* Albert Maltz, Ring Lardner, and *New Orleans'* Herbert Biberman were imprisoned as unfriendly witnesses before HUAC. Noir directors Joseph Losey and Abraham Polonsky (*Body and Soul*) were blacklisted as were writers Robert Rossen (*Blues in the Night/Strange Love of Martha Ivers/Body and Soul*), Carl Foreman (*Young Man with a Horn*), Dashiell Hammett (*Maltese Falcon*), and Arthur Miller (*Death of a Salesman*) and actor Howard DaSilva (*Blues in the Night/They Live by Night*). Blacklisted musical artists included Lena Horne, Artie Shaw, and Leonard Bernstein. Actor John Garfield died suddenly when HUAC demanded he "name names."

Some noir filmmakers went to independent productions (and coproductions) in Europe rather than put up with the xenophobia and paranoia surrounding the U.S. film industry. John Berry moved to France after directing Garfield's last picture, *He Ran All the Way.* Welles and Joseph Cotten (under contract to Selznick) appeared in Carol Reed's 1949 British noir film *The Third Man*, shot in wartorn Vienna with an international cast and crew, independently coproduced by Reed/Korda/Selznick. Jules Dassin, director of *Brute Force* and influential semi-documentary police procedural *Naked City*, was blacklisted. Zanuck sent him overseas to direct *Night and the City* (with Widmark) in London; he made crime film *Rififi* in France. Dmytryk made *Obsession* (*The Hidden Room*) in Britain. Siodmak returned to Europe and directed *The Rough and the Smooth* (*Portrait of a Sinner*) in Britain. Joseph Mankiewicz shot *The Barefoot Contessa* overseas.

While some talented industry professionals made it out and salvaged their careers overseas, McCarthyism nevertheless took its toll. Veteran crime producer Mark Hellinger (*The Killers, Brute Force, Naked City*) died. Noir director Lewis (*Gun Crazy, Big Combo*) suffered a near-fatal heart attack. Dmytryk's wife Jean Porter who starred in musical comedies and Gene Kelly's wife Betsy Drake were blacklisted; Kelly was sent to Europe by his studio MGM, which hurt his career. Noir cinematographer James Wong Howe was "graylisted," along with Lewis Milestone (*Strange Love of Martha Ivers*) and Edward G. Robinson (*Double Indemnity, Illegal*). After *Gang War, Impact, D.O.A.,* and *The Thief,* noir producers Harry and Leo Popkin's careers ended.

Screenwriter Ben Hecht recalled, "Walking at dawn in the deserted Hollywood streets in 1951 with David [Selznick], I listened to my favorite movie boss topple the town he had helped to build. The movies, said David, were over and done with. Hollywood was already a ghost town making foolish efforts to seem alive. . . .

But now that the tumult was gone what had Hollywood been?"[47] By the early 1950s, as noir message films declined, Zanuck (who had produced 1930s gangster films), shifted to widescreen color formats. When Budd Schulberg and Elia Kazan pitched their hard-hitting social realist drama *On the Waterfront*, Zanuck turned it down in favor of more upbeat, spectacular color pictures.

By the mid-1950s, film noir had "ground to a halt," as Paul Schrader explains. "There were a few notable stragglers, *Kiss Me Deadly*, the Lewis/Alton *The Big Combo*, and film noir's epitaph, *Touch of Evil*, but for the most part a new style of crime film had become popular. As the rise of McCarthy and Eisenhower demonstrated, Americans were eager to see a more bourgeois view of themselves. Crime had to move to the suburbs. The criminal put on a gray flannel suit and the footsore cop was replaced by the 'mobile unit' careening down the expressway. Any attempt at social criticism had to be cloaked in ludicrous affirmations of the American way of life. Technically, television, with its demand for full lighting and close-ups, gradually undercut the German influence, and color cinematography [was] the final blow to the 'noir' look."[48] Film noir adopted a lighter "high-key" aesthetic in its visual style, while ideological constraints suppressed noir. After the HUAC hearings, Motion Picture Producers Association president Eric Johnston insisted: "We'll have no more films that show the seamy side of American life."[49]

Howard Hawks shifted from noir to Westerns, comedy, color jazz musical, and science fiction. *Blues in the Night*'s Siegel directed *Invasion of the Body Snatchers*. Robert Wise moved from noir to *The Day the Earth Stood Still*. Fred Zinnemann shifted from noir *Act of Violence* to Western *High Noon* and reimagined Pearl Harbor in the powerful melodrama *From Here to Eternity* before directing the sunlit widescreen color Rodgers and Hammerstein musical *Oklahoma!*. Litvak turned to color widescreen *Anastasia* with Ingrid Bergman. Wilder moved from noir to comedy: Marlene Dietrich is a Berlin nightclub singer in *Foreign Affair*; Audrey Hepburn sings to Bogart in *Sabrina*; Marilyn Monroe parodies dark musicals and noir in color Cinemascope *The Seven Year Itch* and sings with a jazz band and gangsters in *Some Like It Hot*; MacMurray reappears in *The Apartment*.[50] Ray shifted from the noir of *They Live by Night*, *In a Lonely Place*, and *On Dangerous Ground* to moody color Western *Johnny Guitar* with melodramatic excess and musical numbers. After noir films *Raw Deal*, *T-Men*, *Side Street*, and *Border Incident*, Mann made Westerns (*Winchester 73*, *The Naked Spur*) and color musicals (*The Glenn Miller Story*, *Serenade*). In 1953, Jean Negulesco, who directed noir *Road House*, *The Mask of Dimitrios*, and *Humoresque* directed bright color widescreen CinemaScope comedy *How to Marry A Millionaire*. It was a far cry from film noir. As musicals grew in popularity, Jack Webb turned *Dragnet* into a color film with nightclub numbers and directed color noir musical *Pete Kelly's Blues*. Webb played the heavy as Lizbeth Scott croons "That Ole Black Magic" in noir *Dark City*. Scott sings in *The Racket* sans shadows. Jane Russell, like Bacall to Bogart, serenades Mitchum in *His Kind of Woman*.

A Lighter Film Noir Jazz Musical: The Strip

The Strip (1951), in the Korean War period, is a fascinating mix of black-and-white film noir and jazz musical with a star-is-born subplot. *The Strip* was promoted as an "all-time musical" with an "all-star cast."[51] Its opening voice-over narration and on-location shooting on the Sunset Strip, however, evokes *Naked City, Dragnet,* and *Sunset Boulevard*. Mickey Rooney, who struggled to move beyond cheery musical typecasting with *Quicksand* (1950), is cast against type as a returning Korean War veteran and jazz drummer entangled with gangsters and falsely accused of murder in *The Strip*.[52] Like *Blues in the Night, Detour,* and *Young Man with a Horn, The Strip* features a musician antihero with a jazz nightclub singer-dancer girlfriend (femme fatale Sally Forest) ambitiously seeking Hollywood's spotlight. MGM promoted *The Strip*'s jazz music rather than its noir crime sensibility. Its 1950s visual style was different than wartime 1940s noir. Its lighter cinematography reflected television, documentary, and melodrama influences. Publicity featured, "Mickey ROONEY The Musician," playing the drums along with Louis Armstrong, Jack Teagarden, Earl Fatha Hines, Barney Bigard, and the Dixieland jazz of "Basin Street Blues" and Hammerstein's "A Kiss to Build a Dream On." *The Strip* barely recouped its $885,000 cost.[53]

Jazz Noir Musical Amalgam: Glory Alley

Glory Alley was another bizarre musical noir amalgam, an incongruous combination of jazz, ballet, and shrouded noir, defying audience expectations of MGM musicals and its stars. Socially conscious executive Dore Schary had replaced Louis B. Mayer. *Glory Alley* was filmed in November and December 1951 and released in June 1952. Directed by *The Man I Love*'s Raoul Walsh, *Glory Alley* starred *Kiss Me Deadly*'s Ralph Meeker as tormented antihero Socks Barbarosa, a boxer who flees a championship fight, leaving the ring due to a sudden flashback from a violent childhood episode: his abusive father murdering his mother and nearly killing him. To escape the ridicule that follows, he joins the army to fight in Korea and wins the Medal of Honor. *American in Paris* ballet star Leslie Caron is his fiancée Angie, who sings and dances at Chez Bozo, a New Orleans nightclub, while Louis Armstrong works "Blues in the Night" into a hot jazz number with Jack Teagarden at the Punch Bowl bar. Instead of a female-centered color dance musical, *Glory Alley* was a moody noir black-and-white male melodrama. It combined boxing, a war, New Orleans jazz, a seedy cabaret setting, and Walsh's crime style. Like tormented jazz musicians in *Young Man with a Horn* and *The Strip*, *Glory Alley* explores postwar psychic trauma healed by peripheral women. Walsh's gritty film considered courage, valor, character, and patriotism. Filmgoers looking for sweeping romance in a glamorous color musical spectacle like *The Red Shoes* or *An American in Paris* were disappointed. Critics called *Glory Alley* a "ridiculous fiction," a "fatuous little fable . . . supposedly set" on Bourbon Street's "smoky and blues-fogged climate" about a "fellow . . . everybody thinks is a coward because, one night, just before he was to go in a championship prize fight . . . he cut and ran from the ring." They scoffed, "Even after he wins the Medal of Honor in Korea," the "father of his girl still thinks him a coward and refuses to bestow his blessing upon a pending union of the two" until it's revealed that he "has a psychological scar." *Glory Alley*'s music was all that was praised.

Publicity heralded Caron as "The *American in Paris* Girl!" Color noir ads featured black, white, and scarlet (against a muted splash of pale yellow) with the bold red title, "*Glory Alley*" behind Caron kicking her leg up in a revealing black leotard (like Shearer in *The Red Shoes*). With stilettos, a gaudy bracelet and long black gloves, she looks like she is about to do a striptease, recalling Hayworth's glove-peeling "Put the Blame on Mame" number in *Gilda*. Racy taglines clamored: "Street of tough guys . . . hot tunes . . . temptation!" Caron was shown embracing bare-chested hunky beau Meeker (with a muscled arm clad in a black boxing glove), as Armstrong blows his horn.[54] As noir grew increasingly male-centered during this time, the brooding masculinity and marginalization of the female role in *Glory Alley* drew surprising scorn from reviewers: "That cute little French girl, Leslie Caron, who brought such charm and grace to Metro's *An American in Paris*, is wasted miserably . . . stuck with the assignment of playing [a] loyal girl . . . about as pathetic an assignment as we have seen anyone try to handle this year. Except for two welcome chances to shimmy a bit in a Bourbon Street bar, she is given nothing to do but stand by and watch" her man.[55]

Rita's Back: Affair in Trinidad *and* Miss Sadie Thompson

Glory Alley, like many earlier 1940s musical noir films, inhabited an exotic ethnic musical performing space, in this case, the French Quarter in New Orleans. Such locales were often used to convey an illicit noir setting. *Out of the Past* included live jazz in an African American nightspot and an Acapulco Latin jazz club.

Welles's *Lady from Shanghai* was filmed on location in Acapulco and San Francisco's Chinatown. *Lady without Passport* featured Afro-Cuban jazz in a Havana club. Nat King Cole performed jazz in Fritz Lang's exotic *Blue Gardenia* club with Polynesian décor and Pearl Diver mai tais. Foreign locales also offered travelogue allure, a big screen alternative to television. Cain's *Serenade* was a color operatic melodrama filmed in Mexico. After *Gilda* and *Lady from Shanghai*, Rita Hayworth performs in *Affair in Trinidad* and *Miss Sadie Thompson*, shot on location in Hawaii.

Affair in Trinidad (1952) reteamed *Gilda*'s Hayworth and Ford as American lovers in another exotic locale. It was a Beckworth production released through Columbia, directed and produced by Vincent Sherman. Written by Oscar Saul and James Gunn (adapting Berne Giler and Van Upp's story), it costarred choreographer Valerie Bettis, with associate producer Van Upp and editor Viola Lawrence. In this black-and-white film, World War II veteran Steve Emery (Ford) receives an urgent message from his brother in Trinidad but finds him dead when he flies there. He spars with his widowed sister-in-law, Chris (Hayworth), a nightclub singer who mingles with dubious characters. Sparks fly as the couple engages in a tumultuous love-hate affair. As in *Phantom Lady, Gilda,* and *Notorious,* police are suspicious of gangster/club owner Max Fabian and ask Chris to go undercover to spy on him, while Steve jealously objects. Chris solves the case by uncovering a Cold War missile cartel that Fabian was involved with and saving the Western hemisphere from destruction. Fabian dies, and Chris leaves with Steve for the United States.

Filmed January through March 1952 by Joseph Walker, *Affair in Trinidad* was released in late July. Like *Gilda*'s publicity, ads showed Ford slapping Hayworth in the face as she performs in a strapless gown. Taglines clamored: "*She's Back!* With that man from *Gilda!*" and "Don't tell *me* I'm just one more!" Costing over $1 million, *Affair in Trinidad* earned $7 million in the United States alone, outgrossing *Gilda*. Despite its financial success, *Affair in Trinidad* was "pale" in comparison to *Gilda*: its black-and-white cinematography was visually lighter than its shadowy nitrate 1946 predecessor.

Hayworth moved (back) to color pictures, singing the "Technicolor" blues as salacious siren Sadie with José Ferrer as a zealot missionary in a tropical paradise in musical melodrama *Miss Sadie Thompson*. Hayworth's sultry musical number "The Blue Pacific Blues" by Lester Lee and Allan Roberts was nominated for an Academy Award. *Miss Sadie Thompson* was released in 3-D through Columbia in February 1954.[56]

HOLLYWOOD SHIFTS TO COLOR

Film noir style declined after 1953 as studios produced more color films. Hollywood sought to differentiate its cinema product from small-screen television by using widescreen technologies and stereophonic sound; it also relied on color films to meet the industry's "desperate need to lure people away from their black-and-white television sets."[57] In 1950, Technicolor agreed to share its patents after an antitrust decree terminated contracts requiring film producers to use only Technicolor camera equipment, services, and processing for color pictures.[58] This opened the door for color filming. In March 1953 Technicolor announced it would develop film prints of rival "single-negative" processes such as Kodak Eastmancolor using Technicolor to create a "three negative" process. Technicolor would strike three-color separated film strips derived from a single strip of film. Technicolor president Herbert T. Kalmus noted, "Any savings made possible by the use of a single-strip color negative through any black-and-white camera, is therefore available to any producer as part of the Technicolor process."[59] In fact, by 1954, Eastman Kodak's less costly "monopack" single-strip color systems replaced Technicolor's more expensive original three-strip process. The new single-strip color films were easier to shoot (especially with widescreen and CinemaScope films, which required more light), used regular black-and-white cameras, and were more economical, despite offering inferior color compared to the superior hues of the original three-strip Technicolor process seen in *The Wizard of Oz, Cover Girl, The Red Shoes,* and *Gone with the Wind.* (Prestige projects, however, that required enhanced color could arrange for the Technicolor film laboratory to develop Eastman stock using Technicolor's three-color dye transfer process, simulating the look and color of Technicolor's original three-strip process. Hollywood studios often promoted these films as shot in "Technicolor" when they were actually filmed in Eastman and developed by Technicolor.)

By 1954, for the first time, Hollywood produced more color films than black-and-white ones. Fox required that all films shot in CinemaScope be filmed in color, forcing studios like Warner Bros., which had begun filming juvenile delinquent crime film *Rebel without a Cause* in black and white, to reshoot in color. (Black-and-white CinemaScope was finally allowed in 1956.)[60]

The shift from black and white to color changed musicals' visual aesthetic. It was clear the industry was moving to color. Some noir directors and creative talent responded by shifting to musical dramas with darker color noir style. Color noir aesthetic had evolved in painterly Technicolor ballets—*The Red Shoes, Words*

Fred Astaire and Cyd Charisse swivel to "Girl Hunt Ballet—A Murder Mystery in Jazz" in *The Band Wagon*. MGM, 1953

and Music's "Slaughter on Tenth Avenue," *The Pirate, On the Town, An American in Paris, Singin' in the Rain,* and *The Band Wagon.* Toulouse Lautrec's art in *Moulin Rouge* and Vincent Van Gogh's in *Lust for Life* were part of the new aesthetic. Critics praised Huston's atmospheric *Moulin Rouge* for its "magnificent" design and photography. It created a "tangible artist's world inhabited by stylized figures" and featured an "unforgettable" opening can-can dance sequence emerging from "an Impressionist's canvas" as "composition flows vibrantly into life."[61] *The Band Wagon* parodied film noir in Astaire's "Girl Hunt Ballet—A Murder Mystery in Jazz" as Charisse's femme fatale slides across the floor.

Zanuck noted that CinemaScope "adds new dimension" to musicals. He explained, "Even a heavy, downbeat, depressing story can be lifted if it contains a really strong, violent sex situation. . . . *Moulin Rouge* is not a success because it deals with Toulouse Lautrec and his paintings . . . a wonderful, colorful background," but rather because of his illicit affair with a "prostitute" and "other women." He praised "sex" and "showmanship."[62]

Color musicals, Westerns, and melodrama gained in popularity, while censorable noir films were denigrated. A brighter, high-key style replaced the chiaroscuro look and feel of hard-boiled wartime noir films. In a changing industry, even crime films were shot in color—*Rebel without a Cause, Dragnet, Dial M for Murder, Rear Window, Black Widow,* and *Serenade*. In 1954, Fox shot color crime film *Black Widow* with former musical star Ginger Rogers as a femme fatale Broadway star (but without noir shadows). Hitchcock's 1954 *Rear Window* with its shadowy visual design and dramatic low-key lighting, convey the claustrophobic confines of wheelchair-bound photographer L. B. Jeffries' (Stewart) apartment building, thereby retaining a noir aesthetic even in color and widescreen. Joseph H. Lewis's 1955 noir film *The Big Combo*, inspired by the story of Al Capone and Elliot Ness, was originally to be filmed in Eastmancolor. Instead, it was independently produced by star Cornel Wilde and shot in black and white by John Alton in noir style. *The Big Combo* beautifully harkened back to chiaroscuro blacked-out wartime 1940s noir with stark shadows, deep-focus cinematography, and a bluesy jazz score. Filmed on a soundstage with very little light, black velvet, and a fog machine, Alton created a stunning fog-shrouded silhouette finale. But *The Big Combo* was panned by critics. *Mildred Pierce* producer Jerry Wald observed that no 1950 picture earning $4 million had gangster crime or "violence as its theme or basic subject."[63]

By 1954, the industry was almost unrecognizable. Breen retired from the PCA that year, and censorship consequently eased. As Breen received a lifetime achievement award at the Oscars in 1954, the "twenty-sixth Academy Awards play[ed] more like a grim wake than a joyous celebration." Film historian Thomas Doherty writes: "The controlling gaze of television, the extinction of the short film, the risky gamble on CinemaScope, and the retirement of the long-serving chief of the censorious Production Code Administration—all seemed to punctuate the end of a Golden Age, a shimmering epoch when Hollywood held a monopoly over the moving image, when throwaway shorts garnished a beautiful motion picture menu, when the square-shaped motion picture screen was plenty big enough, and when the moral universe projected by the medium was patrolled by a watchful sentinel."[64]

Hollywood itself was a fading star, experiencing a steady decline following its peak in 1946. Observers noticed an "uneasy" industry as Paramount (newly divorced from its theater chains) and Warner Bros. cut employment.[65] Production at Warner Bros. actually came to a halt in spring and early summer 1953. Film historian Ron Haver notes that "in mid-July, Jack Warner announced that the studio, which had been dormant since March, would resume production the following week" with the filming of *A Star Is Born*,[66] much influenced by the highly successful *The Red Shoes*.

Britain's *The Red Shoes* had started an unexpected new trend in the American film industry, with studios hiring European ballet dancers for dramatic musicals. In 1953, *Red Shoes* star Shearer made her Hollywood film debut in MGM's beautiful color noir musical drama *The Story of Three Loves*, reprising her role as an aspiring ballerina who loves to dance to the point of dying for it (this time because of a heart condition). Fellow British star James Mason plays the arrogant Lermontov-style ballet impresario for whom she auditions. *The Story of Three Loves* combined stars from several noir musicals, including *Young Man with a Horn*'s Douglas and *Glory Alley*'s Caron. It won an Oscar for Best Color Art Direction. *Variety* applauded its Technicolor that "makes everything shine the more," its performances, and Gottfried Reinhardt's opening episode "The Jealous Lover" set to Rachmaninoff's "Rhapsody on a Theme of Paganini." Critics praised Sadler's Wells choreographer Frederick Ashton for "some topnotch dance arrangements."[67] Mason had the opportunity to turn in another virtuoso performance as a self-destructive noir antihero opposite Garland the next year in Cukor's *A Star Is Born*.

After *The Story of Three Loves*, Shearer, however, declined further dancing roles in films because she was married and began having children, like so many women channeled back into domestic life after the war.[68] Asked if she avoided Vicky's *Red Shoes* fate by retiring from the screen and stage in favor of domestic life, she replied, "No, leaving the ballet was entirely my own wish. . . . I was a leading ballerina with the Sadler's Wells (now Royal) Ballet for twelve years and, by the early '50s, had also been given a taste of straight acting. I realised that this interested me much more than the narrowness and self-absorption of a classical dancer's life. . . . I was now married, with the first of my four children, and I greatly valued normal family life."[69]

The Barefoot Contessa

In *The Barefoot Contessa* the beautiful philandering dancer-turned-screen star Ava Gardner is gunned down by her war-scarred husband, like disabled Brad killing off singer Kay in *Blues in the Night*. Yet Gardner's heroine is depicted as an idealistic dreamer rather than a femme fatale. Bogart plays her director/mentor/confidante. *The Barefoot Contessa* was filmed in "Technicolor" by *The Red Shoes*' Jack Cardiff on location in Italy with exquisite Mediterranean cinematography evocative of *The Red Shoes* and costarred *The Red Shoes*' Marius Goring.[70] Like in *The Red Shoes*, noir musicals, and noir crime or gothic thrillers, marriage is depicted as a dangerous, and often deadly, nightmare. Bogart even obliquely refers to *The Red Shoes* when he says "life is not a fairy tale" and mentions Hans Christian Andersen, reminding us that "The Red Shoes" ballet was based on Andersen's tale. Bogart also removes Gardner's shoes at the end of the film, as Goring's Julian does to Shearer's Vicky in *The Red Shoes*' finale before she dies. Featuring a noir-style voice-over narration with a flashback structure told from multiple points of view (as in film noir and Welles' *Citizen Kane*), *The Barefoot Contessa*, shot from early January to late March 1954 (as *A Star Is Born* was being filmed), promoted a barefoot Gardner (holding her shoes) as *"The World's Most Beautiful Animal!"*[71] *The Barefoot Contessa* opened in New York on September 29, 1954, the same day *A Star Is Born* premiered in Los Angeles.

A Star Is Born

In 1954, *Seven Brides for Seven Brothers* (MGM) and *There's No Business Like Show Business* (20th Century-Fox) were escapist musicals that celebrated love, fortune, happiness, and success. Another 1954 musical, Warner Bros.' *A Star Is Born*, presented a dark alternative to the idealized world of upbeat musicals. Directed by George Cukor, *A Star Is Born* "musicalized" film noir in a remarkable hybrid of musical and noir styles that deglamorized stardom and success. It was a downbeat backstage melodrama about jazz singer Esther Blodgett (Judy Garland in a triumphant return to the screen) renamed Vicki Lester (evocative of Vicky in *The Red Shoes*) who rises to fame as a Hollywood musical star, yet struggles in a troubled ill-fated romance with self-destructive mentor Norman Maine (James Mason) who discovers her, then is driven to suicide consumed by his own demons.

The quintessential noir musical, *A Star Is Born* innovatively capitalized on limitations of new technology to rechannel noir style and a tragic backstage story into a widescreen color noir musical with distinctive artistry. Cukor, art director Gene Allen, designer George Hoyningen-Huene, and cinematographer Sam Leavitt cultivated extraordinary color noir design for the picture. *A Star Is Born's* color noir visual aesthetic and brooding existential tenor combined elements of *Blues in the Night* with *The Red Shoes*, subverting more typical escapist musical conventions.

Color Noir Style in *A Star Is Born*

From its opening scene, *A Star Is Born* establishes a bleak tone. Thematically, film noir deals with corruption and the underside of society. Noir characters and their environment are ambiguous; normalcy is only a facade. Star Norman Maine's apparent success onstage is countered by his drunken antics backstage. Matt

Libby (*Blues in the Night's* unfaithful trumpeter Jack Carson), the press agent, is also not the friend to Maine that he first seems. His vengeful antipathy for Maine is cloaked by his amicable appearance in public because he is in it for the money (it's his job), as Maine painfully discovers at the racetrack (after returning from the sanitarium). Maine's acquaintances expose the harsh reality of his Hollywood experience—he never had any real friends.

Obsession and alienation typically characterize noir figures. Like protagonists in 1920s and 1930s gangster films, the self-destructive noir antihero struggles against what film scholars Alain Silver and Elizabeth Ward term an "undercurrent of social alienation," "loss of self-control," and "inability . . . to distinguish between benign and malign as he moves through the complex noir underworld."[72] Paul Schrader describes noir films of the 1950s as being characterized by "psychotic action and suicidal impulse" as reflected in the noir hero's battle with the "forces of disintegration."[73] Norman's obsession is his drinking (which is countered at times by his love for Vicki). His alienation is apparent at the racetrack as well as after Vicki/Esther's premiere when he stands apart from the others. The most dramatic example, however, is his isolation as he waits for Vicki to return from work. He is confined indoors putting golf balls, playing solitaire, and taking phone messages for her (while being mistaken for the butler).

This dark tone and pessimistic mood of film noir is also evident in the psychological deterioration that lands Norman in a sanitarium as well as Vicki's resulting emotional instability. There is a kind of circular determinism so that "everything that goes around, comes around" (in Matt Libby's words). This cinematic moral retribution (or "compensating moral values") was reinforced by Hollywood's Production Code that demanded that criminals get their just due in the end. This is seen in *A Star Is Born* when Esther/Vicki goes to the studio after sacrificing her former happy existence with Danny's band for a chance at fame and success: she ends up at the turnstiles at the foot of two sets of stairs, bringing her right back where she started. The turnstile bars (evocative of Welles's *Lady from Shanghai*) symbolize the trap inherent in the pursuit of stardom. This circular pattern resurfaces when Vicki returns to the benefit at the Shrine Auditorium (after Norman's death) and performs at the same place where she first met a drunken Norman. Her past returns to haunt her when she sees the red heart he had drawn on the wall backstage during their first meeting. This noir fatalism also manifests in the destructive nature of their romance—regardless of how hard she tried, "love alone" could not help Norman (as she painfully admits to studio boss Oliver [Charles Bickford] in her dressing room after performing the ironic "Lose That Long Face").

In addition to featuring action typical of noir—drinking, gambling, fighting, and suicide—in *A Star Is Born*, many of the settings are likewise evocative of film noir, such as the Downbeat bar, jail cells, the sanitarium, a funeral, and other dark, claustrophobic interiors. The use of heavy shadows throughout *A Star Is Born* follow noir conventions of expressionistic high contrast and drew on Warner Bros. visual style and lighting of the 1930s and 1940s.[74] This extreme contrast between light and dark (i.e., black-and-white) images is most clearly represented in the typical noir setting: nighttime in the American city. This setting is established immediately with *A Star is Born* in red against the dark panorama of Los Angeles' city lights at night. Another expressionistic influence in film noir is the use of oblique and vertical lines that splinter a screen, making it restless and unstable. This slicing of space within the frame creates tension, as in the opening sequence of *A Star Is Born*. Musical conventions are turned upside down. Darkness and chaos replace lavish costumes and sets. Shots of the black sky are juxtaposed with a close-up of searchlights shorting out and exploding—bringing out the stark contrast. Cukor then cuts to black cars with bright headlights, which are shot to approach at a tilted angle. This shot is juxtaposed with shots of the frenzied crowd outside,[75] angled shots of the exterior of the Shrine auditorium (with crisscrossing diagonal lines and vertical columns), the brightly lit celebrities dressed in black and white, and finally the dark—almost completely black—shots of Libby and studio boss Oliver inside the auditorium. Their conversation is photographed in extreme contrast, first from behind in complete shadow, then from the front with starkly lit faces against a black background. Norman is similarly photographed in complete shadow as he attempts to go on stage from the wings. Esther runs into this black shadow in an attempt to get him off stage before a spotlight illuminates in bright white light. This type of noir contrast, splintering lines, and deep shadows are used throughout the film.

Geometric patterns of light—or barred shadows—are often used in film noir to visually symbolize captivity. When Norman is in the sanitarium, sharp diagonal splinters of light cut through the black shadowed staircase from which he descends to see Oliver. This piercing of compositional space in the frame has the same effect as the chain mesh glass on the sanitarium windows and the prison bars behind Vicki and Norman as they are married: the noir character is trapped. Extreme camera angles also create this visual effect, as when Esther—not yet "Vicki"—sits in the chair of the makeover room. The three cosmetic scientists are shot through a wide-angle lens at an extremely low angle to denote power and create Esther's sense of helpless vulnerability. Mirrors are also used in this scene to dissect Esther into cubistic parts like an insect—a visual metaphor of what they are doing to her.[76] Mirrors and other reflective surfaces, such as water, are also used to reveal the contradicting duality of noir characters and their environment (i.e., appearance versus reality). Esther applies her lipstick in front of a mirror after calmly handling a potential minor disaster and admits how she was really trembling with nerves. Norman throws Libby into a shattering mirror in his dressing room, emphasizing the false nature of their relationship and their deep-seated hatred.

Much of the high contrast of German expressionist and noir films is made possible by black-and-white film. *A Star is Born*, like many postwar musicals, is filmed in color. However, Cukor's color composition throughout the entire film reinforces this noir contrast (usually with black or dark navy, whites, and various muted tones such as gray). The exception used throughout the film is the color red. Red pops in Vicki's lipstick, the neon light flashing outside the Downbeat bar, the stage curtain at Vicki's preview, her dress while visiting the studio, her red satin dressing gown as she sings "It's a New World" to Norman in the dark hotel room after they're married, and in the red carnations (against black-and-white tuxedos) when Esther sings "Gotta Have Me Go with You." There are red lights and red walls backstage as a Degas-like ballet dancer's piercing scream is heard. The audience is clad in black, white, and red with scarlet programs. The walls in the background of the dark bar when Vicki sings "The Man That Got Away" are red in contrast to her navy blue dress that blends in with the black shadow. The color evokes "noir" feelings of passion, blood, and danger (as in "Stop!"). But red, in contrast, also evokes a vibrant life, paralleling in color the standard noir black-and-white contrast. Scenes noticeably absent of red are absent of life, including Norman's decaying bedroom, which is a muted beige (including his pajamas), or Vicki in her sitting room after his death (the first time her lips are not red but a sickening orange). Cukor's color strategy is altered in the final scene at the Shrine. After the dark scene in Vicki's sitting room, this scene contrastingly opens with color, costume, and music. This scene is followed by another contrast, this time between the dark interior of the auditorium and the single white spotlight onstage. Vicki's tearful "Mrs. Norman Maine" tribute in the final scene is evocative of *The Red Shoes* finale where Lermontov tearfully announces Vicky's tragic inability to go on.[77]

Designing *A Star Is Born*: Capitalizing on New Technology

Ironically, the imperfections of the new single-strip color process unexpectedly aided the film's color noir visual style. As film restorationist Ronald Haver suggests, "The wide range and delicacy of color available with the sophisticated Technicolor three-strip method were replaced by the more primitive and garish effects of single-strip WarnerColor, with its much more restricted palette."[78] Art director Gene Allen explained the effect this had on the film: "You didn't have the separation of colors we were used to. We didn't have the grays and the interesting rich blacks and darks. It was kind of muddled up: darks were too dark; where light faded off, it went to green; blues would pop through, so that even on the grayest day the skies would be the brightest blue. Anything that was a cool gray turned blue. And the color was hard—it didn't have the richness and the softness that Technicolor had. If the exposure wasn't absolutely right on, everything would go red. We really had to control what we did and be very careful. It was a moody picture at times, and Cukor wanted to play it for mood. But when you did, the light fell off in the dark; instead of going to rich darks that you can control, they became shadings of green, and this was a problem. Then, we found that the film, even with all our efforts at controlling the color, was just too overcolored, because the Eastmancolor was erratic. So Cukor, Huene [who had worked on Huston's 1952 Technicolor noir musical melodrama *Moulin Rouge*], and myself started a process right then of eliminating color; *we damned near did a black-and-white picture* [emphasis added], except for little accents of color. But then when we did color scenes, where there had to be a lot of color, then we did great color, all controlled and related and in good taste."[79] The results were striking and distinctive.

In deciding how to compose images for the film, rather than fill the entire widescreen CinemaScope space of the frame with action in each shot, Cukor and Allen decided to "leave parts of the screen in darkness or to only use a section of the screen. The technique of isolating sections of the screen is used throughout the picture." Thirty years later, recalling his efforts to create a complete version of *A Star Is Born*, Haver explained, "Cukor was a great student of art. He got his ideas for composition, especially for lighting, from his study of paintings. Gene Allen and George Hoyningen-Huene backed him up on it. . . . Instead of using lots and lots of color, which was the thing you were supposed to do in those days, they kept subtracting color. So the primary color scheme is very natural, subdued pastels . . . no blatant anything. It's all very, very dark, even the daylight scenes." Cukor was so serious about achieving this shadowy look that he had a by-the-book Technicolor cinematographer fired for not subduing the lighting enough to make the scenes sufficiently dark. Cukor wanted "low light levels, the impressionistic feeling of the musical instruments, Garland moving in and out of pools of light with the camera following."[80]

Cukor experimented with the new technology to create a noir-like subjective point-of-view. Allen recalled, "Cukor believed in trying to shoot musical numbers as if they were one shot. We had great camera movements." Al Harrell noted Cukor's "fluid camera style for the musical numbers, a style that seemed to avoid cuts, meant choreographing both the musical number and the camera. . . . Cukor's aim was to use the limitations of CinemaScope—while possibly extending those limitations—in order to make a subtly stylish musical that had something deeply moving and dramatic at its core."[81]

"Musical Noir" Style in *A Star Is Born*

No expense was spared in filming *A Star Is Born*, from costumes to lab work. Garland insisted on wearing the same flesh-colored silk stockings Shearer wore in *The Red Shoes*, which had to be flown in from Paris, and they had "enough money to let Technicolor do the lab work and printing."[82] Al Harrell of *American Cinematographer* recognized *A Star Is Born*'s "controlled, darkly picturesque style, 'the musical noir' style," a "dark color scheme" that "gives the movie a weight and resonance that is very atypical of movie musicals."[83] Cukor described the lure of a "spectacular vista of the whole city from this ugly, dreary roof" as Maine urges Esther to pursue her dreams and ambition. The dark twinkling L.A. skyline suggests the manufactured tinsel of the industry and "offers the magic of a 'Hollywood' Los Angeles as opposed to the grim Los Angeles" Esther "inhabits."[84]

A Star Is Born was also a scathing commentary on the dehumanization of the motion picture industry as the studio system declined in the 1950s. Restoration editor Craig Holt notes the story reveals the entertainment industry's "spirit-breaking machinery, and the havoc it wreaks upon people ensnared in it."[85] Washed-up and unemployed, Norman drunkenly interrupts Vicki's Academy Award victory speech. He accidently slaps her in the face in front of all the Hollywood big shots on live television. In many ways, *A Star Is Born* mirrored Garland's own real-life struggles and remarkable comeback. It shattered the utopian world of classical musicals and repudiated its stylistic conventions, such as cheerful colors, bright costumes, high-key lighting, and a joyous musical soundtrack. Even the camerawork was vastly different. The music, composed by *Blues in the Night*'s Harold Arlen (reflecting the influence of Big Band swing), incorporates a great deal of blues elements atypical of conventional musicals—especially in "The Man That Got Away." The lyrics by Ira Gershwin resonate with pain and loneliness. "It's a New World," which expresses hopeful dreams for a joyous future, is performed ironically with the couple sitting in an almost completely blackened hotel room and again when Norman walks toward the ocean to commit suicide. Music foreshadows his tragic noir fate as the waves crash onshore.

"The Man That Got Away"

Cukor shot the four-and-a-half-minute "The Man That Got Away" number as a single continuous take with no edits as Garland sang "full-out" without lip-synching. Cukor recalled, "I wanted the camera to follow her, always in front . . . sometimes she would go to the side and almost disappear out of the frame . . . all in one long take, for the whole musical number. It isn't easy for an actor or actress to carry a long take—you have to be strong. I wanted to do it with Judy because I knew she could sustain it."[86] In "The Man That Got Away," which evokes *Blues in the Night* and harkens back to the beautifully stylized black-and-white photography of the jam session in *Jammin' the Blues*, "what we did was have the actors in the foreground turn their backs to the camera and go out of focus," Allen explained, "so that the actors in the background could be in focus."[87]

Screenwriter Moss Hart's description of the after-hours bar setting where Esther sings "The Man That Got Away" captures the noir musical mood: "The word

Garland sings "The Man That Got Away" redesigned in shadow for Cinemascope in *A Star Is Born*. Warner Bros., 1954

club is a misnomer. Dive would be more apt. It is a typical musician's hangout—a place where the boys feel truly at home—where they can play as they wish to their heart's content—not set orchestrations for smooth dancing—but improvising, taking off—the kind of place where a new sort of music is born or a Benny Goodman or Bix Beiderbecke emerges, full blown. There are not too many patrons at this hour, but a number of the Glenn Williams aggregation are scattered among the tables, and on the little bandstand a foursome of the Williams Orchestra has taken over. Dan McGuire is at the piano, the drummer behind him, and on each side of him are the clarinetist and the trumpet. In front of them stands Esther. Her eyes half-closed, she begins to sing a low blues—first straight, then as she reaches the second chorus, a wild improvisation begins—throbbing and bizarre."[88]

Arlen collaborated at the piano with Gershwin on a "Dive number" for Garland. Arlen played a song he'd originally worked on with Mercer that began: "I've seen Sequoia, it's really very pretty, the art of Goya and Rockefeller City." Gershwin penned new lyrics that transformed Arlen's music into the most striking memorable song in *A Star Is Born*, "The Man That Got Away." Gershwin's lyrics vividly embody the film's spirit: "The night is bitter / The stars have lost their glitter, / The winds grows colder . . . suddenly you're older. / And all because of / The man that got away. / No more his eager call, / The writing's on the wall; / The dreams you dreamed have all / Gone astray. / The man that won you / Has gone off and undone you. . . . You've been through the mill / The road gets rougher, / It's lonelier and tougher . . . Ever since this world began / There is nothing sadder than / A one-man woman looking for / The man that got away."

"The Man That Got Away" sequence was reshot numerous times and finally redone entirely with different lighting, composition, film stock, and costumes near the final days of production. It was worth the effort. It became one of the most famous scenes in a noir musical, with haunting parallels to Garland's real life. When Mason's fading, self-destructive screen idol hears Esther sing "The Man that Got Away" in the dark empty dive, he is mesmerized: "I've never heard anybody sing just the way you do. That's what star quality was . . . that little something extra. Well, you've got it. Now, what are you doing wasting your time singing with this band?"

Esther replies as Garland might: "Wasting my time? I'm not wasting my time. You don't know how many years it's taken me to get this far. Washing out my gloves in crummy hotel rooms. Winning a contest on the radio. Singing in joints. I can remember my first job singing with a band. Then, one-night stands clear across country by bus. Putting on nail polish in the ladies' rooms in gas stations.

Esther leaves Danny's band to marry Norman, who commits suicide in shadow in *A Star Is Born*. Warner Bros., 1954

Waiting on tables." Although a young aspiring singer, she's a woman who has seen it all: "Wow, that was a low point. I'll never forget it, and I'll never, never do that again. No matter what. But I had to sing. I somehow feel most alive when I'm singing."

Esther's poignant words capture Garland's resilience and perseverance despite challenges onscreen and off. They echo the hardships of singers and musicians on the road. Her life revolves around music and she's willing to pay any dues to perform with a band, get that big break, and cut a hit jazz record. She's an independent woman who's content singing. Maine, in contrast, is obsessed less with his art than with achieving stardom. He is ruthlessly ambitious, willing to abandon the musical ensemble to achieve grander heights.

Vicki lives to sing, as Vicky in *The Red Shoes* lived to dance and as jazz musicians live to play the blues in *Blues in the Night*. But fame and wealth bring only heartbreak and tragedy to Garland's Esther in this "backstage" noir musical. Highlighting the artificial nature of show business, Esther was rebranded "Vicki," as in real life a young singer named Frances Gumm became a star called "Judy Garland." While a significant portion was regrettably cut from *A Star Is Born* following its premiere, Jack Warner assured Hart in a February 25, 1954, telegram: "All re-takes have been made on Downbeat Club dialogue and really are wonderful. What amazing improvement by breaking up scene from Club to parking lot to process in car. All dialogue remains exactly as you wrote it. Know you will be happy to hear this." Cukor was pleased. "We have redone the terrace of the Mocambo" nightclub "and I must say, it seems mighty nice. I think we have generated a lot of sex. She looks attractive and the whole thing is an improvement over the original. We've already done the Downbeat Club and the parking lot, and it comes off with a lot of zip and pep," he wrote to Hart. "She looks perfectly charming in a new Jean Louis dress, and I know that this too is an enormous improvement over the way we first did it—it has fun and spirit. It's been like pulling teeth because Judy really has been under the weather. Walt Disney is breathing down James' neck so we have to get on with it."[89]

Production of *A Star Is Born*

As musicals became the rage in the 1950s, Cukor's *A Star Is Born* was actually a musical variation on his 1932 star-is-born drama *What Price Hollywood?* and Selznick/Wellman's nonmusical 1937 version. It was produced by Garland's husband Sid Luft's independent production company Transcona Enterprises, formed with Edward L. Alperson, partnered with Warner Bros., which provided some of the financing and was given the option to cut the film if production costs exceeded its initial budget of $1.5 million.[90] *A Star Is Born* was filmed from October 12, 1953, through February 13, 1954, with additional retakes and shooting continuing through late July 1954. Production for the film was grueling and expensive. Art director Gene Allen replaced Malcolm Bert and Lemuel Ayers. Garland suffered from exhaustion, anxiety attacks, and drinking problems, eventually needing a two-week "rest and rehab." Mason suffered a brief illness adding further delays and later reshot a fight scene.[91]

Technological and marketing decisions by Warner Bros. contributed to the filming running behind schedule and over budget. Jack Warner initially wanted to film *A Star Is Born* in 3-D, then scrapped this idea to showcase the studio's new WarnerScope anamorphic widescreen process with WarnerColor (Eastmancolor monopack) stock. Unsatisfied with the inferior results of the new technology, Warner decided that "the story is too intimate for WarnerScope" and began film-ing in widescreen three-strip Technicolor. But after eight days of shooting, the studio—impressed with the huge success of 20th Century-Fox' new anamorphic CinemaScope widescreen process used in *The Robe*—shot test footage, and pro-ducers ultimately chose to switch to CinemaScope with multitrack stereophonic sound. They discarded $300,000 of three-strip Technicolor footage already shot, instead going with single-strip WarnerColor film to be developed with the Tech-nicolor dye-transfer process. *A Star Is Born* was Warner Bros.' first CinemaScope picture and only the third film shot in Hollywood using the new process. *A Star Is Born*'s budget rose to $4 million, and production ran nineteen days behind schedule by Thanksgiving. "The Man That Got Away" was completely redesigned and reshot in February 1954. Garland's costume (and MGM designer Mary Ann Nyberg) was replaced, and Columbia designer Jean Louis (famed for her gorgeous gowns for Hayworth in *Gilda*) redesigned Garland's wardrobe to one more flatter-ing in the new anamorphic CinemaScope format and WarnerColor process.[92]

Director Cukor left for Europe near the end of production. Dance director Jack Donahue and choreographer Richard Barstow directed musical numbers with Roger Edens (uncredited) in Cukor's absence, including "Born in a Trunk" med-ley and "Lose that Long Face" (eventually cut from the film for general release after its premiere).[93]

Premiere, Promotion, and Reception of *A Star Is Born*

Two huge premieres were planned, the scale of which had not been seen since the glory days of the 1930s. *A Star Is Born* premiered in Los Angeles on Septem-ber 29, 1954, and again on October 11 in New York, finally to be released October 16, 1954. The *New York Times* reported (much like the opening scene of the film itself), "Crowds of enthusiastic onlookers swirled around. . . . The glare of flood-lights and popping of flash-bulbs provided customary background for the event . . . covered by television cameras, radio broadcasters, Armed Forces Overseas radio, press and newsreel photographers. The sidewalks in front of the two the-atres were carpeted in the traditional red velvet and searchlights sent shafts of light high in the sky over Broadway."[94] Like *The Red Shoes*, *A Star Is Born* was roadshowed at prestigious venues, selling advance tickets in cities across the country. Color noir posters in black, white, red, and blue promoted Garland as a childlike star in a close-up with crisscrossing searchlights behind. With typical noir misogyny, ads showed Norman slapping Garland in the face (clad in her Oscar gown). Publicity advertised the film's cost at $6 million. Its actual $5,020,000 cost was second only to Selznick's *Duel in the Sun,* the most expensive picture produced in Hollywood at the time. *A Star Is Born* earned $4,634,000 domestically and $2,176,000 internationally, for a total of $6,810,000—barely recouping its staggering cost.[95]

After viewing the widescreen "Technicolor" CinemaScope noir musical on September 29, 1954, in its complete 182-minute original premiere form, *Variety* wrote: "*A Star Is Born* was a great 1937 moneymaker and it's an even greater picture in its filmusical transmutation. . . . Judy Garland glitters with that stardust which in the plot the wastrel star James Mason recognizes. . . . From the opening drunken debacle at the Shrine benefit to the scandalous antics of a hopeless dipsomaniac when his wife (Garland) wins the Academy Award, there is an intense pattern of real-life mirrorings."[96]

Praising the New York premiere, the *Times* announced: "Those who have blissful recollections of David O. Selznick's *A Star Is Born* as probably the most affecting movie ever made about Hollywood may get themselves set for a new experience that should put the former one in the shade when they see Warner Brothers' and George Cukor's remake of the seventeen-year-old film" in "one of the grandest heartbreak dramas that has drenched the screen in years." They have "really and truly gone to town in giving this hackneyed Hollywood story an abundance of fullness and form . . . laid it out in splendid color on the smartly used CinemaScope screen." Its spectacle and musical numbers were lauded as the "finest things in the show. And a show it is, first and foremost" with "lush surroundings," "grandeur," "poignance," and performances that "make the heart flutter and bleed." It was a "brilliantly visualized . . . tragic little try at love in an environment that packages the product." Critics applauded the Arlen/Gershwin music, especially "The Man That Got Away" as a "fine, haunting torch-song." Bosley Crowther raved, the "sense of an artificial milieu wraps the whole thing, as in cellophane—all in colors that fill the eye with excitement. It is something to see, this *Star Is Born.*"[97]

But the studio cut the film to a 154-minute version for release to enable more screenings per day. Cukor and Garland, as well as the public audience, were unhappy about the cuts. Angry filmgoers wrote letters complaining that they were outraged to be charged expensive roadshow ticket prices for a much shorter film, which they felt had been "butchered," and wanted to see the original version. Unfortunately, the cut footage was removed from the picture and destroyed. Cukor—

who was not involved in postproduction or in shooting the later upbeat musical numbers incongruous with the darker, brooding dramatic sequences he had shot—did think the film could be trimmed, but in a more nuanced and artful way. (It was partially restored in 1983 to 176 minutes.)

In 1954, *A Star Is Born* was nominated for Academy Awards for Best Actress, Best Actor, Best Color Costume Design, Best Color Art Direction, Best Song ("The Man That Got Away"), and Best Scoring of a Musical Picture (musical director, Ray Heindorf). Garland had just given birth to her son before the Awards and was recovering, so NBC installed a camera in her hospital room and built a tower outside her window to broadcast her acceptance speech if she won. When Garland lost, it was considered one of the biggest upsets in Oscar history. Thousands sent telegrams, including Groucho Marx, who wrote, "Dear Judy: This is the biggest robbery since Brinks."[98] *A Star Is Born* presented a disturbing, unglamorous portrait of Hollywood. It's a world where Hollywood fame produces not happiness but egomania, addiction, self-loathing, and suicide. It's a dark vision for a musical.

Dark Musical Melodrama

From Young at Heart to West Side Story

After the appearance of *A Star Is Born*, brooding musical melodramas such as *Young at Heart* (1954), *Love Me or Leave Me* (1955), and *Pete Kelly's Blues* (1955) fused elements of jazz noir and realism with a star-is-born clash between romance and career (or crime). Experimental variations on noir-styled musical melodrama such as *Sweet Smell of Success* (1957), *A Face in the Crowd* (1957), *Elevator to the Gallows* (1958), and *West Side Story* (1961) revealed a studio system further unraveling and films changing as film noir and noir musicals declined by the late 1950s. Hollywood went after an emerging teenage market, as a new generation flocked to see Frank Sinatra with Doris Day in *Young at Heart*.

YOUNG AT HEART

Warner Bros. remade Michael Curtiz's 1938 black-and-white melodrama *Four Daughters*, which had made a star out of John Garfield, as a new color musical melodrama called *Young at Heart*. *Young at Heart* was produced by *Blues in the Night* noir veteran Henry Blanke (who produced the original and *The Maltese Falcon*) shortly after thirty-nine-year-old Garfield's tragic death while under pressure from HUAC to name names. Gordon Douglas, another noir crime veteran, directed it. Julius Epstein and Lenore Coffee (who had also worked on the original) scripted the film, and Liam O'Brien adapted it.[1]

Young at Heart opens as a sunny musical vehicle for perky, blonde Doris Day, attesting to the popularity of domestic melodrama adapted as color noir musicals in the postwar television era. Reprising Garfield's moving 1938 performance, second-billed Frank Sinatra transforms *Young at Heart's* cheerful opening into a noir musical melodrama with his downbeat entrance 35 minutes into the film. It was Sinatra's first singing role after his dramatic Oscar-winning role in *From Here to Eternity* revitalized his career. Like Day and Priscilla Lane, Sinatra started as a band singer. He sang with the Harry James and Tommy Dorsey bands, becoming a huge success during the wartime musicians' strike as a solo vocalist. In 1944, he introduced himself as the "hoodlum from Hoboken" on Armed Forces Radio and sang "Long Ago and Far Away" from the noir musical *Cover Girl*. He performed with Gene Kelly in *Anchors Aweigh* (1945) and *On the Town* (1949), married Ava Gardner, and then suffered vocal hemorrhage. Another real-life star-is-born character, his career declined even as his wife became a celebrity.

In *Young at Heart*, Sinatra played a gritty part, as he later would do in *Man with the Golden Arm* (1955), *The Joker is Wild* (1957), and *Pal Joey* (1957). Sinatra's bitter performance as emaciated self-destructive jazz musician Barney evoked *A Star Is Born*'s Norman Maine. As Garfield had before him, Sinatra stole the picture (and the girl). He captivates beautiful Laurie (Day), his friend Alex's (Gig Young) fiancée, with a mesmerizing rendition of "Just One of Those Things" in a deserted late-night dive, recalling the melancholy mood of *A Star Is Born*'s "The Man That Got Away." Barney marries Laurie, sweeping her away from her loving suburban family home to a life on the skids as wife of a musician-gambler who faces tough times in New York (recalling *Blues in the Night*'s antihero). He eventually tries to kill himself in a car crash on a dark snowy night. *Young at Heart* shifts from a scene of familial bliss to a seedy world of bookies and jazz music in the urban jungle, breaking Day's heart. The nuclear family in suburbia is depicted as far more pleasant than city life in the Big Apple, a theme reflecting the mood in postwar suburban baby-booming America. The film surprisingly ends with the couple singing together in celebration, crooning to their child who is born with her family in suburbia.

Like the antiheroes in *Blues in the Night* and *Young Man with a Horn*, Sinatra's tormented piano player/composer in *Young at Heart* strives for jazz music artistry but never achieves fame. He writes music for his less-gifted friend Alex who uses Barney's compositions and arrangements to achieve success on Broadway while Barney struggles to make a living. This mirrors the real life of many talented black jazz artists who arranged or composed for renowned big band leaders—often white—who paid handsomely for their artistic expertise. Even prolific maestros like Ellington used the work of lesser-known brilliant and openly gay arranger/composer Billy Strayhorn, who penned "Lush Life" and Duke's signature "Take the 'A' Train."

Young at Heart evokes the moody film noir atmosphere, capturing Sinatra/

Hardboiled jazz musician Frank Sinatra sings the blues and attempts suicide in *Young at Heart*. Warner Bros., 1954

Barney's heartbreak vividly brought to life in Cole Porter's melancholy lyrics. The dingy club becomes a metaphorical cage when shadows from a skylight form splintered crisscrossing diagonal bars across the ceiling of the dark empty room, a claustrophobic interior reminiscent of the low-key after-hours setting in *A Star Is Born*. Sinatra bids farewell to Laurie who is about to marry Alex in minor-key blues: "So good-bye, good-bye, bye, bye, goodbye baby, and amen. Here's hoping we meet now and then. It was great fun, but It was just one of those things."

Sinatra's anguish and false bravado as he sings of his defeat alone at the piano, created a noir musical milieu like that in *Blues in the Night* and *A Star Is Born*. Day suddenly appears as an ethereal apparition in the doorway behind him just as he finishes singing his blues and turns from the piano to take a drag on his cigarette.[2] Day's sunny suburban world of musical cheer contrasts with Sinatra's brooding blue-toned alienation in a noir collision of opposites. Like in *A Star Is Born*, Sinatra's antihero leads Day's upbeat performer into a darker existential world. In *Young at Heart*, Laurie leaves upbeat composer Alex, quits singing, and becomes the pregnant domestic spouse of a suicidal husband.[3] Just as women left the workforce and returned home after World War II, Day is happier staying at home singing with her family rather than pursing a profession.

Young at Heart's color noir publicity featured black, white, red, and muted tones showing Sinatra's suicide attempt behind the wheel. He is shown wearing a noir-style fedora and trench coat with a cigarette dangling from his mouth; his expression is morose, as sleet and snow pelt the windshield of his car. Ads shouted that it was shot in "WARNERCOLOR printed in TECHNICOLOR." Reviews called Sinatra as Barney a "rude and bitter misfit with splendid talents in the musical line" that "does the most disrupting and is most radically reconstructed in the end." In the original film *Four Daughters*, Garfield dies at the end of the movie. Critics noted that *Young at Heart's* version allowed Sinatra's "hard-luck character" to live and "recover from his attempt at suicide." They critiqued Day's upbeat heroine as "sometimes much too bubbly," but admired Sinatra's unvarnished antiheroic performance: he "put quills on the misfit before they blunt him to conformance in the end." They also praised Sinatra's troubled composer/musician singing the blues in an after-hours nightclub, calling his rendition of "Just One of Those Things" one of the film's finest numbers.[4]

Young at Heart exemplifies the changes in the 1950s that channeled noir films with music into color musical melodrama.[5] The Hollywood studio system was unraveling and independent production soaring; widescreen and color films competed with television, and less expensive single-strip Eastmancolor and Cinema-Scope led to the creation of noir musicals. Warners' noir crime talent shifted to color musicals. In 1953 (prior to remaking *Four Daughters* as their color musical *Young at Heart*), Douglas and Blanke shifted from noir to backstage musical melodrama *She's Back on Broadway*, shot in Warnercolor in noir style to simulate the red color scheme and stylized backstage ballet performances of *The Red Shoes* in a theatrical Broadway setting (though less imaginatively). It featured leggy blonde star Virginia Mayo (in a sexy red dress), tormented Garfield-like stage director/ex-lover Steve Cochran, Carnival costumes, jazz/tap-dance sequences (atop a piano), and even a performance of "Blues in the Night." However, the choreography, music, stars, and cinematography were pale in comparison to The Archers' vibrant three-strip Technicolor French Riviera and ballet sequences of *The Red Shoes*.

Douglas and Blanke reteamed for *Young at Heart*, filmed July to September 1954, a year after *A Star Is Born* began filming, completing production just as *A Star Is Born* premiered. Those making noir musical films made around the same time were well aware of the themes and scripts of other projects, especially those at the same studio. After Sinatra was considered and rejected as box-office poison for *A Star Is Born*, his bluesy, downbeat song in the bar in *Young at Heart* evokes Garland's "The Man That Got Away," a star comeback vehicle coinciding with his revived career. As *A Star Is Born* showcased Garland, *Young at Heart* featured re-cording stars Day and Sinatra singing music by George and Ira Gershwin ("Some-one to Watch Over Me"), Cole Porter ("Just One of Those Things"), Harold Arlen and Johnny Mercer ("One for My Baby"), Ray Heindorf ("Til My Love Comes Back to Me"), Sammy Fain ("There's a Rising Moon for Every Falling Star"), and Johnny Richards and Carolyn Leigh ("Young at Heart"). *Young at Heart* composer/conductor Ray Heindorf worked on noir musicals *Blues in the Night*, *The Man I Love*, *Young Man with a Horn*, *A Star Is Born*, *Pete Kelly's Blues*, Kazan's melo-drama *A Streetcar Named Desire*, and Hitchcock's *Strangers on a Train*. Just as *A Star Is Born* was produced by Garland's husband Sid Luft's Transcona Enterprises, *Young at Heart* was a musical remade in color and produced by its singer star's spouse's independent company. Day's husband was Martin Melcher who owned Arwin Productions and worked with Warners. *Young at Heart* promoted its re-cording stars and hit records as ancillary merchandise, publicizing Day's songs for Columbia Records and changing the film's title (from *Four Daughters*) to capi-talize on Sinatra's popular hit "Young at Heart."[6] *Young at Heart's* serious noir musical melodrama storyline with a piano player/antihero attempting suicide (not surviving in the original film) prompted *Motion Picture Herald* to note its incongruously upbeat title upon its December 1954–January 1955 release. After dying in *From Here to Eternity*, Sinatra—who by this time had considerable clout after winning an Oscar and experiencing recording and film success—did not want to perform another death at the end of *Young at Heart*.[7] *Young at Heart* cost $1,653,000 to make and grossed $3,102,000.[8] Across town, MGM emulated War-ner Bros.' success.

LOVE ME OR LEAVE ME

Film studios looking for an audience found one in color period spectacles. Biog-raphy was also popular, especially musical biographies. Portraying the lives of jazz singers tapped into both the postwar trend in realism and the influence of film noir. *Love Me or Leave Me* was a film that took advantage of Doris Day's success in *Young at Heart*. Day hit her stride in a sexy, hard-hitting dramatic performance opposite gangster/lover James Cagney in this 1955 MGM color noir musical. The film, a biopic of singer Ruth Etting, was directed by Charles Vidor (*Cover Girl, Gilda*) and produced by Joe Pasternak. Etting ambitiously pursues her showbiz career from Jazz Age dance hall girl to Broadway's Ziegfeld Follies and Hollywood. She marries "The Gimp" Snyder (Cagney), a violent hoodlum who drives her to drink. Etting leaves him for her piano player, who is in turn shot by her former lover. Thus, the film offers plenty of noir backstage crime as well as the ever-present love triangle. Evoking Warners' *Blues in the Night,* it was originally titled *Singin' the Blues* (and *The Ruth Etting Story*). In casting Day and Cagney—two iconic Warner Bros. stars—MGM turned the tables back on Warner Bros., who had cast former-MGM musical stars Garland and Sinatra in *A Star Is Born* and *Young at Heart.*[9]

Biopics depicting a shady crime milieu were problematic with censors, who would omit or alter particularly frank biographical facts. Day later recalled a violent rape scene with Cagney that was omitted due to censorship concerns.[10] Finding the right stars also took time. Bogart and Widmark were considered for the role of Snyder. Jane Powell, Jane Morgan, and Ava Gardner were considered for Etting. (Gardner was placed on suspension for refusing the role because she was "afraid it would be just another fairly standard biography.")[11] Etting refused to approve an August 1954 screenplay draft that suggested she and Snyder were having an affair early in her career, when they had actually been married. When Etting insisted the script be altered, the PCA responded: "This presented the Code problem of the breakup of her marriage to The Gimp and the suggestion that she eventually marries her piano player." Since Etting's marriage in fact ended because of Snyder's vicious nature and not for "romantic reasons" (i.e., to marry someone else), it was possible to circumvent the Code's ban on divorce. According to *Variety* editor Joe Schoenfeld, Etting and Snyder threatened "to sue Metro if it portrayed them not married, which would be tantamount to telling the world that they had lived together 'in sin.' Now the company is caught between the Code and the threat of a lawsuit, but with still no solution to the crux of the drama." Breen sent a letter to *Variety* denying the columnist's accuracy. Schoenfeld replied: "If the facts as I wrote them . . . are incorrect as pertaining to your office, then some of the people associated with this picture at Metro are sadly misinformed." The film was shot from early December 1954 to mid-February 1955. It premiered in late May and opened June 1955, earning $4.1 million.[12]

Color noir publicity in black, white, red, and muted tones featured scantily attired Day opposite gangster Cagney in a "*Life-inspired drama from dance hall to Ziegfeld Follies!*" MGM's "*dramatic musical*" in "CINEMASCOPE *and* COLOR!"[13]

Gangster James Cagney delivers "rough stuff" pursuing singer-dancer Doris Day backstage in *Love Me or Leave Me*. MGM, 1955

The *New York Times* commented: "In the Thirties it was common knowledge along Broadway that the popular singer Ruth Etting was something of a brow-beaten slave of her husband, an ex-Chicago mobster named Martin Snyder, better known as The Gimp. Miss Etting's friends finally helped her to get a divorce, after which The Gimp expressed his sentiments by dispatching a couple of bullets into the man who later married her. Needless to say, the pretty details of this little show-world idyl found their way into any number of gangster movies. But real names were never used, and finally the story of Miss Etting and The Gimp went out of fashion and out of mind." The *Times* added that MGM remembers this "none-too-delectable affair" in *Love Me or Leave Me* "with music" using "real names" with Day as "blonde," "bewitching" Etting and Cagney with "verve," "virtuosity," and "propitious skill" giving "hardboiled muscler" The Gimp "vividness and gutter gallantry," making him "sufferable" so it's "possible not only to stand him but to like him."[14]

Variety observed: "The off-beat aspects of the strange real-life relationship of Etting and . . . Snyder has been caught with an honesty and realism that borders on creating mixed emotions. . . . Doris Day as Etting, is so consumed by ambition as to blot out the nefarious antecedents of 'The Gimp,' so ably played by James Cagney. His personation of the clubfooted Chicago hoodlum and muscle-man is the Cagney of the Warner Bros. gangster pictures of the early 1930s—hard-bitten, cruel, sadistic and unrelenting. It becomes difficult betimes to know for whom to root. Their 'marriage' is a strange thing. Her recourse to the bottle; her dull-eyed acceptance of the somewhat unholy nuptial alliance; her consuming ambition to scale the heights; her careful decorum vis-à-vis pianist-arranger Johnny Alderman (well played by Cameron Mitchell); the patience of the agent (Robert Keith, another good job); the dogged faithfulness of Harry Bellaver as the dimwit stooge-bodyguard, and the rest of it, make for an arresting chunk of celluloid. . . . In CinemaScope and color, it's a rich canvas of the Roaring 20s with gutsy and excellent performances."[15]

Critics noted that Cagney and Day made an "uncommonly interesting" "dramatic couple for a musical film." Comparing Cagney to his crime persona in Warners' gangster films, they observed that when he "slaps Miss Day in the face, the audience reacts to the shameful violence with genuine and audible gasps. It's as real as when the old *Public Enemy* squashed a grapefruit in Mae Clarke's face." MGM's color CinemaScope noir musical was called "expensive and atmospheric of the era of night clubs and booze" in a "stinging but entertaining" film.[16] *Love Me or Leave Me* received an Oscar for Best Story and was nominated for Best Actor (Cagney), Screenplay, Sound Recording, Song ("I'll Never Stop Loving You"), and Score.

In March 1957, *Variety* reported that Etting filed a $1 million libel suit against Hearst's *Cosmopolitan* regarding an April 1956 publicity story on Day's performance in *Love Me or Leave Me*, which described her in noir tagline fashion as "a famous girl singer of the twenties who fell in love with a bad man, became an alcoholic, and inspired a murder."[17]

PETE KELLY'S BLUES

Back across town, like MGM's *Love Me or Leave Me*, Warner Bros.' *Pete Kelly's Blues*—with Jack Webb, Peggy Lee, Ella Fitzgerald, Janet Leigh, Edmond O'Brien, and Lee Marvin—was a color CinemaScope noir musical set in the 1920s Prohibition era. Based on NBC's short-lived 1951 radio series, *Pete Kelly's Blues* illustrates the shift from classic film noir to postwar color musicals inspired by radio and television. Noir film/radio actor-turned-TV star Webb was a supporting player in such noir films as *He Walked by Night, Sunset Boulevard,* and *Dark City* and became a huge television star as Sgt. Joe Friday in the 1951 police procedural series *Dragnet,* based on the radio series. Webb gained so much clout from his television success by 1954 that Warners paid Webb $800,000 to direct *Dragnet* as a 1954 color noir feature film with musical numbers (and complete creative control). Then he produced, directed, and starred in the costly widescreen color noir musical *Pete Kelly's Blues,* written by *Dragnet's* Richard Breen. Color noir crime film *Dragnet* featured the Red Spot bar with neon lights and jazz ambiance, frequented by gangsters. The Herm Saunders Trio performs "Foggy Night in San Francisco." Pete Kelly's Blues Radio Orchestra jazz combo in the film *Dragnet* appears in *Pete Kelly's Blues.*[18]

Mid-1950s noir musicals like *Pete Kelly's Blues* were further variations on *Blues in the Night. Pete Kelly's Blues* opens in New Orleans and moves to a Jersey City railcar where a man wins a cornet in a crap game. Like *Blues in the Night, Pete Kelly's Blues* features a jazz band, gangster violence in a speakeasy roadhouse, a bluesy jazz vocal as its title song, and the demise of a musical performer in a mental hospital. Peggy Lee plays a jazz singer and abusive gangster's moll who is violently beaten by thugs, goes crazy, and is institutionalized (like *Blues in the Night* and *A Star Is Born* characters). In a mesmerizing moment, Ella Fitzgerald exhibits her vocal jazz artistry in an evocative rendition of "Pete Kelly's Blues" in her shrouded roadhouse on the other side of the tracks, reminiscent of the way Gillespie sings "Blues" in jail. Webb's cornet player Pete Kelly plays jazz in Kansas City gangster speakeasies, but he never reaches the level of Ella's style. Directing himself, Webb composed an awkward lengthy shot of Kelly (himself) *watching* Ella rather than showing her singing, suggesting a missed opportunity to show more of her artistry. Unlike tormented antiheroes in *Blues in the Night* and *Young Man with a Horn,* Webb's musician doesn't sing the blues or pursue a musical art form; he doesn't seek fame or success. Like the band in *Blues in the Night,* or Esther when she played with Danny's jazz combo on the road in *A Star Is Born,* Kelly is just happy for his band to have a gig, even in a cheap illegal gangster dive that gets raided by the cops. But he's not a musical genius/antihero creating jazz as art.

Pete Kelly's Blues was filmed from March to May 1955 in WarnerColor Cinema-Scope. Its Prohibition setting targeted nostalgic older audiences with gritty big-screen color spectacle not available on TV. It appealed directly to women with glamorous costumes and numbers and to combat-hardened war veterans with crime, gangsters, and violence. Color noir publicity for *Pete Kelly's Blues* simulated black-and-white noir (with a wash of steel blue like for *Blues in the Night*) and splashes of scarlet red (and muted pale yellow), proclaiming "*CinemaScope*" and "*WarnerColor.*" Warner ads deliberately made blonde star Leigh resemble Doris Day, who was gaining success at MGM in *Love Me or Leave Me* in her sexy new role. *Pete Kelly's Blues* publicity taglines announced: "Warner Bros. present the story of a jazz-man of the wide-open 20's . . . caught in the crossfire of the blazing .38's!" alongside an image of coatless, hatless Webb with an open collar and unfastened tie, cigarette and cornet in hand. Below, a shadowy black-and-white gunfight is in process, with inserts of platinum blondes Leigh and Lee singing. (Fitzgerald featured more prominently in black and bright scarlet ads that targeted African Americans where she is shown with a black-and-white image of Webb looking more "ethnic" and blowing his horn.)[19]

Released August 1955, *Pete Kelly's Blues* had all the trappings of jazz noir. *Variety* wrote: "Jazz addicts (usually highly opinioned) may have a special interest in the musical frame. Beyond this special-interest factor is a melodramatic story that catches the mood of the Prohibition era." They described it as a "gangster picture (without the cops)" "woven" with "Dixieland" music and a "smalltime bootlegger-racketeer." Lee "scores a personal hit with her portrayal of a fading singer taken to the bottle." In the same way that *Blues in the Night* was dismissed, *Pete Kelly's Blues'* lavish, nostalgic Jazz Age widescreen color musical also fell flat with critics. They complained it was *Dragnet* made into a widescreen color musical, calling it "*Webb Plays the Blues*" and an "incredible waste of tantalizing music and decor designed for the sole purpose of letting Jack Webb strut his stuff almost exactly as before." He "simply swaps his *Dragnet* badge for a cornet and triumphantly battles some prohibition-era Kansas City mobsters. The picture should have been a knockout." Its "superb assortment of period settings and costumes, garishly tinting a CinemaScope screen" with "tingling atmospheric detail," a "smattering" of "authentic background jazz," and Fitzgerald and Lee singing the blues in poignant pathos, should have been a "perfect set-up for that rarity—a sturdy picture about dedicated musicians." Instead it's "plain jailhouse."

Critics knocked its sensationalized violence, "random brutality," and Webb's directing, but praised its "musical trimmings," particularly Fitzgerald's blues vocals. They liked the "story of jazz" (reminiscent of *Blues in the Night, Syncopation,* and *New Orleans*): "About five minutes (out of ninety-five) suggest the picture this might have been. Take the ingenious prologue, the funeral of a Negro cornetist in the bayou country. Or take the fleeting scenes when the wonderful Ella Fitzgerald, allotted a few spoken lines, fills the screen and sound track with her strong mobile features and voice. The grand title ballad, by Ray Heindorf and Sammy Cahn, should be remembered long after the picture is forgotten. For Sergeant Friday— or Mr. Webb—has deliberately passed a cheap musical counterfeit."[20] Despite Fitzgerald's remarkable bluesy jazz version of its title song and Lee's moving performance, the film was disappointing. It seemed an empty shell of big-budget widescreen color instead of an authentic jazz noir reimagining of the Roaring 20s Jazz Age. Nonetheless, Pete Kelly's Blues, which cost $1,525,000, was a commercial success that took in $3,496,000 and spun off an NBC television series in 1959.[21]

SWEET SMELL OF SUCCESS

Unlike the color widescreen spectacle of Pete Kelly's Blues, just two years later— in film noir's last gasp—other films featured a harsh, grittier look at backstage themes in black and white. Jazz melodrama Sweet Smell of Success (1957) marked British director Alexander Mackendrick's American film debut. It was independently produced by Burt Lancaster, Tony Curtis, James Hill, and Howard Hecht (Hecht-Hill-Lancaster, Norma-Curtleigh Productions)[22] and released by United Artists. It presented a bleak vision of backstage corruption and McCarthy-era informing in a brooding black-and-white documentary style. Influential noir cinematographer James Wong Howe shot striking images on location in New York nightspots. Independent producers Lancaster and Curtis were gorgeous leading men, well known for their romantic roles and sex appeal.[23] While Trapeze (featuring Lancaster and Curtis in a love triangle with Gina Lollobrigida) was set in glamorous Paris in color, Sweet Smell of Success deglamorized Lancaster and Curtis as opportunistic antiheroes in searingly unattractive roles in Manhattan's high society.

Sweet Smell of Success was based on Ernest Lehman's 1950 novella, Tell Me About It Tomorrow! It was adapted for the screen by Clifford Odets, Lehman, and director Mackendrick. It depicted ruthless, power-hungry New York Globe Broadway gossip columnist J. J. Hunsecker (portrayed by Lancaster with icy perfection— the character was based on Walter Winchell) and slick double-dealing press agent Sidney Falco (Curtis, evoking Matt Libby in A Star Is Born) and their corrupt ambition. It captured the manner, dialogue, and lifestyle of hustlers lusting for power, fame, and a fast buck as they comingle with senators and starlets at the 21 Club. Sweet Smell of Success exposed sleazy big-time operators corrupted by fame and power, "savagely" dissecting a "sordid" world of frenetic malice, venal bribes, payoffs, manipulative schemes, and evil "machinations" facilitated by J. J.'s "avid coterie" of crooks. The film cooly examined a nocturnal urban jungle. Punchy dialogue included Lancaster's caustic line: "I'd hate to take a bite outta you. You're a cookie full of arsenic." Cinematographer Howe applied petroleum jelly to Lancaster's glasses to enhance his menacing stare. Elmer Bernstein composed the score, with jazz music composed by Chico Hamilton and Fred Katz and performed by the Chico Hamilton Quintet—Hamilton, Katz, Paul Horn, Carson Smith, and John Pisano (with bassist Buddy Clark sitting in on a jam session).[24] Jazz and musicians, unlike most of the other characters, are presented positively in *Sweet Smell of Success* as they were in *Blues in the Night* and *Jammin' the Blues*.

Like in *The Red Shoes* and other star-is-born narratives, an older mentor tries to break up a young couple's marriage because of his repressed desire for the young woman. Sick with ego and jealous rage, Hunsecker tries to destroy the young jazz musician, Steve Dallas (Marty Milner), who is engaged to his nineteen-year-old sister Susie (Susan Harrison). He plants false press stories that Steve is a Communist who smokes marijuana, thus getting him fired from the club—after Steve calls J. J. a "national disgrace" full of "phony patriotism." Hunsecker entices Sidney Falco with promises of getting his stories in print to plant narcotics on Steve, the only innocent person in the film. Like a mob godfather, J. J. calls in favors, getting crooked cop Harry Kello (Emile Meyer) to brutally beat Steve and arrest him on false charges. Evoking the forbidden romance in *West Side Story* (simultaneously being produced on Broadway but not yet filmed) and Paul Muni's incestuous relationship with sister Ann Dvorak in *Scarface*, J. J. plans to vacation with Susie after breaking her engagement.[25] Hunsecker loses his sister's loyalty and their relationship, admitting "You're all I've got in this whole wide world" before coldly arranging with Falco to ruin her fiancé. Susie allows J. J. and Falco to destroy each other, then walks out to join Steve at the hospital.

Sweet Smell of Success originally ended with Susie accusing Sidney of rape and Sidney being murdered by Hunsecker but was changed to appease censors. In May 1949, producers inquired if Lehman's story posed any problem for the PCA. Breen insisted the story was "unacceptable" due to its depiction of incest and marijuana. After Breen retired in 1954, his PCA successor Geoffrey Shurlock still considered it problematic in July 1956. By January 1957, its negative depiction of police lieutenant Kello was allowed (after adding an honorable policeman), and it received a PCA seal of approval without substantial changes.

There were tensions on the set. When Hecht-Hill-Lancaster purchased the story in 1955, writer Lehman was supposed to direct. Lehman scouted locations in spring 1956, but then the producers fired him (noting United Artists was resistant to having a first-time director, although Hill admitted he never intended for Lehman to direct). Sinatra and Welles were considered for leads, but Lancaster and Curtis sought the leads for themselves. Robert Vaughn was set to play Steve, but he was drafted. It was shot on location in New York from November 1956 through March 1957 (with additional scenes shot through May). It was a contentious shoot. At one tense moment, Lancaster threatened to hit writer Lehman, who retorted: "Go ahead, I need the money."[26] Clifford Odets rewrote the script, with many last-minute changes that created delays—filming was postponed for ten days in late February because of revisions. Lancaster and Mackendrick clashed over the ending and portrayal of Steve in the film. Young Susan Harrison was overwhelmed by the star's/director's/producers' intense personalities.

Publicity promoted *Sweet Smell of Success* with sensational taglines: "They know him—and they shiver—the big names of Broadway, Hollywood and Capitol Hill. They know J. J.—the world-famed columnist whose gossip is gospel to sixty million readers! They know the venom that flickers in those eyes behind the glasses—and they fawn—like Sidney Falco, the kid who wanted 'in' so much, he'd sell out his own girl to stand up there with J. J., sucking in the sweet smell of success! This is J. J.'s story—but not the way he would have liked it told!" Against a backdrop with ominous images of Lancaster and Curtis, posters for *Sweet Smell of Success* warned: "Beware these Gentlemen of the Press!"[27] The film was released in June 1957. Viewers and critics objected to its unsympathetic roles for favorites Lancaster and Curtis. However, it was praised as one of the year's best films by *Time* and *New York Herald-Tribune,* which reported that it would not recover its $1.3 million production cost. Eventually it came to be celebrated as a cinematic milestone for boldly referring to the blacklist. *Sweet Smell of Success* was among eighty-two films blocked by the U.S. Information Agency from screening in twelve countries in May 1959 for "painting a false picture abroad of the United States."[28]

1957: *JAILHOUSE ROCK* AND *A FACE IN THE CROWD*

Noir icon Humphrey Bogart died in 1957. Hollywood's classical studio system was also dying, and black-and-white film noir and noir musicals were in decline. Color films were influenced by noir and noir musicals, yet they were distinct from the 1940s noir cycle. Big bands burdened by economic constraints declined after the war. Musicals in the early to mid-1950s featured jazz recording artists Sinatra, Garland, Armstrong, Day, Carmichael, Ellington, Holiday, Fitzgerald, and Lee. Though jazz reached new heights in artistry and virtuosity, popular music began to shift. A growing youth market embraced rock 'n' roll, which had developed from African American rhythm-and-blues, which had in turn come from the blues and jazz. Jukeboxes were the rage.[29] Hollywood films now targeted youth even more than before. By 1956, ABC-Paramount Theatres president Leonard Goldenson advised developing "new young stars" to "help induce today's young audiences to become regular customers," as well as producing more "pictures for women," and "aggressive pre-selling of pictures before they are released to theatres" to "maintain leadership over television."[30] *Jailhouse Rock*, shot in black-and-white CinemaScope, was geared to the youth market. Instead of *Blues in the Night's* ensemble, it was a rock 'n' roll vehicle for Elvis Presley. Like in *Blues in the Night*, *Jailhouse Rock's* antihero (though not a leader of a jazz band) gets into a fight in a bar and ends up in jail where he discovers his talent for blues music. But instead of forming a combo and pursuing jazz artistry with a group, Presley cuts a record, performs on television, and pursues individual stardom in Hollywood, where fame (as in *A Star Is Born, The Red Shoes*, and *Blues in the Night*) leads to unhappiness and a downbeat ending.[31] Elvis also belts the blues tune "Trouble" in New Orleans with a jazz band in *King Creole*, again evoking *Blues in the Night*.

In the same year, another black-and-white, jail-to-fame film came from the pen of Budd Schulberg and was directed by Elia Kazan. *A Face in the Crowd* is about drunken, philandering antihero, Larry "Lonesome" Rhodes (Andy Griffith), who plays the blues on his guitar in jail and is discovered as a "man on the street" by radio reporter Marcia Jefferies (Patricia Neal), who rises as a television producer and makes him a television idol. Lonesome becomes a power-hungry "prepackaged" country star. Rather than being a real artist, he is a fraud who is commercially exploited. He, in turn, uses his fame to manipulate and exploit everyone around him. In the end, with both his love life and career in tatters, as he looks out on the spectacular view from the patio balcony of his Manhattan penthouse in drunken self-absorption, he complains that nothing grows so high up—all his plants die because the air's too thin—as the wind howls and blows the dirt around. He has literally reached the top, but the top is bleak, and he is no happier there than he was on the bottom—on the street. Money, power, and fans cannot prevent his swanky high-rise penthouse from becoming a creepy den of alcoholism, drug abuse, polygamous sex (corrupting minors), fraud, and greed. He even tries to control the political landscape with his influence and manufactured Americana that seems hokey and harmless but is actually dangerous and insidious, a comment on media, fascism, and the Red Scare.

Unlike the nostalgic Jazz Age period settings and color spectacle of noir musicals *Love Me or Leave Me* and *Pete Kelly's Blues*, Kazan's brooding black-and-white film was a scathing indictment of fame, artifice, television, contemporary postwar society, and the corrupt power of a corporate media machine and those who control it. It is likewise an indictment of the machine's capacity to manufacture screen idols, to manipulate and mislead millions of people on "live" television. *A Face in the Crowd*, like *Jailhouse Rock*, depicted the meteoric rise and tragic off-screen life of music stars. But unlike in *Blues in the Night*, or even *Jailhouse Rock*, *A Face in the Crowd*'s corrupt antihero does not care about music at all (certainly not playing or singing as a creative art form as was the case with *Blues in the Night's* musicians). Rather, the appearance of authenticity, that "real" quality sought by the characters in jazz-blues noir musical *Blues in the Night* is exploited for commercial gain. *A Face in the Crowd* is all about stardom and the media's capacity to corrupt, and, like *Sweet Smell of Success* and Kazan's topical *On the Waterfront*, it is an intense male melodrama with a blistering social realist critique rather than a musical or a 1940s-style film noir. However, musical noir and noir musicals inspired innovative films overseas that adapted the style of U.S. films.

FOREIGN FILMS: *SALÓN MÉXICO, ELEVATOR TO THE GALLOWS, AND THE H-MAN*

Noir musicals inspired films outside the United States. Emilio Fernández' Mexican *cabaretera* melodrama *Salón México* featured stunning noir cinematography by Gabriel Figueroa. Taxi dancer-prostitute Mercedes (Marga López) struggles to support her younger sister amid shadowy streets, tenement slums, and Latin dance sequences in Mexico City's famed cabaret nightclub-dance hall until abusive pimp-gangster-toxic lover Paco (Rodolfo Acosta) guns her down in the dark as she stabs him after he beats and torments her.

The American experimental conventions of musical noir films were so recognizable that they influenced postwar films abroad—especially after the Occupation in Europe and Japan. By 1958, the *New York Times* noted an overseas crime trend inspired by American noir films: "Gallic producers are continuing to turn out their gangster and murder-suspense films . . . influenced by American movie makers, now . . . being deftly done à la Francaise" with young directors in features "reminiscent of such noted American thrillers as *Double Indemnity* and *The Postman Always Rings Twice*." In 1958, twenty-five-year-old Frenchman Louis Malle earned the esteemed Louis Delluc film prize for directing *Elevator to the Gallows* (*Ascenseur pour l'échafaud*, or *Lift to the Scaffold* in the U.K.), a film that "blueprints" the "perfect crime" in which "fate takes a hand." In it, a murderer involved in an illicit love triangle is trapped in an elevator while his car is stolen by a juvenile delinquent couple who commit a murder for which he is subsequently blamed. *Elevator to the Gallows* anticipates the French New Wave, which paid homage to Hollywood film noir, its iconic jazz milieu, and even PCA censorship so influential to film noir in emulating the constraints of Hollywood's Production Code in the doomed fate of its murderous adulterous romance.

American Miles Davis's melancholy jazz score was an essential element in the poignant French noir-style melodrama made famous for its blue music. Davis was a key figure in the "birth of the cool" and blues-based hard bop that grew out of smaller jazz combos and bebop, following the swing era. Davis, Dizzy Gillespie, Charlie Parker, Thelonious Monk, and John Coltrane were jazz icons of the postwar period. In December 1957, Davis, who was especially known for his somber blue tones, his mysterious "prince of darkness" persona, and his "Round Midnight" solo at the 1955 Newport Jazz Festival—vividly captured the downbeat spirit of film noir with his haunting soundtrack for *Elevator to the Gallows*. Davis, who had never written a film score, improvised a brooding theme of pain and loneliness for Malle's "James M. Cain–style" murder story (in the vein of *Double Indemnity*). It was a clear example of the influence of hard-boiled American film noir and jazz on postwar French New Wave films. Davis recalled, "Since it was about a murder and was supposed to be a suspense movie" we used an "old, very gloomy, dark building where I had the musicians play. I thought it would give the music atmosphere." Images of Davis playing in the dark, with tendrils of cigarette smoke rising from his trumpet, as well as images of tormented femme fatale Jeanne Moreau searching all night in vain for her lover on the streets of Paris were shown on French television to promote the jazz crime picture. The score's moody sadness conveyed the doomed affair. Many African American musicians sought refuge from racism back home in the Paris jazz scene of the late 1950s, and Davis's real-life relationship with his lover in Paris had just ended.[32] Photos of Davis performing live at Birdland in 1958 evoke images from film noir. His innovative *Elevator to the Gallows* score influenced his distinctive jazz style with Coltrane on the 1959 masterpiece *Kind of Blue*.

Musical film noir even influenced Japanese science-fiction films such as director Inoshiro (Ishiro) Honda's *"kaiju eiga"* color spectacle monster movie, *The H-Man* (1959). The abundant rain pouring down on late-night Tokyo streets, the shadowy musical numbers, the alluring women in smoky nightclubs, gangsters and their molls, and the low-key moody atmosphere all are typical of film noir. The film was cut, censored, and dubbed for the U.S. market, and, when it was released, the Hollywood trade magazines actually remarked on how "American" the film was. It captured Cold War radiation fears with color footage of a hydrogen bomb exploding and extraordinary special effects by Eiji Tsuburaya, with special meaning to the Japanese who actually experienced it. *The H-Man* was produced at Japan's famed Toho studio (where Akira Kurosawa directed postwar master-works *Rashomon, Ikiru, Seven Samurai, Yojimbo*) and released in the United States by Columbia.[33] These Cold War fears and a changing culture and film industry paralleled those seen in postwar America.

FROM *SERENADE* TO *WEST SIDE STORY*

In the U.S., as the studio system declined by the late 1950s and 1960s, PCA censorship continued to ease in the absence of Breen. As the Code became more lenient, noir films dissipated. The decline of censorship, ironically, contributed to the decline of film noir because there was less need to work around the Code by using the noir approach of innuendo and suggestion. In filmmaking's ever-evolving environment, film noir—exemplified by Cain's *Double Indemnity, Mildred Pierce, The Postman Always Rings Twice,* Chandler's *The Big Sleep, Farewell My Lovely/Murder My Sweet,* and *The Blue Dahlia* during the war years—was ebbing by the time Henry Blanke (*Blues in the Night*) produced a film version of Cain's novel *Serenade* for Warner Bros. This brightly lit 1956 WarnerColor musical melo-drama shot outdoors on location in Mexico was directed by noir veteran Anthony Mann, though it was distinctly non-noir. The book had been banned from filming for a decade due to its homosexuality. *Serenade* evaded the salacious aspects of Cain's book to appease censors. This milder version of Cain's story starred singer Mario Lanza, whose gay lover was transmuted into an older wealthy heiress (Joan Fontaine) with whom he has an affair.

In this new, somewhat more open, climate, aspects of American culture such as tolerance of racism and use of nuclear weapons were challenged. *Giant* (1956) and other films depicted interracial couples and overturned the PCA's objection, further contributing to the Code's easing. Like *The H-Man,* U.S. postwar noir films—Raoul Walsh's *White Heat* (1949), Lang's *The Big Heat* (1953), Robert Aldrich's *Kiss Me Deadly* (1955), and Welles' *Touch of Evil* (1958)—had dealt with Cold War anxiety and paranoia. Like the gun battles and fistfights prevalent in wartime noir films, apocalyptic explosions were frequently depicted in 1950s noir, each thus conveying the era's most prominent preoccupations. *Kiss Me Deadly* ends as a radioactive atomic blast detonates. *Touch of Evil's* ticking time bomb is an explosive culmination of the classic film noir period. In 1959, Robert Wise's noir-style heist film *Odds Against Tomorrow* included bluesy jazz performances by Harry Belafonte but depicted an apocalypse. Its trailer promoted the musical crime film as "This is More Than a Story. . . . It's an Explosion!" with images of a huge blast and mushroom cloud suggesting a bleak atomic Armageddon. Cold War fears were reimagined in John Frankenheimer's paranoid *The Manchurian*

Candidate (1962), as Korean War veterans Sinatra and Laurence Harvey grapple with posttraumatic nightmares and Communist brainwashing. Stanley Kubrick's *Dr. Strangelove or: How I Learned to Stop Worrying and Love the Bomb* (1964) ends in global annihilation as atomic bombs explode to the tune of Vera Lynn's 1939 World War II lament "We'll Meet Again."[34]

Joseph Mankiewicz's social realist adaptation of Tennessee Williams' *Suddenly, Last Summer* (1959) depicted homosexuality, sexual assault, and cannibalism, seriously challenging even a much more lenient PCA. Social realist films *Border Incident* (1949), *The Lawless* (1950), *Odds against Tomorrow*, *Shadows* (1959), *Paris Blues* (1961), *The Naked Kiss* (1964), and *A Man Called Adam* (1966) dealt with issues of race, ethnicity, and sexual identity, reexamining the American dream against an evolving civil rights cultural terrain, as would be seen in *West Side Story.*

WEST SIDE STORY

Amidst this new terrain, composer Leonard Bernstein, who had scored Kazan's social realist *On the Waterfront*, was signed in June 1955 to compose a Broadway musical version of Cain's *Serenade*, adapted by Arthur Laurents, but it stalled after Jerome Robbins dropped out. So, Bernstein collaborated with Laurents and Robbins on a different theater project, this one about a contemporary *Romeo and Juliet*-style couple set in the inner city. *West Side Story* burst onto the American cultural scene in a blaze of glory, coinciding with a time when civil unrest threatened to rupture the social fabric. Their *Romeo and Juliet* project evolved when they heard about Chicano gang wars in Los Angeles and shifted the story to New York.

Origins of West Side Story

Bernstein, Laurents, and Robbins thus created the incomparable 1957 Broadway musical *West Side Story*, which captured the era's tumult and volatility.[35] Its ill-fated interracial romance and murder of an idealistic youth by a rival gang member resonated in its postwar cultural context.[36] Its contradicting duality subverted the romantic utopian ideals seen in escapist musicals to reveal a dark turbulent underside as in film noir and noir musicals.

In 1949, director-choreographer Jerome Robbins initially conceived what later became *West Side Story* about a Jewish versus Catholic *Romeo and Juliet*-style plot called *East Side Story*. He approached Bernstein in 1949 to collaborate with Laurents on a modern, tragic musical that does not resemble opera. A protégé of Agnes DeMille, Robbins was struggling to elevate and expand the potential of dance in the musical beyond the depiction of subconscious states to dark actu-

alities, for example, to enact a murder.[37] As Manhattan's infamous East Side tene-
ments were torn down and New York's gang activity moved west, the musical's
locale also "moved from the Lower East Side with its religious mix to the Upper
West Side with its racial mix."[38] *East Side Story* thus became *West Side Story*. Tackling serious social issues with music by a jazz-influenced, classically trained composer and kinetic dance that conveyed violence and emotional turmoil, *West Side
Story* defied expectations for a Broadway musical. Bernstein recalled, "Everyone
told us . . . it was suicidal. I don't know how many people begged me not to waste
my time on something that could not possibly succeed. After all, how could we
do a musical where there are two bodies lying on the stage at the end of the first
act and everybody eventually dies . . . a show that's so filled with hatefulness and
ugliness?"[39] Such "hatefulness and ugliness" drew on cultural tensions in postwar America.

An Era in Flux: The Postwar Cultural Context

West Side Story was very much a product of its time: it articulated the cultural
shifts of postwar America, an America of Cold War xenophobia, the Red Scare,
and growing civil rights protests. In 1948, just prior to *West Side Story*'s 1949 inception, President Truman desegregated the military, laying the groundwork for
civil rights integration. The establishment of the North Atlantic Treaty Organiza-
tion (NATO) in 1949 signaled the loss of the notion of an America able to go it
alone. Film historian Robert Ray has noted how the Korean conflict from 1950 to
1953 was the first 20th-century war America did not win, thereby shattering the
nation's sense of invincibility.[40] In 1955, Winston Churchill and jazz icon Charlie
Parker died; President Eisenhower suffered a heart attack; and the Montgomery,
Alabama, bus boycotts were underway following the "Brown vs. Board of Educa-
tion" Supreme Court decision. A kind of national conformity was the response
to the anxiety and the nuclear fears surrounding the arms race, the space race,
and the Berlin Crisis in 1961. At the same time, increasing civil rights for African
Americans and immigration concerns for Hispanics by the late 1950s and early
1960s made the New York City white ethnic (Polish) and Puerto Rican gang racial
issues in 1961's *West Side Story* topical, with sit-ins in 1960 and Freedom Rides
in 1961. *West Side Story*'s move from stage to screen coincided and expressed postwar sociopolitical tensions. Both the xenophobia and the civil rights dissension
were articulated in *West Side Story*'s innovative dance. Bernstein's music captured the tumult and expressed America's anxiety about the Cold War; ironically,
in real life, the composer was being harassed by HUAC while composing *West
Side Story*'s score.

West Side Story *on Stage*

Bernstein had been especially inspired by the opportunity to infuse jazz and Latin American rhythms into his symphonic score. New York was the center of a burgeoning Latin jazz scene in the 1940s through 1960s. Along with bebop, Latin jazz and Afro-Cuban rhythms were enormously popular after the war. Bernstein ingeniously adapted the classical Shubert house band at New York's Winter Garden Theatre by doing away with the violas to create an elaborate Latin American percussion section. Sondheim, friend and protégé of Oscar Hammerstein II, was hired as *West Side Story*'s lyricist in October 1955 after auditioning for the musical version of Cain's *Serenade*. Sondheim was previously a television writer influenced by the postwar 1950s trend toward realism; his first Broadway play was *West Side Story*. Sondheim was young, hip, and talented; he wrote clever lyrics with a darker edge that would become more prominent in his later work. Librettist Laurents used made-up street slang for dialogue in *West Side Story*, fearing contemporary phrases would become outdated.[41]

Bernstein's stunning music and Robbins' innovative dance made the dark musical come alive on stage in 1957. Songs from Bernstein's score immediately became popular hits. Much of the story and action were told through dance and music rather than dialogue. Its unhappy musical ending set a precedent on Broadway, and there was more dancing than in any previous musical. Noting the challenges and complexity of composing a downbeat crime musical, Bernstein explained the "chief problem" is "to tread the fine line between opera and Broadway, between realism and poetry, ballet and 'just dancing,' abstract and representational" where "not even a whisper about a happy ending was heard."[42]

From Stage to Screen: Film Production of West Side Story

As *West Side Story* was produced onstage, Hollywood was facing tremendous industrial restructuring as the studio system on which classical musical films were so economically and creatively dependent had to divest from theater exhibition chains by 1959. MGM—noted for its musicals—was the last to comply with this ruling. PCA censorship had weakened after Breen's departure in 1954 and was liberalized in 1956. Classical escapist musicals such as those of Rodgers and Hammerstein were still being produced through the 1950s. In the 1960s, this trend continued in hefty-budget musical blockbusters that nostalgically sought to recapture a hopeful, youthful innocence.

Many did not know what to make of such an unusual dark musical as *West Side Story*. When they tried to sell the screen rights to *West Side Story*, stage producer

Harold Prince claims, "nobody wanted it."[43] However, according to a September 12, 1960, production budget, the Mirisch Company paid $350,000 for the story rights to film it.[44] Ernest Lehman adapted it into a screenplay, and it was independently produced and directed by Robert Wise (codirected by choreographer Robbins) with Mirisch, and released through United Artists.[45] The film was shot early August 1960 through early February 1961 in New York City and at Samuel Goldwyn Studios in Hollywood. It was budgeted at $4,029,600. Its estimated final cost was $7 million.[46]

Reimagining noir musicals as well as the stage production, the film of *West Side Story* combined musical romance with youth-oriented gangster antiheroes (inspired by film noir style) to produce a social-realist dark musical that illuminated contemporary sociocultural tensions. The story was about self-destructive antihero, Polish gang member Tony (Richard Beymer), who falls in love with Puerto Rican immigrant Maria (Natalie Wood), leading to tragedy. Rather than working to produce a show as in classical backstage musicals or performing in a musical noir jazz nightclub, the rival New York street gangs featured in the story sing and dance as they prepare for a rumble (fight) where they beat and kill each other to Bernstein's riveting music. Tony has left his Jets gang and gotten a job, but, as in gangster films and film noir, there is no real escape from his history of violence. Tony has a well-known "rep," like notorious hoodlums and famous stars, "bigger than the whole West Side." Maria's brother, Sharks gang leader Bernardo (George Chakiris), kills Tony's best friend and Jets leader Riff (Russ Tamblyn). In revenge, Tony kills Bernardo. Bernardo's girl Anita (Rita Moreno) is taunted and roughed up by the Jets. Tony is gunned down by Maria's former fiancé.[47]

West Side Story's film adaptation showcased technology, something that new advances in filming had over television. It was shot in Super Panavision 70, large-frame format (and 35 mm) by Daniel Fapp (with second unit photography by Robert Relyea) and used Technicolor (single-strip dye-transfer processing). This prestige production was granted a large budget based on its previous theatrical success. It was released (like *The Red Shoes* and *A Star Is Born*) in roadshows to emulate a musical theatrical stage event. At the same time, the film borrowed from conventional low-budget B films such as in gangster/noir crime films. Like gangster and B noir crime films, this dark musical has an ensemble cast that deviates from more classical musicals in lacking a single major musical star—all the key characters are youths, and the majority are violent, self-destructive male antiheroes, as in *Blues in the Night*. Musically, the film incorporates darker thematic elements, denoting the influence of noir and lyricist Sondheim. The infu-

sion of Latin jazz rhythms into Bernstein's classical score and the dynamic experimentation of Robbins' dance combine to rearticulate opera as a dark musical.

Several filmmaking trends informed *West Side Story*'s screen adaptation. Partially shot on location in New York, it coincided with runaway production from
Hollywood in the "age of television." To enhance spectacle and compete with
television, Hollywood also expanded filming beyond the standard 35 mm to large-
frame 70-mm formats.[48]

As studios faced declining revenues, *Variety* noted in 1956: "There were two
ways movies could outflank television: (1) do what television could not do in the
matter of spectacle (form) or (2) do what television could not do in the matter of
controversial images or narrative (content). In short, 'make 'em big or make 'em
provocative.' During a decade notorious for conservatism and conformity, the
motion picture industry, with a vigor born of desperation, became more technically innovative, economically adventuresome, and aesthetically daring than
at any time in its history."[49] This prestige adaptation trend, influenced by television and the New York stage, combined theatrical realist style with topical subject matter to capitalize on more lenient Production Code censorship after 1954.
Hollywood was also looking to capture a growing new baby boom audience of
young teens.

Targeting Teenagers: The Youth Market

In an effort to appeal to an emerging youth market, studios sought a new demographic consumer group: teenagers. Doherty explains that by 1955, although
Hollywood "initiated its courtship of the teenage audience with great reluctance;
by 1960, it had become a devoted suitor. Delinquent dramas, dean-agers, *Rock
around the Clock*, adolescent werewolves, and the sanitized spawn of Presley-
Boone had in turn and cumulatively asserted the singular value of teenage movie-
goers. Within a few short years the teenpic, a motion picture targeted at teens
even to the exclusion of their elders, had become the most marketable of movie
commodities."[50] Even gangster films and 1940s–1950s noir B films, such as *They
Live By Night*, were reformulated into juvenile delinquency films to capitalize on
the emerging youth market, as in *The Wild One, Rebel without a Cause, Blackboard
Jungle*, and *Jailhouse Rock*. Early juvenile delinquency films included *Are These
Our Children?*, and Dead End Kids pictures, *Dead End, Angels with Dirty Faces*,
and *They Made Me A Criminal*. Juvenile delinquency films had been discouraged
by the PCA and, like gangster films, banned by the OWI and Office of Censorship
during World War II. In 1943, they were a controversial social topic. *Where Are*

Your Children? with Jackie Cooper and *Youth Runs Wild* in Val Lewton's RKO noir B unit (when Wise was there) were both projects that faced OWI scrutiny.[51] *West Side Story*'s Tamblyn (Riff) played a juvenile delinquent in 1949 noir *Gun Crazy*.

In 1958, the PCA initiated a campaign against juvenile delinquency films, getting the studios to "avoid making movies on the subject . . . except in a serious and mature vein." By July 1961, industry analysts noted, "Violence in Films Seen on Decrease: Juvenile Delinquency Scripts Drop as a Result of Drive. Films about juvenile delinquency have almost vanished. The disappearance of the inexpensively made pictures filled with youthful crime and sex has been the result of a campaign by the movie industry."[52] *West Side Story* was a "serious" prestige spectacle and "theatrical event" that was able to maneuver around this restriction. *West Side Story*'s lavish presentation was a savvy production strategy to comply with yet circumvent censorial restrictions on taboo subjects including but not limited to juvenile delinquency. The American family is presented in the film as either dysfunctional or nonexistent with the youth gang acting as a surrogate family. Young lyricist Sondheim subverted traditional notions of gender, the nuclear family, sexual orientation, childhood innocence, mental health, and patriotism. In the Jets' "Officer Krupke" number, he wrote: "My father is a bastard, my ma's an S.O.B. My grandpa's always plastered," which was censored for the film and changed to "My Daddy beats my Mommy, my Mommy clobbers me. My Grandpa is a Commie," referring to the Red Scare. His lyrics focus on real social issues also featured in crime dramas: alcoholism, psychological instability, and domestic abuse. He comments on drug abuse, homosexuality, and the collapse of the American family. "My Grandma pushes tea. My sister wears a mustache, my brother wears a dress . . . that's why I'm a mess!" He wrote: "Our mothers all are junkies, our fathers all are drunks . . . we're punks; we never had the love . . . every child oughta get. / My parents treat me rough. With all their marijuana, they won't give me a puff. They didn't wanna have me, but somehow I was had . . . that's why I'm so bad."[53] Sondheim, Laurents, Bernstein, and Robbins were homosexual (as were other noir musical creative talents such as *A Star Is Born*'s Cukor, *Lady in the Dark*'s Leisen, and *The Red Shoes*' Walbrook). To the degree that it was possible at the time, they explored issues of sexual orientation, cultural/ethnic/sexual identity, and the problems confronted in a homophobic postwar society by oppressed minorities.[54]

Criminal behavior is at the forefront of *West Side Story*: murder is choreographed; gang rape is implied in the ominous candy store[55] scene, where Anita is taunted and attacked by the Jets. Yet, these racially motivated violent actions are suggested, stylized, choreographed, and performed to music, a provocative twist on the classical musical, which usually deals with an idealized rendering of the "American dream" mythology. Taboo sex, violence, profanity, and juvenile crime were permitted in the film because it was a prestige Broadway stage adaptation. "A boy like that," Anita warns, "who'd kill your brother," she sings bitterly, "will bring you sorrow" and "leave you lonely. He'd murder your love; he murdered mine." Evoking postwar xenophobia and its ethnic strife and intolerance, she says, "Stick with your own kind!"[56] *West Side Story* was applauded for its dark themes that resonated with the times.

Dark Musical Style in West Side Story

Though not the first dark musical, *West Side Story* was heralded as innovative in combining divergent styles: stark realism, the dark shadowy style of film noir, serious "messages," classical tragedy, and musical romance. It effectively integrated location shooting of dance numbers on the streets of New York with enclosed studio photography on a Hollywood soundstage. Director Wise insisted, "The picture had to open in New York City . . . in its milieu," but (as in wartime film noir) the remaining nocturnal settings "could be done in the studio. Because at night you see what you want to see. You see what you light." Wise was a veteran noir thriller director and proponent of the hard-hitting realism style at RKO. Wise was not known as a musical director, although he got his start as a sound editor on the Astaire-Rogers films. Wise himself later referred to *West Side Story* as a "noir musical."[57]

West Side Story used noir cinematic conventions of low-key, high contrast, chiaroscuro lighting and visual design (versus bright, thematically upbeat "flat" high-key musicals). It thus conveys an oppressive, claustrophobic environment with dark, cavernous interiors and nocturnal urban settings: alleys, concrete freeway underpasses, shadowy bedrooms and basements, and the cramped confines of the after-hours candy store. While Warner Bros. was producing vanguard noir musical *Blues in the Night*, Wise was editing *Citizen Kane* (1941) and *The Magnificent Ambersons* (1942) for Welles at RKO. He then directed *Curse of the Cat People* (1944) in Val Lewton's B horror unit, followed by noir films *Born to Kill* (1947), *The Set-Up* (1949), and *Odds against Tomorrow* (1959, with jazz numbers). Wise's experience with grim noir realistic backgrounds influenced *West Side Story*'s stylization from actual city streets to later studio scenes. The film's crew had to beg and bribe a wrecking company to delay demolition of the older buildings where the opening dance sequence was to be shot so they could utilize its grittily "realistic" setting. (It's now the site of Lincoln Center.)

Drawing on Wise's black-and-white B film noir background, *West Side Story* was inevitably also a social, cultural, industrial, and generic product of its own time. The Technicolor musical aesthetic created a highly stylized version of stark realism: muted tones, deep shadows, and dark mise-en-scène—where the exception is a predominant use of the color red. Flashing red police sirens under the freeway at the shadowy rumble suggest blood and danger as dead bodies lay on the concrete in a fenced cage. Bright red walls reveal the dance as a site of racial conflict and, paradoxically, of love. A noir-inflected approach to color was also used in color noir musicals *The Red Shoes, A Star is Born,* and *Love Me or Leave Me.* These, in turn, influenced later "neo-noir" films *Chinatown, Blade Runner,* and *LA Confidential* as well as dark serious musicals *New York, New York, Round Midnight,* and *Moulin Rouge.* Wise described *West Side Story*'s approach to color as "a musical set in a real background not a never-never land; a tough side of New York City requiring a good, strong color scheme to accommodate darker areas of the film realistically, but not too flamboyant except in the gym with the red walls. We tended to use low-key colors." The result evokes a black-and-white film with moments of bright color for thematic punctuation. Wise sought out Linwood Dunn, an associate from RKO who did the optical work for *Citizen Kane* and *The Magnificent Ambersons.*[58]

Wise explained, "Once you got through the rumble at the beginning, the whole antagonism of the two gangs ending up in a fight, the rest of the story onstage and in the film is told at sunset and at night. There was no more daytime stuff in it. The studio wanted me to shoot the entire thing on a soundstage, and you couldn't do it. I finally convinced them that if I could do the whole daytime opening in New York, all the rest could be done in the studio."[59] The milieu is increasingly dark and stylized, composed of flashing neon and reflective surfaces. Repeatedly, chain link fences slice the foreground to represent the fragmentation and splintering apart of romance, the gangs, and their youth. The film's color noir visual style undermines the possibility of a conventional musical happy ending.

West Side Story uses extreme camera angles, especially in the opening shot— a straight down aerial view of an oppressive gray New York skyline to constrict rather than expand space. Wise's soundtrack uses silence and the ambient traffic sounds in lieu of a symphonic score—more like noir, gangster, and urban crime films than the musical. It deviates from classical musical scores, such as the buoyant opening of Donen and Kelly's *On the Town* shot on location in New York.[60] Instead of the sweeping shots typical of the classic musical style, Wise used extreme, Dutch, or low angles evocative of the horror genre and German expressionist films, even in the dance sequences. In directing his first musical, Wise unexpectedly combined dramatic noir style and musical conventions, all to good effect.[61]

WEST SIDE STORY'S RECEPTION

The dark musical was a huge hit with the public, at home and abroad. While its racial tension, gang violence, and doomed teen affair resonated with a young, ethnically diverse audience in the emerging era of civil rights, it also appealed to adults with its romance, spectacle, music, and dynamic dance numbers reminiscent of classical musicals. Critics called the film a "musical advance" with "drama, dance, and music," a "sparkling" and "moving" "cinematic masterpiece" as well as a "starkly realistic crime film." They compared it favorably to *On the Waterfront* for which Bernstein had written the score. The *New York Times* wrote "Always there is the palpable frame of a concrete and crushing reality enclosing the action on the screen . . . kids kill one another in a violent rumble" of "mutual hatreds and distrust" of "ethnic groups." Its "ironic and tragic" ending was called a "piercing and haunting demonstration of social folly and human waste" that does "more than entertain and provide an emotional catharsis." It makes a "conspicuous advancement of sophistication through the musical film and opens the door to wider expression of more serious and mature themes in this genre." This "juvenile gang feud could not be classed as a musical comedy. It was much too violent and poignant," "essentially tragic in mood, " "harsh" and "stinging" with a "gang of tough kids [lounging] in a playground like young panthers in a wire-fenced cage."[62]

Variety called it a "beautifully-mounted, impressive, emotion-ridden" and "violent musical" with "realism" and a "stark" approach to a "raging social problem" that "may set the pattern for future musical presentations" against a "seething background" of "rival and bitterly hating youthful Puerto Rican and American gangs" in a "savage and tender admixture of romance and war-to-the-death." Robbins's choreography was "breathtaking." Dancing numbers were called the "most spectacular ever devised and lensed, blending into story" and "action" that is "electrifying to the spectator." The "brutality of the juv gangs . . . vent upon each other the hatred they feel against the world. Here is juvenile delinquency in its worst and most dangerous sense." They said that Wise "catches the spirit in devastating fashion" and that "technically, it is superb; use of color is dazzling, camera work often is thrilling, editing fast with dramatic punch, production design catches [the] mood." Leven "scores as production designer." *Saturday Review* called it "a triumphant work of art." The *Hollywood Reporter* called it a "magnificent

show, a milestone in movie musicals, a box office smash. It is so good that su-
perlatives are superfluous. Let it be noted that the film musical, the one dramatic
form that is purely American and purely Hollywood, has never done better"; it
applauded its "daring design" with "seeping hopes and hates," "joy and humor
profusely illuminating the stark story" with "kinetic excitement" that "seizes the
spectator" and does "not let go until" the "very end . . . almost a traumatic experience." They wrote that Wise "makes evident everywhere his special gifts for poetic realism," "natural excitement," and "poignance" as "dance is used as part of
the story . . . imbedded in the action" of "all its turbulent events."[63]

West Side Story swept the Academy Awards, earning ten, including Best Picture. It grossed $19.5 million in North American rentals.[64] It also did well abroad,
running a full year (1.5 million viewers) in Tokyo. It was the strongest overseas
box office hit in United Artists' history, playing for four years at the George V
Theatre in Paris, the longest run in French film history.[65] It was rereleased in
1968 and again reached a youth market, much as in 1961, who were part of the
growing countercultural climate of the decade.

West Side Story was a transitional film, moving from the classical to postclassical Hollywood era. *West Side Story* and later dark musicals were distinct,
different from—yet inspired by—the original 1940s–50s noir musical cycle. Tremendous changes affected Hollywood in the 1950s. The classical studio system
was completely dismantled by the end of 1959, and big-budget independent production was the new thing. *West Side Story* brought social realist experimentation
to the evolution of musical noir for the emerging postclassical period.

CHAPTER SEVEN

The Legacy of the Noir Musical

Although *West Side Story* enjoyed phenomenal popularity, musical comedies were generally more successful. After *West Side Story*, Wise produced and directed *The Sound of Music* (shot in Technicolor on location in Austria), which made over $72 million dollars in North American rentals in 1965, more than any film up to that time.[1] Nicknamed "The Sound of Money," its tremendous success spurred studios desperate for profits to produce epic upbeat musicals. Musicals of all types had to compete with television and foreign art cinema. At the same time, the postclassical film industry increasingly relied on international markets where musicals were not always popular.

At first, film historian Mark Harris notes, "color was reserved for musicals, Westerns, scenic spectacles, and fantasy, while black and white, which was considered more realistic, was used for anything serious, adult, or controversial." He explains that this division was often "forced on filmmakers by the fact that the inconsistencies of color-processing labs were still yielding sloppy, overbright, unrealistic hues [and] was followed by directors until 1966, when the conversion of network television to color (and the refinement of processing techniques) led studios to abandon black and white entirely within a matter of months."[2] Dark musicals, when they were produced, fused the black-and-white tradition of serious themes with the color tradition of spectacular presentation.

A new generation of filmmakers (nicknamed the "Young Turks") began an American cinema renaissance by emulating the growing popularity with baby boomers and art cinema audiences of innovative French New Wave (François Truffaut's *400 Blows*, Jean Luc Godard's *Breathless*) and Italian art cinema (Federico

Fellini's *8½*, *La Dolce Vita*, Antonioni's *La Notte*). In the "sex, drugs, and rock-n-roll" era, classical musicals and jazz were associated with an older generation (parents) and old Hollywood. The new generation gravitated toward socially taboo content. Mike Nichols' sexual convention-challenging black comedy *The Graduate* and Arthur Penn's hip outlaws *Bonnie and Clyde* demonstrate that the Code was all but dead by 1967. The PCA and Production Code were discarded in 1968 and replaced by a rating system. The Code was undeniably gone by 1969 as is evident in *Easy Rider*, *Rosemary's Baby*, and *The Wild Bunch* that were released that year. Corporate mergers transformed Hollywood's film industry and production climate. The full impact of these mergers was not felt until the 1970s. Sentimental big-budget musicals declined along with the major studios as provocative art cinema targeted a growing counterculture by the late 1960s and early 1970s.

POSTCLASSICAL DARK NEO-NOIR MUSICALS

Hollywood's classical studio system, film noir, and noir musicals had declined by 1959 in a changing cultural/industrial climate. But they had a big impact on the darker postclassical musicals that appeared after 1960. Film noir and (noir) musicals had benefited from the studio system's in-house resources and wealth of contract talent. Postclassical films were distinct from the original films noir. The new darker musicals that emerged reimagined noir musicals such as *Blues in the Night, The Red Shoes,* and *A Star Is Born*, responding to the trend toward European art cinema in an experimental New Hollywood, paying homage in an ever global arena. Postclassical dark musicals include *Paris Blues* (1961), *All Night Long* (1962), *I Could Go On Singing* (1963, Garland's last film), *Ballad in Blue* (1964), *A Man Called Adam* (1966), *Cabaret* (1972), *The Harder They Come* (1972), *That's the Way of the World* (1975), *New York, New York* (1977), *All That Jazz* (1979), *Pennies from Heaven* (1978/1981), *The Cotton Club* (1984), *The Singing Detective* (1986), *Round Midnight* (1986), *Bird* (1988), *The Fabulous Baker Boys* (1989), *Mo' Better Blues* (1990), *The Mambo Kings* (1992), *Kansas City* (1996), *The Big Lebowski* (1997), *Dark City* (1998), *Moulin Rouge!* (2001), *Chicago* (2002), *Dreamgirls* (2006), *Chico and Rita* (2010), and *Black Swan* (2010). By 1966, *New York Times* critics recognized the 1940s and '50s musical crime film as a unique phenomenon. They held up *Blues in the Night* as an exemplar of the form, linking it to *Casablanca* and *Young Man with a Horn*, as well as later experimental films with troubled musician antiheroes and a downbeat jazz atmosphere.[3] Issues of civil rights, ethnicity, gender equality, and sexual identity that are hinted at in film noir musicals are more fully revealed in postclassical dark musicals.

PARIS BLUES

In *Paris Blues* (1961), made the same year as *West Side Story*, Paul Newman gives a moody performance as jazz trombonist Ram, a talented musician and aspiring composer—like the antiheroes in *Blues in the Night*, *The Red Shoes*, *Young Man with a Horn*, and *A Star Is Born*—who is famous, but unhappy. His jazz partner Eddie (Sidney Poitier) grapples with African American identity in Paris in self-imposed exile from the bigotry in his home country. Teacher/activist Connie (Diahann Carroll) cajoles him to return to make things better politically. Small-town divorcee Lillian (Joanne Woodward) pursues an intense affair with Ram (real-life husband Newman), but his music career prevents the couple from uniting. Serge Reggiani plays junkie guitarist Michel. "Wild Man" Armstrong blows in a lively jam session and Ellington's vibrant jazz score—"Mood Indigo," "Take the 'A' Train," "Paris Blues"—brings the film to life. Directed by Martin Ritt, adapted by Walter Bernstein, and based on Harold Flender's 1957 novel about American musicians abroad, *Paris Blues* was shot by Christian Matras on location in Paris. It was independently produced by Sam Shaw (Diane Productions-Jason-Monica-Monmouth-Pennebaker) and released through United Artists. Bernstein had worked with *Blues in the Night*'s writer, Robert Rossen, and Ritt served in World War II, joined Kazan's Group Theater, and worked in television. Both men had been blacklisted before they worked abroad on this film exploring interracial relations in a jazz combo of international musicians.[4]

A MAN CALLED ADAM

Inspired by musical noir, experimental low-budget *A Man Called Adam* vividly captured atmospheric jazz melodrama in a film independently produced by its star Sammy Davis Jr. with Trace-Mark Productions (Ike Jones, James Waters, Joseph Levine). It was released by Embassy Pictures, which also distributed foreign films such as Federico Fellini's *8½*. It was filmed on location in New York with low-lit, black-and-white cinematography by Jack Priestley. African American star Davis was a member of the Rat Pack, a group of actors originally centered on Bogart, then headed by Sinatra. The film featured a fine jazz score by Benny Carter, with Louis Armstrong, Nat Adderly, Ossie Davis, Cicely Tyson (who later married Miles Davis), Johnny Brown, Lola Falana, Jeanette Dubois, Peter Lawford, Frank Sinatra Jr., and Mel Tormé swinging in "All That Jazz." The director was Leo Penn,[5] a World War II veteran who was blacklisted after starring in *The Best Years of Our Lives* (1946) and noir films *Fall Guy* (1947, written by Cornell Woolrich), *Not Wanted* (1949, produced by Lupino), and *The Undercover Man* (1949). He eventually became a television director.

Harsher than *Paris Blues*, *A Man Called Adam* takes advantage of declining PCA censorship with hard-hitting socially conscious themes. Davis plays hard-drinking jazz trumpeter Adam Johnson who gains fame and reaches artistic musical heights while destroying everything and everyone around him. In a time of civil rights activism, reformer/activist Claudia (Tyson) tries to help Adam with his addictions, psychic demons, and racial resentments. The cinematography subjectively depicts his turbulent world, descent into drugs and alcohol. Adam collapses onstage (after his relationship crumbles) and he's carried off to die. Its jazz noir ambiance conveys seedy dives, corruption, and jam sessions rather than a star's glamorous world, despite his success. Like *Sweet Smell of Success*, it allegorically suggests the blacklist in the activities of agents and publicists. Lawford as a high-powered agent blackballs Adam (for insulting him), which forces the musician to endure humiliating racism and violence in the segregated South in order to get a gig.

A Man Called Adam was recognized by critic Howard Thompson for tackling racial issues: "In the background, as smoke swirls, ice cubes rattle and music throbs sweet, cool or red-hot, is a racial intermingling of black and white as right as the rain." Yet, suggesting harsh low-budget noir, he criticized *A Man Called Adam* as "technically crude," its jazz musician/antihero so "flamboyantly masochistic" and "self-pitying" that "not even Mr. Davis can render [him] sympathetic or palatable." Its strength was in the way it focused on a "small patch of intriguing terrain—the night-blooming world of bandstand performers—sticks to it like glue and plays it, quite literally, from the inside out, which is more than any other jazz drama has tried in years." He explains, *A Man Called Adam* "dares—that is the only word—to unfold a simple and tender love story" between two black leads as if "it were the most natural everyday thing in the world. This is rare in the world of film."[6]

CABARET

Wise's *Sound of Music*, set in the Austrian Alps during World War II, marked the end of an era in film musicals. After "The Sound of Money," a series of big-budget musicals flopped as the Vietnam War induced national cynicism, and grittier films prevailed in a post-PCA era. *Bonnie and Clyde* (1967), *The Wild Bunch* (1969), *Easy Rider* (1969), *Butch Cassidy and the Sundance Kid* (1969), *M*A*S*H* (1970), and *Cabaret* (1972) all allegorically critiqued the Vietnam War. In 1972, Bob Fosse's dark modernist musical *Cabaret* (adapted from the 1966 Broadway stage) incorporated music and Nazis, but it was not *The Sound of Music*. *Cabaret* was a disturbing, experimental musical endeavor. As World War II was a catalyst for film noir, the violence of the Vietnam War created a cultural climate ripe for "neonoir." With the end of the Code, graphic neo-noir films like Roman Polansky's *Chinatown* gained popularity in the New Hollywood era. His supernatural gothic neo-noir film *Rosemary's Baby* revolved around the deeply corrupting power of ambition. Coppola's gangster epic *The Godfather* was a neo-noir blockbuster that made $86.3 million.[7] Like musical noir, *The Godfather* included musical performances and a star-is-born subplot involving an ambitious jazz crooner with ties to the mob (loosely modeled on Sinatra). Brando's Godfather famously made studio moguls an "offer they can't refuse."

As censorship waned, dark musicals expressed the growing cynicism related to the Vietnam War and political assassinations. Neo-noir musicals were subversive aesthetically and socioculturally.[8] The film version of modernist neonoir musical *Cabaret* starred Liza Minnelli and Joel Grey.[9] Jay Allen adapted the Broadway show written by Joe Masterhoff with music by John Kander and lyrics by Fred Ebb. Set in Weimar, Germany, in 1931 in a burlesque cabaret called the Kit Kat Club, it was based on Christopher Isherwood's 1946 *The Berlin Stories* (which included *The Last of Mr. Norris* and *Goodbye to Berlin*) and John Van Druten's 1951 dramatic play *I Am a Camera* (filmed in 1955). In 1969, independent company Allied Artists, moving from smaller-budget noir films like *The Big Combo*, paid $1.5 million (more than any of its other properties up to that point) for the screen rights to *Cabaret*. Allied Artists distributed the film in partnership with television company ABC Pictures. ABC Pictures was headed by Martin Baum who hired Broadway producer-composer Cy Feuer. Feuer got Fosse, protégé of Robbins, to direct. Minnelli sought the Broadway role before being cast in her Oscar-winning screen role. Grey reprised his Tony-winning sexually ambiguous Master of Ceremonies.

Despite its 1930s setting, *Cabaret's* dark modernist vision captured the late 1960s–early 1970s political and countercultural spirit. Its unusual love triangle subverts musical romance and matrimonial union. It openly depicts homosexuality and bisexuality. It also attacked the Nazis and anti-Semitism. Bawdy, suggestive choreography mocked glamorous beauty, classical musical numbers, and traditional musical stars and aesthetics. Naive American singer/dancer Sally (Minnelli) works in a German cabaret while dreaming of Hollywood fame. She entangles herself in sexual affairs that defy classical romance and end in failure—and an abortion. Sally never attains stardom, happiness, romance, or success. *Cabaret* ends with a disturbing lack of resolution. Its social context is ominous and profound: something terrible is about to happen as the Nazis rise to power. Darkness is coming, paradoxically brought by fair-haired, fresh-faced Aryan Hitler youth. *Cabaret* depicts a rebellious atmosphere of booze, promiscuity, and indulgent excess capturing the milieu of the Weimar era and late 1960s. Sally—oblivious and unconcerned—doesn't realize what's going on around her, an allegory for America's naiveté as a nation.

Cabaret's cinema style is less shadowy than other dark musicals, yet it conveys bleak existentialism. Fosse contains visuals to create a claustrophobic mise-en-scène (rather than expansive space as in classical musicals). The Kit Kat Club stage where cabaret dance numbers comment on life beyond its walls is small and cramped. Montage editing stylishly crosscuts between the stage and the disturbing action on the streets of Berlin.

In an era of runaway production, *Cabaret* was shot on location in West Berlin, Bavaria, and Munich for $5 million from late March through July 1971. It opened in New York in February 1972 to rave reviews. The dark musical was described by *Variety* as "most unusual," noting its "literate, bawdy, sophisticated, sensual, cynical, heart-warming, and disturbingly thought-provoking" nature and "sleazy cabaret" milieu. Reviewers noted that it "never seems to talk down to an audience." The *New York Times* critics called it "not so much a movie musical as . . . a movie with a lot of music in it," noting its "willingness to isolate its musical stage—even to observe it from behind the heads of a shadowy audience in the foreground . . . down to the last weary transvestite and to the least of the bland, blond open-faced Nazis in the background." Fosse was considered to play a "major creative role in the evolution of American film musicals" by the *Washington Post*.[10] *Cabaret* was a smash hit. Other directors such as Martin Scorsese began to consider making dark musicals with Minnelli. *Cabaret* made $2 million in two months, the highest-grossing film in Allied Artists' history.[11] It earned Oscars for Best Director, Actress, Supporting Actor, Cinematography, Art Direction, Sound, Scoring, and Editing (losing Best Picture and Screenplay only to Coppola's *The Godfather*).

ALL THAT JAZZ

All That Jazz (1979), directed, choreographed, and scripted by Fosse and produced and cowritten by Robert Alan Aurthur, autobiographically captured Fosse's manic workaholic pace as he directed musical *Chicago* on stage. Like Fellini's middle-aged filmmaker Guido (Marcello Mastroianni) in *8½*, self-absorbed director/choreographer Joe Gideon (Roy Scheider) looks in the mirror. He needs drugs, Visine, "Alka-Seltzer," and Vivaldi to face his bloodshot reflection. He creates

great art, but grapples with death, his identity, and manic lifestyle. While directing a Broadway musical, finishing a film (*Lenny*, running over budget), juggling
relationships with his mistress (Ann Reinking), his ex-wife (Leland Palmer), and
his daughter, he smokes cartons of cigarettes, drinks heavily, and takes drugs. *All
That Jazz* exposes ugly truths about stardom and the American Dream. It opens
with Broadway lights. Gideon talks to beautiful blonde "Angel of Death" (Jessica
Lange) in a white bridal veil as he rehearses numbers and rejects dancers auditioning for his new show. He pops pills and squirts eye drops, all with a cigarette
dangling from his mouth: "It's showtime, folks!" George Benson's funky rock-
inspired jazz-guitar vocal subverts musical idealism: "The neon lights are bright
on Broadway / But when . . . you ain't had enough to eat the glitter rubs right off
and you're nowhere." Fosse deglamorizes backstage life and the manufactured
"razzle dazzle." Singer/dancers struggle through dehumanizing casting calls.
Sex is leveraged for ambition, suggesting prostitution. Gideon propositions desperate auditioning dancers who stroke his ego. Rejected dancers hurl expletives
as they flee down pitch-black stairwells. He recalls his philandering to the Angel
of Death, evoking Lermontov in *The Red Shoes*. Victoria can't dance, but he casts
her to have sex. "Look, I can't make you a great dancer," or even "a good dancer.
But I can make you a better dancer."

Breathtaking montage editing by Alan Heim and a brooding style and fluid
cinematography by Giuseppe Rotunno (who shot *8½*) capture the putting-on-a-
show narrative. Fosse manipulates point of view, time, and space through fragmentation, exaggeration, repetition, and abstraction in choreography, cinematography,
and editing to push conventions to the limit. Fosse's distinctive choreography and
musical direction infuse every move, step, leap, bend, swivel, and jump. From
extreme low-angle close-up shots of slippered feet and muscled legs sliding across
the floor to sweeping overhead tracking shots of movements on stage, the dancers and the artistic production of the musical evolve, transform, and improve,
despite Gideon's self-destructive manic lifestyle. His suggestive choreography
shocks the show's uptight financial backers—much like "sordid" film noir, jazz,
and early gangster pictures mortified censors. Near-naked dancers, intricately
intertwined in Fosse's elaborate racy choreography, perform in the dark using
flashlights as stark low-key, high-contrast spotlights in the shadowy expanse of a
black unlit room. Instead of culminating with a big Broadway production number
from *Chicago*, Ben Vereen sings "Bye Bye Life" as Gideon dies of cardiac arrest.

Fosse exceeded Columbia's budget before the finale was shot; 20th Century-
Fox financed the rest. The film was released through Columbia/Fox. Color posters
simulated black and white with the title in white marquee lights against a plain

black background. Ads featured color noir black, white, and scarlet. Taglines exclaimed: "All that work. All that glitter. All that pain. All that love. All that crazy rhythm. All that jazz." Many compared *All That Jazz* to *8½*. Like Fellini's exploration of midlife anxiety—about making the film you're watching—Fosse reexamined his life when he feared his ability and life were ending. *Variety* called it "self-important," "egomaniacal," "compelling," and "wonderfully choreographed," as it celebrated Fosse's "energetic" life, loves, career, and "preoccupation with death." It praised Scheider's "superb" performance filled with "nervous energy."[12]

THAT'S THE WAY OF THE WORLD

Dark behind-the-scenes musical *That's the Way of the World* (1975) featured music by Earth, Wind & Fire, promoted as a black rock band. It was independently produced and directed by Sig Shore, written by Robert Lipsyte, with cinematography by Alan Metzger and released through United Artists. It was Shore's directorial debut after producing "blaxploitation" *Superfly*, which targeted an African American audience in a revisionist neo-noir with riveting funk music. The cynical musical neo-noir was a remarkable, unlikely amalgam. Film critic Robert Firsching called *That's the Way of the World* a "cult favorite" that "went belly-up at the box-office." He said further: "That's a shame, because what other film offers viewers Harvey Keitel as a record producer who skates at an all-black disco rink, Bert Parks as a child molester, and squeaky-clean singer Jimmy Boyd ('I Saw Mommy Kissing Santa Claus') as a hardcase junkie? Other treats on hand include the manager of a Christian pop band threatening to stick an ice pick in Keitel's ear and appearances by noted disc jockeys Murray the K and Frankie Crocker. Amidst all of this insanity, Cynthia Bostick's female-lead turn as a Joplin-like junkie singer named Velour is lost. The film ends with a number of Earth, Wind and Fire songs, but by that point most viewers will be in bad-movie shellshock."[13] Like *Superfly*, noted for its Curtis Mayfield R&B soundtrack, Earth, Wind and Fire's *That's the Way of the World* soared up the charts to become a number one soundtrack album.

Schrader's "Notes on Film Noir" tapped the disillusionment of the time: there was the 1972 Watergate break-in, Nixon's resignation in 1974, and the fall of Saigon in 1975, which ended the Vietnam War. Just a few months before *That's The Way of the World*'s quiet unveiling, Steven Spielberg's commercial blockbuster *Jaws* opened "wide" in June. Its success transformed Hollywood's "high concept" summer action blockbusters. In contrast, *Los Angeles Times*' Kevin Thomas observed of *That's the Way of the World*, "opening virtually unannounced . . . hampered by a vague, unexciting title [the film] turns out to be a witty morality play satirizing the corruption of the recording industry." The "final irony" of a "film about the almighty, all-American hype, is that it hasn't received enough hype itself to reach the audiences it deserves." Taglines for *That's the Way of the World* clamored: "Simple truths for the ways of the world," "There are two sides to every hit record!" and "Where were you when the stardust hit the fan?" *Box Office* noted "catchlines" for its modest opening: "Payola, Flyola, Drugola—That's the Way of the Record World . . . From the Same Wonderful Folks Who Gave You Watergate."[14] *That's The Way of the World* was an extraordinary but underrated neo-noir variation on a musical that exposed the seamy side and constructed artifice of the entertainment industry, like another dark musical, *New York, New York.*

NEW YORK, NEW YORK

Martin Scorsese's gritty neo-noir crime films *Mean Streets* (1974), *Taxi Driver* (1976), and *Raging Bull* (1980) were iconic of Hollywood's renaissance. His films fostered greater interest in the visual style and cinematic conventions of film noir, as neo-noir films proliferated in the 1970s onward. His revisionist jazz neo-noir musical *New York, New York* starring Liza Minnelli and Robert DeNiro paid homage to classical noir musicals, what he himself described as "musical film noir."[15] Scorsese said he wanted to "make a different kind of film . . . a mix of *The Man I Love*, Raoul Walsh's forties film noir with music . . . all Gershwin songs . . . a little touch of *Road House*" and "Technicolor films"—but "update it" to "take the characters as far as possible, way beyond genre conventions of the musical into the obsessive behavior of a noir."[16]

Laszlo Kovac's cinematography reimagined color noir visual style, moving from rich Technicolor hues to deep shadows in rain-soaked nightspots in a moody palette of black, white, red, and muted tones inspired by *The Red Shoes*, *The Man I Love*, *Road House*, *My Dream Is Yours*, *On the Town*, *Young Man with a Horn*, and *A Star Is Born.*

The narrative of *New York, New York* centers on two talented musicians: bigband singer Francine (Minnelli), who meets volatile, self-destructive saxophonist Jimmy (DeNiro) during V-J Day celebrations in 1945 Times Square. Like in *A Star Is Born* and Day's noir musicals, Minnelli's heroine Francine rises to recording stardom while DeNiro's antihero destroys their relationship and his own career because of his jealous insecurity, which evokes the returning veteran noir antiheroes of the 1940s and '50s. The pair pursues their showbiz careers. She becomes famous singing commercial Broadway show tunes, while he plays dissonant bebop and starts his own jazz club. In the end, they part.

The big-budget homage to classical Hollywood is set in the postwar era with "period" costumes and demythologizes escapist musicals with their idyllic romances and hopeful pursuit of the American dream. The theme song "New York, New York" was penned by *Cabaret*'s Kander and Ebb—"blues are melting away . . . a brand new start . . . If I can make it there, I'll make it anywhere. It's up to you"—suggests bold aspirations in the Big Apple. But like *The Red Shoes* and *A Star Is Born*, the film reveals the price of fame, in the end severing the musical's classical romantic union. It is an ambiguous, downbeat ending. Yet, the resilient heroine moves away from an abusive relationship. The final parting ends with a shot inspired by beautiful color noir style on a nocturnal rain-slicked city street reminiscent of classic noir musicals.

Scorsese encouraged extensive improvisation on the set, working closely with DeNiro and Minnelli—they had to go to the hospital after a violent fight scene. But Hollywood musicals, even dark ones, were better planned than improvised. The final cut ran 4 1/2 hours. "And it worked," Scorsese said. "But it wouldn't be for the theatrical audience. Once we started cutting and finally got it down to two hours, forty-five [minutes] that was when we were in the ballpark area. I reshot the key things, a couple of things at the end, because up until that point, I had been so close to the subject matter . . . that I couldn't see how they should end as characters . . . Really, in a way, I didn't shoot an ending, and we knew it. So we just waited. It was really that kind of a picture."[17]

New York, New York fused jazz musical nostalgia with modernistic neo-noir in the aftermath of Vietnam and Watergate. Rock sax "Big Man" Clarence Clemons of Bruce Springsteen's E Street Band played jazz musician Cecil Powell in DeNiro's bebop club. With painstaking attention, veteran production designer Boris Leven (*Sweet Smell of Success/West Side Story*) recreated the early color noir look. *Wizard of Oz, Gone with the Wind,* and *A Star Is Born* hairdresser Sidney Guilaroff and *Bonnie and Clyde/The Godfather, Part II* costume designer Theadora Van Runkle strikingly remade Minnelli to incarnate her mother Judy Garland. Liza used Judy's old dressing room; her father was moved to tears at her resemblance. *New York, New York* revived big band jazz music with *Cabaret*'s Minnelli, Kander, Ebb, and Ralph Burns.

Scorsese's dark musical was generally panned by critics. Overall, they didn't know just what to make of it. Its unusual amalgam was called a "flawed musical drama . . . imitating the old studio style as it encompassed his new ideas on what a serious musical could be." Les Keyser noted the "whole project, unfortunately, suffered from the same vertigo, a dizzying confusion of fantasy and documentary, romance and realism." The film's incongruous fusion of brooding themes in a nostalgic period musical was an unexpected combination from Scorsese and

DeNiro after *Taxi Driver* and *Mean Streets*. Mary Pat Kelly called it *"The Red Shoes* with boxing gloves . . . Love does *not* conquer all. Jimmy writes a bluesy tune and Francine adds the lyrics: Together they create the song 'New York, New York' as a tribute to the talent each one recognizes in the other. But their differences are too great; they must part . . . some judge it too dark for a musical and too musical for a serious drama." Like *Blues in the Night*'s Depression-era populism, it's about "two creative people who are struggling," Scorsese explained. "They don't know where their next meal will come from, and it's worse because they're on the road. The film deals with a relationship, and how it grows, and then gets destroyed, and hopefully in the end is resolved." *Variety* warned of the film's "abrupt, downbeat ending that halts the picture just as it might be getting better," knocking its "schizophrenic shifts." Minnelli, evoking Garland in *A Star Is Born*, explained: "It was the hurt that made her a star. She put everything she had been through into her songs. Jimmy Doyle loved Francine, but he was a musician, and that was his priority, and he left her. But I think to be a great star, that isolation, that pain is a necessary part."[18]

The *Village Voice*'s Andrew Sarris thought the dark musical was a failure because of its mixture of "*Taxi Driver* and the Cukor-Arlen-Garland-Mason *A Star Is Born*. . . . It is mixed moods and delirious dialectics—two crucial ingredients for box office poison . . . to integrate a realistically raunchy character with a romantically gossamer genre." *Film Comment* aptly titled a 1977 interview with Scorsese: "Taxi Dancer." DeNiro's Method acting created modernist critical distance, while Minnelli's moving performance and musical style clashed with DeNiro's style. David Thomson observed, "De Niro's drive prefers private, sinister ecstasies to the wholesome bliss of the 1940s Musical. He makes the musical noir." Scorsese planned and started work on *New York, New York* before *Taxi Driver*, but he was committed to film *Taxi Driver* first. He considered shooting *New York, New York* like earlier films à la *Mean Streets*, as "a two-million-dollar, straight low budget picture" but "strictly a love story." After the success of *Taxi Driver*, it was budgeted at $7.2 million, growing into the big-budget independent Hollywood production by Irwin Winkler and Robert Chartoff released through United Artists.[19]

There was some critical appreciation of what Scorsese was trying to do. Many compared *New York, New York* favorably to *A Star Is Born*, praising its music and "romance vs. success rivalry" evoking "The Man That Got Away." Some critics appreciated the film's neo-noir revisionism, what seemed a "bright, welcome change of pace from a man who had built an early reputation on dark films about Catholic guilt and cathartic violence . . . proved to be not a traditional film musical but a modernist commentary on the traditional musical, a grueling, desperate romance set against a backdrop of stunningly stylized sets and lush music of the 1940's." Film scholar Richard Glatzer suggests that the "combination of raw, improvised drama with artful cinematic expressionism was not new to Scorsese—his gritty *Taxi Driver* was a no less stylized film—but critics were shocked to find the director's idiosyncratic emotional violence invading the sacrosanct realm of the musical." Nevertheless, critics complained, "Whenever someone says, 'New York, New York,' we automatically think: 'What a wonderful town, The Bronx is up, And the Battery's down. . . .' But that song isn't even in the movie." The "volatile, unrelenting" antihero "reaches out murderously to get at his pregnant wife and beats her." Improvised "bared-nerve scenes . . . shock one with the emotional violence of two people who love each other but ultimately have no place in each other's lives."[20]

Scorsese admitted, "George Lucas came down to look at the rough-cut and said we could add $10 million to the box-office receipts if we'd give the film a happy ending and have the man and the woman walk away together. He was right, but I said it just wouldn't work for this story. I knew that he was going for something that was extremely commercial, but I had to go another way." Released just four weeks after Lucas's record-breaking, trend-setting blockbuster *Star Wars*, *New York, New York* far exceeded its budget and earned a disappointing $6 million (some cite $13 million). By comparison, *Star Wars*, which cost $11.5 million, grossed $193.5 million domestically—even more than another industry trendsetter, Steven Spielberg's *Jaws* (which was the highest-grossing picture of all time just two years prior at $129.5 million).[21] The publicity campaign for Scorsese's 1940s musical romance targeted women, but women were not enthralled by DeNiro's antihero beating his pregnant wife into labor, then deserting her in the hospital without even seeing their newborn son. At the same time, male fans of the grisly (albeit misogynistic) violence and salacious sex of *Taxi Driver* and *Mean Streets* couldn't fathom why on earth Scorsese was doing a musical.[22]

The film's generally negative reception revealed how little interest there was in backstage musicals by 1977. One critic complained about the period atmosphere, saying Scorsese "means to recall the lost sights and sounds of post-World War II" films, but "after one has appreciated the scholarship for about an hour or so, admiring [DeNiro's] manic intensity [one] begins to wonder" what the director is up to. Vincent Canby concluded: "The original genre is really not interesting enough to have had all of this attention to detail spent on it."[23] Costly unusual musicals and provocative modernist experimentation declined as summertime special-effects blockbusters like *Jaws* dramatically changed the film industry, and expensive, risky musicals were avoided.[24]

New York, New York and *A Star Is Born* were restored to their precut glory in 1981 and 1983 respectively. After initial reservations about combining lyricism with gritty hard-edged themes, many reappraised *New York, New York*, including the restored production number, "Happy Endings," which cost $350,000 to shoot. *American Cinematographer* applauded *New York, New York* and *A Star Is Born*'s "musical noir" style. The *Los Angeles Herald Examiner* acknowledged the stunning audacity of the "*idea* of a film noir musical."[25]

PENNIES FROM HEAVEN AND THE SINGING DETECTIVE

British writer Dennis Potter experimented with innovative musicals *Pennies from Heaven* and *The Singing Detective*, inspired by classic film noir and noir musicals like *Blues in the Night*. Potter's postmodern British BBC and Hollywood productions reimagined dark musicals in completely different cultural, industrial, and reception contexts, reimported into American film adaptations. Drawing on classical Hollywood cinema, film noir style, and noir musicals, Potter wrote *Pennies from Heaven* as a series for the BBC over several weeks in 1977, energetically combining neo-noir style, musical fantasy, melodrama, and black comedy in an absurd variation on dark musicals (reenvisioning American film genres), employing Depression-era 1930s popular music in a period setting. Potter himself referred to *Pennies from Heaven* not as a conventional musical, but as a drama with music. It has even been called an "anti-musical." He immediately breaks with convention by dispensing with the imaginary "fourth wall" between the viewer and the character and jarring the audience out of its narrative reverie—eliminating efforts to become absorbed in the unfolding sexual conflict between passionate hero, Arthur (Bob Hoskins), a traveling sheet music salesman, and his frigid wife Joan (Gemma Craven) in the privacy of their suburban bedroom. When Arthur's sexual advances are rejected, he interrupts the fight with Joan and unexpectedly (as lighting shifts dramatically from high-key to low-key shadows) turns toward the camera not to sing but to lipsynch a female voice on Elsie Carlisle's recording of "The Clouds Will Soon Roll By." From this point on—at the juncture between dream/fantasy and "reality"—it becomes clear that anything is possible in his story.

Potter had to convince everyone that such a bizarre transgression would work, including reluctant director Piers Haggard, who initially wanted to alternate between shooting black-and-white sequences of everyday narrative reality/action with color sequences for musical fantasy dream sequences. Potter insisted on doing it entirely in color. *Pennies from Heaven* combines in-studio video sequences with location sequences on film. Haggard worked with lighting director Ken Westbury and cinematographer Dave Sydenham to achieve a striking dreamlike "halo" quality in the musical fantasy sequences.

With *Pennies from Heaven*'s success, Potter formed independent production company Pennies from Heaven Limited (PFH) in 1978, moving to Hollywood to script a film adaptation and interact with the American film industry. His high-profile move into independent production, transatlantic engagement with the Hollywood film industry in the screen adaptation, and big-budget return to the BBC (appropriating a pastiche of American cinematic conventions) with *The Singing Detective* enhanced his auteur status. Inspired by film noir and Hollywood musicals, Potter aesthetically, generically, and commercially imported dark musicals, then re-exported them back to Hollywood. Ironically, his 1981 American film adaptation of *Pennies from Heaven*, directed by Herbert Ross for MGM, was an abysmal failure with critics as well as audience in the United States and abroad. The film, visually darker than the series, has exquisite color neo-noir cinematography. Moody images by legendary production designer Ken Adam (who designed Stanley Kubrick's *Dr. Strangelove* and *Barry Lyndon*) paid atmospheric homage to film noir and Edward Hopper's painting *Nighthawks* with an impressive shrouded dance number by gangster Christopher Walken across a bar in a pool hall. In trying to turn Potter's series into a lavish Hollywood musical, MGM spent an extravagant $20 million, but the film only made $7 million—a record-breaking loss that accelerated the studio's eventual postclassical decline. A disappointed Potter realized that writers wielded little power in movies and that MGM didn't quite get what he had created in a different media context. Neither did the audience, nor for his *Gorky Park* (1983), another commercial failure.

Potter's Hollywood experience afforded him creative carte blanche on *The Singing Detective* when he resumed writing for the BBC in 1985. While the original *Pennies from Heaven* series had cost £800,000 to produce at the BBC, *The Singing Detective* was budgeted at £2 million (with Australian coproduction seed money from ABC). Potter was influenced by his exposure to American film and popular culture, absorbing and adopting new ideas related to a comparatively fragmented writing and production process ("developed" in pieces), appropriating Hollywood film, advertising, and fiction conventions. His dark musical *The Singing Detective* was continually rewritten during production as it progressed (at one point Potter even completely rewrote 7 1/2 hours of material at director Jon Amiel's request), rather than using the BBC convention of simply directing a prewritten script. It had three different producers (Kenith Trodd, John Harris, and executive producer

Rick McCallum) and was shot entirely on film at Amiel's insistence. Unlike *Pennies from Heaven*, Potter was present and active on the set for *The Singing Detective*— Amiel encouraged his involvement in the production and postproduction editing process.[26] *The Singing Detective* looked much more like a film noir, opening with a dark night shot of a woman's dead body in the water and the bluesy jazz theme from *Blues in the Night*.

In *The Singing Detective*, Potter infused his own narrative aesthetic into his protagonist, a physically and psychologically decrepit 1940s detective pulp fiction writer named Philip E. Marlow (Michael Gambon in a dual role as the author and the character)—like Potter, afflicted with arthritic disease and growing up in the Forest of Dean.[27] Invoking his illness in a complex flashback narrative and refor- mulating traditional genre practices, Potter creates a postmodern tour-de-force that draws on film noir, hard-boiled detective pulp fiction (appropriating Raymond Chandler's Philip Marlowe character), musical, mystery, thriller, action-suspense, melodrama, situation comedy, comic books, advertising, and 1940s popular songs in a cynically bizarre variation on dark Hollywood musicals. *The Singing Detective*'s intricate flashback structure fuses fantasy with oppressive reality into a dense amalgam: integrating Marlow's present, past, fantasies, guilt, dreams, wishes, nightmares, premonitions, and the narrative of his 1940s pulp fiction novel in his reenactment of the novel.

Potter's activation of different generic patterns is more complex in *The Singing Detective* than in *Pennies from Heaven*—there are fewer songs and it is considerably darker in theme and style. Thematically, the series focuses more on pain, para- noia, and psychological trauma than on the dreamlike optimism of *Pennies from Heaven*. However, whereas the protagonist played by Hoskins dies (is executed) at the conclusion of *Pennies from Heaven*, there arises a happier ending in *The Sing- ing Detective*. The young healthy trenchcoat and fedora-clad detective Marlow of the ailing writer's fiction fantasy joins the real world in the hospital ward—engaging in a neo-noir action shootout with the hoods who are stalking him—then kills the older diseased Marlow (the writer) to emancipate and cure him (fusing the two characters and the two realities) and walks out of the hospital with his ex-wife (Janet Suzman). Stylistically, *The Singing Detective* combines strikingly beauti- ful and disturbingly visceral photography—an assault on the senses. The sleek, stylized neo-noir images of Marlow's 1940s detective novel are hauntingly evoca- tive, his childhood Forest of Dean is sweeping and epic, the musical sequences are exaggerated and absurd, while the hospital is caustically hideous and graphic (Frances Hannon's make-up makes the skin crawl). It ends with Vera Lynn's World War II song "We'll Meet Again," featured in Kubrick's *Dr. Strangelove*.

Potter's interaction with the American film industry influenced his dark musicals adapted into Hollywood films. (*The Singing Detective* was also adapted as a Hollywood film starring Robert Downey Jr. based on Potter's screenplay in 2004, a decade after his 1994 death.)[28] Potter's twist on film noir and Hollywood musicals reflects a refreshing, unpredictably bizarre sensibility, relocating noir musicals from modern to postmodern terrain. As Potter completed *The Singing Detective*, Scorsese played an instrumental role in another dark 1986 musical, the remarkable transatlantic jazz neo-noir *Round Midnight*.

ROUND MIDNIGHT

Modest Franco-American coproduction *Round Midnight* (1986) brought the sights, sounds, and spirit of "jazz noir" to life in an evocative star-is-born narrative with a stylish nocturnal milieu and a sublime soundtrack. *Round Midnight* was coproduced by French independent companies Little Bear and P.E.C.F., written and directed by French director Bertrand Tavernier, cowritten by David Rayfiel, produced by *New York, New York*'s Irwin Winkler, and funded and distributed by Warner Bros. Set in Paris in 1959, Tavernier's atmospheric film (its title derived from a Thelonious Monk composition) boasted extraordinary color neo-noir visual design and a brooding blues score by Herbie Hancock. Inspired by the lives of American jazz pianist Bud Powell, saxophonist Lester Young, and French jazz enthusiast Francis Paudras, the dark musical centers on the friendship of African American bebop maestro Dale Turner, an aging, hard-drinking, drug taking, past-his-prime tenor sax player (Dexter Gordon) and his Parisian graphic illustrator fan Francis (François Cluzet), who tries to keep the musician from destroying himself. Both protagonists are tormented self-destructive antiheroes whose personal lives are messes. But they create great art. Just as The Archers cast a dancer rather than an actress for *The Red Shoes*, *Round Midnight* starred not an actor as its flawed antihero but a working musician: 6′5″, 63-year-old tenor sax man Gordon.

The Dark Side of Fame

Tavernier's film eloquently conveyed an unvarnished realism in its exploration of the dark side of success and the unglamorous life of bebop-era jazz musicians in a brilliant homage to earlier "jazz noir" films. *Round Midnight* vividly evoked the atmospheric world of jazz noir in a way that transcended earlier films, drawing on noir musicals such as *Blues in the Night*. (Gordon interpolated "Blues in the Night" into his tune "Society Red.")[29] It captured Paris' postwar jazz noir milieu inhabited by bebop artists Gordon, Davis, Powell, and Young with jazz musicians Hancock, Bobby Hutcherson, Wayne Shorter, Ron Carter, Tony Williams, Freddie

Hubbard, John McLaughlin, Billy Higgins, and Cedar Walton and bluesy jazz vocals by Lonette McKee and Sandra Reaves-Phillips.

Tavernier recalled that the project originated over dinner with Scorsese and Winkler. Scorsese asked what his "dream movie" would be if given total creative freedom. Tavernier replied: "a story about American jazz musicians in Paris in the late 50's." Winkler offered to produce it. *Round Midnight* recalled Davis's haunting blue tones and loneliness in *Elevator to the Gallows*. One version of the story claimed that Warners agreed to finance the project because Clint Eastwood was a jazz fan. Its final $3 million cost was $470,000 below its $3.5 million budget.[30]

In this variation on the dark side of fame and the talented self-destructive antihero, African American jazz saxophonist Dale (Gordon) is in an advanced state of addiction to alcohol and drugs. Although he has achieved great recognition for his musical artistry, he had to go to France to be fully appreciated. He plays his sax "sweetly" at the Blue Note to avid applause but is unhappy, desperately seeking his next drink or fix, even stealing to get it. (Gordon told Tavernier: "I would steal, but never beg.")[31] He is locked in his room by his handlers, not paid like the other musicians, and not given any drinks. Even his passport is locked away because of his binges and encounters with the police. His addiction is killing him. His friend Hershell is also dying back in New York. (Hershal Evans was Young's sax companion in Count Basie's band.) When Dale finally returns to America, it's implied that he dies of drug abuse. Meanwhile, fantastic jazz music surrounds him—and the audience.

Like in archetypal noir musical *Blues in the Night*, passion and obsession become a kind of dark musical prison in *Round Midnight*. "My life is music. My love is music. And it's twenty-four hours a day," Dale tells the shrink at the hospital he's sent to. "That's a heavy sentence to face," *Film Quarterly*'s Michael Dempsey observed. "It's like something that will not turn off . . . not let go of you."[32] Like *Blues in the Night* and *The Red Shoes*, *Round Midnight* subverts the idealism, happiness, success, and aesthetic of classical musicals. Playing jazz for art's sake is shown to be painful, especially when accompanied by traumatic memories of war and racism.

Tavernier reveals a disturbing side of fandom and its compulsive obsessive behavior in Dale's fan-turned-friend, Francis. A French graphic illustrator whose wife has left him, Francis deserts his young daughter to crouch obsessively in the rain and shadows outside the Blue Note, listening to Dale play through the air vent because he has no money. The scene evokes the poignant personal challenges depicted in European art cinema, such as François Truffaut's French New Wave classic *The 400 Blows* (1959) and Vittorio De Sica's Italian neorealist masterwork

The Bicycle Thief (1948). At one point Francis even meets his estranged wife to ask for money to move to a bigger apartment so Dale can live with him. "It's a very violent scene," Tavernier explains. "It's somebody who is so childish and immature that he is telling the woman whom I think he still loves that he has never been inspired by her. So he *hurts* her all the time. I think the scene is very important because it brings out the dark side of his character."[33] As Francis and Dale walk along New York's East River for the last time before he dies, Dale says, "You know, Francis, there is not enough kindness in the world." Gordon came up with the line after a musician on the set quoted the 1944 film noir *The Mask of Dimitrios*.

Dale's pain becomes more understandable when he powerfully recounts his memories of World War II brutality and racism: "I remember it rained pitifully that day. We were an all-Negro unit, with all-pink officers. One day at inspection this captain found a photo of my wife, who was lighter-skinned and much prettier than his. So then he made one of those funny remarks and I hit him in the head, which really wasn't the way white folks were treated in those days. So then I found myself in the Camp Polk stockade where they started to do drum paradiddles on my head—for some time. Yeah, I got lucky. I found this Jewish doctor from New York. Wow. Without him it would've been a catastrophe. He got me out of the army. You know, it just occurred to me that bebop was invented by the cats who did get out of the army." Tracking shots show rows of World War II army barracks, images evoking Alain Renais' haunting 1955 documentary *Night and Fog* about Nazi concentration camps.

Round Midnight's *Design*

Round Midnight featured production designer Alexandre Trauner's (*Paris Blues, Le jour se leve, The Apartment*) moody art direction, inspired by film noir and color noir. Trauner observed, "The film's title itself dictates the color style." It opens in stark black and white in an oppressive hotel room that gradually transforms into muted color noir shades of brown. Tavernier poetically conveys downbeat themes with exquisite design in what he described as "subdued, cold colors, with lots of dark areas, film noir style. This was, in part, in deliberate reaction against the current widespread practice of over-lighting everything, as though theatrical movies were made with television in mind. So much is lost, whole areas of imagination, because of this TV style of lighting. It's often been said television provides a training ground similar to what B movies used to be, but it's not really true. What was so great about B movies were their lighting; that made up for all the weaknesses." Tavernier recalled *Out of the Past* director Jacques Tourneur saying,

"Lighting gives a scene dignity." In conceiving *Round Midnight*, Tavernier screened noir films shot by John Alton for his cinematographer Bruno de Keyzer so he could achieve "shots lit with only one light source" using a "minimal amount of light" as in film noir. Together they created extraordinary results with specific ideas about color schemes, keeping in mind that "the most important thing is what to leave out." As in Cukor's color noir design strategy for *A Star Is Born*, Tavernier and Trauner tried to eliminate and subtract colors to emphasize certain hues. Tavernier said, "We mapped out very precisely the kind of shapes and colors we wanted, especially the use of blue-gray to make it cold . . . like the color of cigarette smoke. We wanted to evoke the feeling of a black and white photograph, so Trauner painted everything in those cool colors."[34]

Round Midnight's *Musical Noir Style*

Tavernier was much inspired by American cinema: film noir, John Ford, William Wellman, Sam Fuller, Delmer Davies. He praised *The Big Sleep*, Michael Powell, French auteurs (Jean Renoir), and Italian cinema. Tavernier compared Dexter Gordon to Bogart and Mitchum. Tavernier welcomed Gordon's insight on his performance and dialogue on the set. "Dexter Gordon was tremendous, very literate with a sharp sense of humor, a great knowledge of film, and incredible admiration for actors like George Sanders, Richard Burton and James Mason. Dexter said Mason sounded like tenor saxophone. He contributed 30 or 40 lines to the film." When jazz musicians gather for a recording session, film buff Wayne Shorter recounts how *Red Shoes* composer Julian tells impressario Lermontov that his music has been stolen. Tavernier recalled the jam sessions recorded live and a "shot of Billy Higgins at the drums, just waiting for Dexter's next move. No actor could come up with something like that."[35]

The minor key of bluesy jazz is central to this experimental film that drifts between French and English. After a drunk passes out on the floor of the club, Dale tells the bartender: "S'il vous plait, I would like to have the same thing he had." Its musical neo-noir ambiance is captured in McKee's sultry rendition of George and Ira Gershwin's "How Long Has This Been Going On?" evoking Lena Horne and Billie Holliday. *Round Midnight*'s complex narrative structure parallels its music, reflected in a "free flow of voice-overs, time lapses, flash-forwards . . . laying of one musical number over another." Dale's tormented jazz genius, like *Blues in the Night*'s pianist, is pursuing art for art's sake; he's not selling out his dream, but still he's suffering. Fluid camerawork captured jazz performances, recorded "live" in a downbeat milieu replicating Paris' famed Blue Note club in 1959 (shot at Epinay studios north of Paris.) Tavernier recalled, "In the musical sequences, the camera work *had* to adapt to the music constantly because the music was improvised, and all of it was recorded directly while filming—which no one thought we could manage to do. We never knew in advance what the musicians were to do, how many choruses they were going to take. A number that went on for four minutes in one take might go on for seven in the next. I was lucky to get a wonderful camera operator who is a musician himself and who patterned his camera moves after the harmonic structure of the compositions, so that he could smoothly track along a musician playing a solo and move past him just as he completed it."[36]

Round Midnight's Reception

Critics called *Round Midnight* "masterly." "No actor could do what the great jazz saxophonist Dexter Gordon does" in Tavernier's "glowing tribute to the golden age of bebop." Janet Maslin applauded its "lovely, elegiac" pacing, real-life inspiration, and "tremendous depth of feeling" as Gordon becomes the "very embodiment of the music" with "heavy-lidded eyes," "smoky voice," and "long, graceful fingers" that "seem to be playing silent accompaniment to his conversation." *Variety* praised its "atmosphere," calling it a "rare example of Franco-American filmmaking in the truest sense of the term," a "superbly crafted music world drama" where "colorful images of Dale and Francis briefly turn into the black-and-white, home-movie memories they will someday become." Recalling the sights and sounds of film noir with its melancholy strains of blue jazz, *Los Angeles Times'* Sheila Benson lauded the film's evocative milieu with lonely Paris streets and stark hotel rooms filled with great, serious, "humbling" music, calling it the "first film about jazzmen to be made in their own rhythms; it's a ballad, with repeated themes, long sustained passages and a perfect, delicate gravity. . . . With consummate tact, intelligence and passion, Tavernier lets us understand the cost of such exploration." *Round Midnight* reveals "civilized rage" at the "beauties and horrors of a musician's life" as Dale (Gordon), "complex and magnificent," moves "serenely to his own inner rhythms, ironic, unexpectedly sweet, utterly aware of both his powers and his demons." *Round Midnight* grossed $3,250,000. It won an Oscar for Best Original Score. Despite never having acted, Gordon was nominated for Best Actor, though he did not receive the award. Tavernier recalled, "When the film was released in America, Marlon Brando sent a letter to Dexter in which he said that for the first time in fifteen years he learnt something about acting. Dexter read me the letter over the phone and said, 'After that who needs an Oscar?' "[37] Biographical dark musicals also followed suit, influenced by the verisimilitude of *Round Midnight*.

BIRD

As with the real life jazz musicians who inspired *Round Midnight*, other films also drew on nonfiction stories of actual figures in the jazz world. Dark musical biopics depicted fame's dark side, as in Billie Holiday biopic *Lady Sings the Blues* (1972), *Funny Girl/Funny Lady* (1968/1975), Thelonious Monk documentary *Straight, No Chaser* (1988), *Bird* (1988), and *Ray* (2004). The year after *Round Midnight*, Eastwood produced and directed *Bird* for his Malpaso Productions, released by Warner Bros. It is based on the life of jazz saxophone legend Charlie "Bird" Parker, played by Forest Whitaker. *Bird* reimagines film noir in its unvarnished rendering of the life of the brilliant, tormented jazz maestro. In brooding neo-noir style, it features claustrophobic interior settings. *Bird* "seldom ventures outdoors" and "takes place in the smoky nightclubs where Parker played or in the dimly lighted apartments where his unruly private life unfolded." Critics recognized its "studied, shadowy look, at times so striking that the actors' features can't clearly be seen" and saw the dark atmospheric ambiance as the "most concerted effort to capture the spirit of Parker's music." Critic Janet Maslin noted, "Until Bertrand Tavernier's *Round Midnight*, in which Dexter Gordon served as the purest imaginable embodiment of jazz and its attendant way of life, it might have seemed impossible to convey these things on screen. *Bird*, earnest and immense as it is, reinforces the earlier notion of jazz's elusiveness. Though the music is everywhere in Eastwood's film, heard on the superb soundtrack and seen on every street corner, its essence remains somehow out of reach."[38] Forest Whitaker won the award for Best Actor at the Cannes Film Festival. *Bird* also won an Oscar for Best Sound. Filmed in 52 days for $14.4 million (with an estimated $9 million budget), *Bird* grossed only $2,181,286 in the United States.[39] Other films began to adopt noir musical conventions in surprising ways.

THE FABULOUS BAKER BOYS

Dark musicals even influenced romantic comedies such as *The Fabulous Baker Boys* (1989). The film, written by first-time director Steve Kloves, invoked Bogart and Bacall films of the 1940s. Paula Weinstein acquired it in 1985; three years later, it was produced by Gladden Entertainment and Mirage (which produced Kenneth Branagh's 1991 neo-noir musical suspense thriller *Dead Again*.) It was filmed on location in Los Angeles and Seattle.

The film opens on a gray rainy scene. Dave Grusin's bluesy jazz score conveys an existential sadness that immediately suggests film noir rather than comedy. It begins like the 1981 neo-noir *Cutter's Way*: disheveled, grabbing rumpled clothes the morning after a one-night stand, antihero Jack (Jeff Bridges) leaves a naked stranger between the sheets in cold disregard. He leaves to play a gig at a dive bar with his balding, married older brother, Frank (Beau Bridges). His jazz musician buddy asks him, "Still stompin' at the Sheraton?" Much of the story unfolds in "dark dives," dying piano lounges that Frank and Jack "resort to for work."[40] Michelle Pfeiffer plays the call girl/singer Susie who revives the Baker boys, singing the blues in a fiery red dress while draped across cigarette-smoking Jeff Bridges' piano. Roger Ebert wrote, "Whatever she's doing while she performs that song isn't merely singing; it's whatever Rita Hayworth did in *Gilda*."[41]

Beneath the film's deadpan humor, there is a serious musical drama in which jazz standards recall a noir era. Its "smart, slangy . . . furiously hard-boiled" dialogue, is clearly meant to recall Bogart, Bacall, and Hayworth, "specializing in smoky, down-at-the-heels glamour." The *Washington Post* described it as "nostalgic" with a "passion for Ella Fitzgerald records, film noir and romantic melodrama" that mesh "like a beloved movie from the glory days of Hollywood. It transports you. It's an American rhapsody . . . slinky and cynical, more Bacall than Bacall." *New Yorker*'s Pauline Kael called it a "romantic fantasy that has a forties-movie sultriness" and "melancholy" with "the radiance of the very young Lauren Bacall."[42]

Cinematographer Michael Ballhaus said he deglamorized venues to "create garish, unattractive lighting . . . ugly and cheap, and a little sleazy. Some of the places really looked terrible. . . . You feel it's kind of a cheap crowd, not a great place to be." He explained, "You can still do a lot with light to give the impression that it's an undesirable place . . . almost all of the film is set indoors—in lounges, bars, hotels—the places where the Fabulous Baker Boys earn their keep."[43] *American Film* praised Ballhaus's imagery, noting it "set the standard for modern screen romance" with "some of the most rapturous and moody-blues cinematography around" and a "fierce nostalgia for the romantic scenarios of the '40s" with "new-style romantic fantasies [that] hearken back to the old style."[44] They captured what was special about *The Fabulous Baker Boys*: a "distinctively modern touch" that is "filled with regret—an awareness that the romantic mood it is invoking is a vanished fantasy." Critic Elvis Mitchell observed, "It's as if Jack studied Humphrey Bogart's doomed-hero pose from *Casablanca*, tucked the black-and-white glamour into his head and never let it go."[45]

Publicity described "romance, drama, music and comedy" about a "gifted jazz musician whose talent is being wasted on the lounge circuit" and the "singer who brings new life to the act and causes Jack and Frank to reexamine their relationship to each other and to their music." Ads featured diva Pfeiffer between the

Baker boys, real-life brothers Jeff and Beau Bridges. Evoking the world of noir, they brutally beat each other in a late-night rain-soaked alley trapped against a crisscrossing chain-link fence. The film was budgeted at $11.5 million; released by Fox in October 1989, it grossed $18.43 million.[46] On the heels of *The Fabulous Baker Boys'* success, other films would also revive noir musical aesthetic.

Spike Lee's 1990 *Mo' Better Blues* featured self-absorbed trumpeter Denzel Washington, rival Wesley Snipes, and drummer Jeff "Tain" Watts (with Branford Marsalis, Kenny Kirkland, Terrance Blanchard, and Robert Hurst on its sound-track). It was compared to *Bird* and *Round Midnight.* The Coen Brothers' 1997 *The Big Lebowski* recasts *The Big Sleep* with voice-over narration and outrageous Berkeley-inspired musical fantasies. Alex Proyas' futuristic 1998 *Dark City* offered atmospheric neo-noir style and moody voice-overs. Jennifer Connelly sings with a jazz combo in a murky club. Nostalgic billboards, postcards, and simulated memories resemble classical Hollywood Technicolor musicals. Its tormented an-tihero John Murdoch (Rufus Sewell), framed for a prostitute's murder, asks the detective (William Hurt), "When was the last time you saw the sun out?" comment-ing on the shadowy nocturnal world it recreates—shot in Australia studios.

NEW HOLLYWOOD AND A CHANGING INDUSTRY

Dark musicals continued to change as the industry also continued to change. Business conglomerates outside the media industry absorbed major American film studios. After talent agent Lew Wasserman's 1962 Music Corporation of America (MCA)-Universal merger, Gulf+Western purchased Paramount in 1966. Transamerica took over UA in 1967. Seven Arts acquired Warner Bros., bought by Kinney in 1969. Las Vegas developer Kirk Kerkorian purchased MGM in 1972. Global corporate merger/acquisitions accelerated after a deregulated 1980s–90s era. Gulf+Western became Paramount Communications in 1989, sold to Viacom in 1994. Australian Rupert Murdoch's News Corporation acquired 20th Century Fox in 1985–86. After Coca Cola bought Columbia in 1982, Japanese consumer electronics Sony acquired Columbia in 1989. Time merged with Warner in 1989–90 and Turner in 1996. Disney acquired independent Miramax in 1993 and ABC in 1996.[47] The Telecommunications Act of 1996 further deregulated a con-glomerate media industry, thereby allowing greater concentration of ownership. Transnational corporations acquired major studios and independent production companies (absorbed into subsidiary arms of massive multinational conglomer-ates). The Big Six media conglomerates News Corp/21st Century Fox (20th Cen-tury Fox), Time Warner (Warner Bros./CNN/HBO), Viacom (Paramount/CBS), Sony (Columbia), Comcast (Universal/NBC), Disney (ABC/ESPN/Miramax/Pixar/

168 MUSIC IN THE SHADOWS

ILM) own Hollywood film studios; broadcast television and cable networks; and a vast array of new media industries spanning music, video games, cable satellite systems, theme parks, print publishing, consumer electronics, toy manufacturing, and online media.[48] Films favored in this environment tended to be spectacular, over-the-top blockbusters that appeal to young audiences and that also play well abroad. Conglomeration coincided with a rise in transnational coproductions, global independent film financing, and postmodern homage to classicism as in color neo-noir *The Big Lebowski*, *Dark City*, *Moulin Rouge!*, and *Chicago*.

MOULIN ROUGE!

As the industry consolidated in transnational cartels, its films evolved into increasingly simplistic "high concept" blockbusters. A New Hollywood era of sequels, prequels, trilogies, and global franchises counted on lucrative opening weekends at the box-office. They focused on the bottom line, playing it safe with action movies with heightened digital special effects that were aimed to attract kids. Spin-off toys, games, theme park rides, and commercial soundtracks also contributed to profits. Blockbuster spectacles showcasing digital technology targeted a global audience and were produced abroad. At the same time, there was a renewed interest in the classical and neo-classical film era. Baz Luhrmann's dark musical blockbuster *Moulin Rouge!* was a postmodern neo-noir with brooding color visual design. It concluded his "Red Curtain" musical trilogy (following *Strictly Ballroom* and *Romeo+Juliet*) that evoked *The Red Shoes* and *A Star Is Born*. *Moulin Rouge!* offered a dazzling special effects tour-de-force in a gorgeous visual style. It was cast with huge stars (Nicole Kidman[49] and Ewan McGregor of the *Star Wars* prequel trilogy.) The plot of *Moulin Rouge!* revolves around a tormented creative antihero's doomed love affair set against a lively, but dangerous musical performance setting. As in *Round Midnight's* Blue Note club, *Moulin Rouge!* centered on a famous Paris nightclub. Evoking shady noir musical dives, the Moulin Rouge, an infamous turn-of-the-century Parisian cabaret, is a raucous bar rife with drugs, booze, prostitutes, and illicit activity. Written, directed, and produced by Luhrmann, the Bazmark production (cowritten with Craig Pearce, coproduced with Martin Brown and Fred Baron) featured Kidman as the club's singer/dancer/star/ prostitute and McGregor as the show's writer/singer/antihero. Femme temptress Satine (Kidman) dreams in star-is-born fashion of becoming a real singer and actress—as she is dying of consumption. The actual Moulin Rouge, like the smoky nightclubs of film noir, was notorious for its racy can-can dancers in what Breen would have called a "sordid," "sexually-suggestive" atmosphere. The original club opened in Montmartre in October 1889. Artist Henri de Toulouse-Lautrec was known for his portraits of the club's entertainers. Like antiheros of noir musicals, Parisian bohemians of the 1800s believed in art for art's sake, rejecting wealth and pursuing ideals of love and truth. The Moulin Rouge club inspired several films, notably Ewald André Dupont's 1928 silent melodrama and John Huston's 1952 dramatic color noir musical melodrama biopic of Lautrec starring José Ferrer. In the new global conglomerate production climate, Luhrmann adapted *Moulin Rouge!* as a stylized neo-noir musical (rather than a biopic), an experimental postmodern Australian-American international coproduction depicting a Paris shot entirely in-studio in Australia and Madrid rather than on a Hollywood soundstage.

Moulin Rouge! opens with a beautiful color neo-noir atmospheric sequence and a moody voice-over narration by its tormented antihero that propels the narrative into a neo-noir-styled flashback. *Moulin Rouge!* begins by simulating a silent film in 1900 Paris with Lautrec (John Leguizamo) singing "Nature Boy." Breathtaking tracking shots move swiftly through the (digitally recreated) Montmartre quarter, past a red marquee, and on into the dark claustrophobic room where devastated writer Christian (McGregor) types, reliving turbulent memories, like Bogart in *Casablanca*. Like *Round Midnight*, the sequence begins in black and white, evoking film noir, then bleeds in color gradually until it becomes full-color neo-noir.

Inspired by the myth of Orpheus, Verdi's *La Traviata*, and India's Bollywood musicals, *Moulin Rouge!* provides an industrial critique of postclassical New Hollywood in the era of the blockbuster. Drawing an allegory between the fate of its prostitute Satine and the movie business itself, it crosscuts between a sultry Fosse-esque "Roxanne" tango dance number and an attempted rape sequence of Satine by the stage show's investor. In "exchange" for funding, the investor demands the deed to the Moulin Rouge and "exclusive rights" to Satine. Luhrmann's musical spectacle culminates in a stage show (aptly titled "Spectacular, Spectacular"), as in *The Red Shoes* and classical backstage noir musicals. It mirrors the tragic narrative of the film by exposing the dark side of show business with the death of its star onstage, as the audience applauds on the other side of the curtain.

Luhrmann and wife Catherine Martin, the film's production and costume designer, considered: "Could a musical work? A musical must be able to work in western culture again, and could it be comic-tragic?" *Moulin Rouge!*'s "whole stylistic premise" is to "decode what the Moulin Rouge was to the audiences of 1899 and express that same thrill and excitement in a way to which contemporary movie-goers can relate."[50]

With a vast array of contemporary songs, musically and thematically, *Moulin*

Rouge! subverts Wise's *Sound of Music* and every other musical number it experiments with in wild postmodern abandon. It's an exquisitely stylized color neo-noir celebration of popular culture—while simultaneously critiquing its commercialism and nostalgically parodying, celebrating, and subverting the musical genre. Film critic Elvis Mitchell wrote: "Few films since the gorgeous dreamscapes of the old Technicolor process, in which the dye was printed right on the stock, have cajoled as much out of a single color as Mr. Luhrmann has out of red" in *Moulin Rouge!*. The ambitious production was challenging and incredibly innovative both aesthetically and technologically in the new digital era.[51]

Budgeted at $52.5 million, the movie was shot from October 1999 through April 2000 at Fox Studios in Sydney (where *Dark City* was filmed). It ran beyond schedule and was eventually bumped from soundstages as an even bigger blockbuster (*Star Wars Episode II: Attack of the Clones*) began filming, so additional sequences were shot in Madrid in May 2000. Originally scheduled to open in December 2000, its release was delayed to allow more time for postproduction. Black and streaks of scarlet red dominated color noir posters promoting the dark musical with the doomed couple locked in a torrid embrace against a shrouded nocturnal background and the club's marquee. Despite its style, critics complained that Luhrmann achieved his elaborate visual aesthetic at the service of a "blatantly artificial" formulaic story in a recognizable downbeat musical plot.[52] *Moulin Rouge!* premiered at the Cannes Film Festival and in Los Angeles in May 2001. Released by 20th Century Fox (a global conglomerate owned by Murdoch's News Corporation), *Moulin Rouge!* grossed $179 million. Nominated for eight Academy Awards, including Best Picture and Best Actress, *Moulin Rouge!* won Oscars for Art Direction and Costume Design. It was the first musical nominated for Best Picture in twenty-two years, not since Fosse's *All That Jazz* in 1979. *Moulin Rouge!*'s success revived interest in dark experimental musicals, paving the way for *Chicago*.

CHICAGO

Director/choreographer Rob Marshall and screenwriter Bill Condon adapted Fosse's 1975 Broadway musical *Chicago* with music by Kander and Ebb based on Maurine Dallas Watkins' 1926 play about contemporary Chicago murders. The film *Chicago* (2002) fused neo-noir musical with Prohibition-era crime and tabloid sensation. Fosse's trademark dancer's count "5-6-7-8" picks up *All That Jazz*'s "1-2-3-4." It opens in a stylish homage to noir and dark musical style as a jazz band performs in a smoky, shadowy speakeasy. Martin Walsh's crosscutting montage editing presents a Fosse-inspired cinematic tour-de-force. A tight low-angle shot of black-stockinged legs moves from a black car, up cramped stairwells, through shadowy claustrophobic corridors, and into dark backstage dressing rooms. The camera follows slinky jazz singer/dancer Velma (Catherine Zeta-Jones), a scrappy black-clad brunette who has knocked off her husband and dance-partner sister (entangled with her unfaithful spouse). She stashes the gun, washes the blood off her hands, and swivels into seductive choreography belting out "And All That Jazz." The jazz number is intercut with scenes of another married singer/dancer, Roxie Hart (Rene Zellweger), a sinewy blonde star-struck ingénue, also blowing away sleazy lover Fred Casely (Dominic West) who lied to her, promising to make her a star (for sex), then mocked her, roughed her up, and callously walked away saying, "That's life, sweetheart" just before she guns him down.

Roxie lands in jail with Velma. Husband Amos (John Reilly) realizes he's been duped: "She's up here munchin' on bonbons and tramping around like some . . . floozy!" (Tough molls munched bonbons in gangster films like Mamoulian's *City Streets*.) "You've been . . . jazzin' him!" Like classic noir, "And All That Jazz" uses jazz as sexual innuendo. "I'm gonna rouge my knees and roll my stockings down / I know a whoopee spot where the gin is cold but the piano's hot, a noisy hall, a nightly brawl . . . blow the blues." *Chicago* provided a star-is-born narrative, juxtaposing showbiz celebrity with criminal notoriety and a corrupt legal system. Like *Moulin Rouge!,* it mocks the image-driven, media-dominated consumer culture it portrays. Invoking color noir, Australian cinematographer Dion Beebe presents action against production designer John Myhre's "rich canvas of dark tones and bloody reds" to blend fantasy with a grittier crime milieu in its shadowy opening. *Chicago* uses crime to comment on sensational blockbusters, critiquing media hype that feeds a "thrill-hungry," "low-attention-span" public.[53]

Fosse had considered adapting *Chicago* to film (as did Scorsese, Laurents, and Luhrmann) but instead turned to *All That Jazz*. So, Harvey Weinstein, head of Miramax (acquired by Walt Disney Corporation) began working on it with co-producer Martin Richards (Producer Circle Co.) in 1994. Weinstein and Richards struggled for six years to adapt *Chicago* as fewer and fewer musicals were being made in a male-action blockbuster era. In 2001, first-time director Marshall was signed with Condon writing the script; Zellweger was cast as Roxie. (Minnelli, DeNiro, Joel Grey, Kidman, and Pfeiffer were also considered for roles.) It was filmed from December 2001 through April 2002 in Toronto (with Chicago exteriors). *Chicago* cost $45 million to make and opened in December 2002.[54] It was compared to work by Fosse, Potter, and Luhrmann.

Variety called it an "attempt to resurrect the musical as a contemporary film genre" though "less buoyant" or "inventive" than "unconventional, artistically controversial" *Moulin Rouge!*. Condon's script reimagined numbers as "fruit of a stagestruck chorine's rich fantasy life" intercut with "parallel reality" solving a "fundamental conundrum" to "sell a traditional musical to audiences unaccustomed to characters bursting into song." Critics praised *Chicago's* "superlative" score. It won six Academy Awards including Best Picture.[55]

As the dark musical phenomenon thus persisted, 2010's *Black Swan* reimagined *The Red Shoes* as a psychotic ballerina suffers paranoid delusions when she achieves fame and stabs herself to death.

In an industrial climate marked by international coproduction, experimental postclassical films *Moulin Rouge!*, *Dark City*, *Chicago*, and *Black Swan* fused spectacle with postmodern neo-noir variations on dark musicals. They exemplify and critique the industry's transformation in the digital age, targeting youth with spectacular, over-the-top scenes.[56] These experimental dark musicals combine elements from blockbusters, musicals, and crime films. Amidst rising costs, films are increasingly shot outside Hollywood or abroad with multinational crews. Dark musicals had come a long way from *Blues in the Night*.

EPILOGUE

The beautifully noir cinematography style and downbeat tenor of films like *Blues in the Night* influenced a long series of noir musicals. In an unlikely combination of styles, noir musicals subverted romantic musical idealism and optimism. Like film noir, noir musicals evolved during classical Hollywood's wartime through postwar 1940s and 1950s eras, inspiring an experimental legacy in later neo-noir musicals. Playing with the tradition of noir's earlier Golden Age, filmmakers tried to keep the spirit of black-and-white noir cinema art alive, even in musical films with a color noir aesthetic. Just as film noir was adapted to jazz noir and color noir musical melodrama, noir musicals reveal how noir style evolves and ebbs.

The dark musical film with a distinctive noir-styled visual aesthetic shows how noir style affected a wide variety of different types of films, even those as divergent from noir as color musicals. Filmmakers, stars, musicians, and creative personnel involved in these productions were cognizant of previous noir musicals, referring to innovative pictures like later references to *Blues in the Night*, *The Red Shoes*, and *A Star Is Born*, acknowledging their significance and importance. These films were promoted in similar ways using color noir style posters, even for black-and-white pictures. Dark musicals appropriated noir conventions. They fused musical performance with noir visual style as a brooding black-and-white jazz noir and a moody "color noir" aesthetic emerged. Like in film noir,

aesthetics combined shadowy expressionistic painting with stark realistic photography, elaborate design, low-key lighting, and a stylized mise-en-scène. Fusing fantasy with grittier realism, noir musicals invoked incongruous elements:
brooding melancholy and film noir menace with classical musical romance and
spectacle.

An extraordinary amalgam, noir musicals defied genre, narrative, and stylistic
conventions. Critics rejected *Blues in the Night* for incongruously deviating from
escapist expectations. *The Red Shoes* was initially dismissed, denied a premiere
due to its unusual nature. While director Cukor was overseas, *A Star Is Born* was
expanded to include more upbeat numbers and drastic cuts. Marginalized when
originally released, these films were later recognized as innovative and restored.

This remarkable array of dark musical pictures displayed a cinematic vision
responding to changes in culture, the film industry, censorship, and new technology. It moved from black-and-white nitrate film (*Blues in the Night*) to three-strip
Technicolor (*The Red Shoes*) to Eastman Kodak monopack single-strip color with
widescreen CinemaScope (*A Star Is Born*, processed by Technicolor lab for better color quality). Classical 1940s and 1950s noir musicals inspired postclassical
experimental variations (*West Side Story* shot in 70 mm) as well as neo-noir films
paying homage in later dark musicals (*New York, New York*) and global coproductions (*The Singing Detective, Round Midnight, Moulin Rouge!*). Darker musical
variations invoked noir style and revived downbeat musicals as classical escapist
musicals were made less frequently and eventually fell out of fashion in a cynical
postclassical New Hollywood era.

Darker musicals elevated the status of musicals by taking on serious subjects and realistic downbeat themes. Like film noir, dark musicals involved self-
destructive antiheroes and conflicted working heroines performing to music in
after-hours jazz nightclubs or dancing as an artistic endeavor. Tormented musicians play the blues in *Blues in the Night, Young Man with a Horn,* and *Young at
Heart.* A dancer belts the blues in *Gilda.* A jazz vocalist sings and lives the blues
as aspiring screen star in *A Star Is Born* reimagined in *New York, New York.* A
talented dancer pursues ballet in *The Red Shoes.* As musicians perform jazz in
Blues in the Night, noir musical protagonists strived to create art while struggling
to avoid selling out. These flawed antiheroic musicians-singers-dancers struggle
to achieve fame and fortune on stage or screen trying to capture a mythic ideal
and are miserable once they get there, whether because they have sold out or
because the dream, it turns out, is only a dream. In noir musicals, success does
not bring happiness; rather it contributes to the musical artist's downfall or demise in a subversion of the American dream. Influenced by noir, crime films,

and trends in realism, noir musicals moved beyond escapism to explore the shady side of the spotlight. Noir musicals inverted the hopeful aspirations of the American dream as presented in classical musicals and Hollywood's mythic glamour machine. Featuring underdog survivors, scrappy everymen, or working girls, they questioned what individuals pursuing fame and success are fighting to achieve, and how they, or life around them, are transformed in the process. Like the gangster antiheroes' ill-fated pursuit of success, noir musicals examined identity, artifice, and the struggle for recognition. Individuals pursue their goal of performing artistically and elevating their social class. They encounter romance in their personal life that complicates or interferes with their ambitions. Noir musicals involve the tension between the private sphere and the public sphere, between the realm of dramatic creation and domestic relationships. Downbeat noir musicals experimented with classical formula, employing existential critique more typical of film noir to reveal that fame and its facade of glamour, are not always what they seem. They challenge traditional musicals' romantic myth of success and scrutinize Hollywood's star factory, its manufacture of celebrity personas for consumption by fans, thus exposing how identity is artificially constructed and the personal cost with which it is paid.

Noir musicals shifted from masculine Depression-era narratives like *Blues in the Night* to comparatively female-centered musical noir films during and just after World War II (*Cover Girl, Phantom Lady, Gilda, The Man I Love, The Red Shoes*), followed by musical film noir that once again targeted an increasingly male audience as men returned home (*Road House, Young Man with a Horn, Glory Alley*). *A Star Is Born* combined a female protagonist with a tormented antihero partner, while *Blues in the Night* and *The Red Shoes* included self-destructive love triangles and multiple flawed relationships. Noir musicals highlighted the conflict between intimacy and performing careers. They explored psychic trauma, sexuality, and ethnic and creative identity—to which émigrés and oppressed minorities, including those blacklisted, could relate—inspiring later dark musicals that sought a lucrative youth market.

Dark musicals spawned an amazing legacy. *Blues in the Night, The Red Shoes,* and *A Star Is Born* in particular were surprisingly influential. Warners producer Wallis had little faith in *Blues in the Night*'s ability to make money because its unusual nature did not conform to typical genre formula. Wallis and Warner Bros. were hopeful after seeing the final cut but disappointed with its box office failure as America entered World War II. Yet, films referred to and were inspired by *Blues in the Night*. These dark musicals eventually enjoyed greater success and artistic appreciation. Twenty-five years after its 1941 release, *Blues in the Night* was critically recognized as one of the best films devoted to jazz, influencing a musical crime film trend. The tremendous success of *The Red Shoes* in the United States was unexpected even by its backer; it inspired Hollywood filmmakers Kelly, Minnelli, Cukor, Garland, and Scorsese. *A Star Is Born* influenced *Young at Heart, Love Me or Leave Me,* and *New York, New York.* As it was restored and better appreciated, filmmakers like Scorsese, *American Cinematographer,* and critics recognized the existence of a musical noir style, which influenced later films such as *New York, New York, Round Midnight,* and *Moulin Rouge.*

Serious downbeat drama undermined musical romantic fantasy. Dark musicals were not often made because of their financial risk. Given the unusual, often unsuccessful, fusion of musical escapism with darker thematic and stylistic elements of film noir, it is surprising that such opposing forms as film noir and musicals were combined, resulting in such unconventional musicals—and there were indeed disastrous releases with unfortunate consequences. Noir musicals faced setbacks and suffered at the box office; even their productions were chaotic affairs. But they did produce highly successful hit songs and musical soundtracks. Their atmospheric milieu has continued to fascinate filmmakers for decades, inspiring postclassical neo-noir musicals. Their innovative synthesis of cynical noir style and musical entertainment—seemingly polar opposites—subverted sentimentality, which has contributed to their appeal.

Realism drawn from the lives of jazz musicians and performers—and the experiences of artists, stars, creative personnel, and filmmakers involved in these projects—inspired noir-style musicals. Stories depicted talented performing artists struggling with self-destructive tendencies in narratives that mirrored their own lives. A great deal was riding on creating these remarkable but less-successful films. Filmmakers were so seriously committed to making these out-of-the-ordinary downbeat musicals that their careers and livelihood were affected, suffering as a result if films flopped at the box office. These extraordinary films encountered resistance or failure in troubled productions that actually (or nearly) ended entire careers. Kazan's screen acting career ended after *Blues in the Night;* Whorf moved to directing after *Christmas Holiday.* Garland's expensive and time-consuming *A Star Is Born* failed to revive her Hollywood career.

When Eastman Kodak announced it would no longer be manufacturing or processing low-speed black-and-white film stock or making film cameras, it marked the passing of an era. Classic film noir, atmospheric motion pictures noted for their distinctive visual style, sophisticated black-and-white cinematography, and chiaroscuro shadows, seemed a lost art form. Noir musicals and film noir declined after the fall of the classical studio system. However, the influence and legacy of film noir musicals lived on in an array of incarnations. In a cynical postclassical era, neo-noir color films tapped resurgent interest in film noir with gritty de-glamorized portrayals of backstage musical life more provocative and realistic than conventional escapist musicals. Downbeat musicals distinctively deviated from typical genre formula by refusing to resolve narratives with a happy ending of heterosexual couples walking off into the sunset together.

These atypical dark musical films produced an enduring aesthetic. Brooding red color noir and shadowy jazz noir are instantly recognizable. A downbeat bluesy milieu, after-hours jazz music, antiheroic performers, and Technicolor noir style simulating the feel of chiaroscuro black-and-white film noir were characteristic. These iconic elements emerged as experimental revisionist dark musicals capturing the existential spirit of film noir. They examined psychological obsession, the corrupting power of ambition, and problems of sociocultural repression. Musical noir undermined romance and naive idealism to reveal a harsh, ominous landscape beneath the alluring tinsel of show business. Dark musicals explored recognizable musical noir style conventions in a cinematic world where tormented jazz musicians, blues singers, dancers, and manufactured stars, like crime antiheroes, find that fame is a deceptive trap and success is ultimately an unattainable illusion. Their music is made in the shadows.

Notes

UNC   Universal Collection
USC   University of Southern California Cinema Library Special
               Collections, Los Angeles, California
VAR   *Variety*
WBA   USC Warner Bros. Archive
WP   *Washington Post*
WSC   William Schaefer Collection

CHAPTER I: THE NOIR MUSICAL

1. Films included *Syncopation, Casablanca, This Gun for Hire, Jammin' the Blues, To Have and Have Not, Lady in the Dark, Cover Girl, Phantom Lady, Christmas Holiday, Detour, Club Havana, Gilda, The Big Sleep, Black Angel, Lured, New Orleans, Dead Reckoning, The Man I Love, Road House, Casbah, The Red Shoes, Young Man with a Horn, The Strip, Glory Alley, Affair in Trinidad, Moulin Rouge, A Star Is Born, The Barefoot Contessa, Young at Heart, Love Me or Leave Me, Pete Kelly's Blues,* and *Sweet Smell of Success.*

2. Nino Frank, "Un Nouveau Genre 'Policier': L'Adventure Criminelle," *L' Ecran Francais* 61 (August 28, 1946), 8–9, 14; Jean Pierre Chartier, "Les Americains aussi font des films noirs," *Revue du Cinema* 1 (November 3, 1946), 66–70; James Naremore, "Film Noir: The History of an Idea," *Film Quarterly* 49, no. 2 (Winter 1995–96), 14–17.

3. Raymonde Borde and Etienne Chaumeton, *Panorama du film noir Americain 1941– 1953* (Paris: Editions du Minuit, 1955); *A Panorama of American Film Noir,* trans. Paul Hammond (San Francisco: City Lights, 2002), 9.

4. Sheri Chinen Biesen, *Blackout: World War II and the Origins of Film Noir* (Baltimore: Johns Hopkins University Press, 2005), 1; Paul Schrader, "Notes on Film Noir," *Film Comment* 8, no. 1 (1972), 8–10.

5. Biesen, *Blackout,* 36; Thomas Schatz, *Boom and Bust* (New York: Scribner's, 1997), 236; Janey Place, "Women in Film Noir," in *Women in Film Noir,* ed. E. Ann Kaplan (London: BFI, 1980), 35, 41–42; see Schrader, "Notes on Film Noir; Frank Krutnik, *In a Lonely Street* (New York: Routledge, 1991); James Naremore, *More Than Night* (Berkeley: University of California Press, 2008); David A. Cook, *A History of Narrative Film* (New York: W. W. Norton, 1996, 2004), 377, 404.

6. Schrader, "Notes on Film Noir."

7. Jane Feuer, "The Self-Reflexive Musical and the Myth of Entertainment," *Quarterly Review of Film Studies* 2, no. 3 (1977), 313–26; Feuer, *Hollywood Musical* (Bloomington: Indiana University Press, 1982); Thomas Schatz, *Hollywood Genres* (New York: McGraw-Hill, 1981); Rick Altman, *American Film Musical* (Bloomington: Indiana University Press, 1987); Drew Casper, *Postwar Hollywood* (Malden, MA: Blackwell, 2007); Richard B. Jewell, *The Golden Age of Cinema* (Malden, MA: Blackwell, 2007).

8. Feuer, "The Self-Reflexive Musical," 313–26.

9. Rick Altman, "A Semantic/Syntactic Approach to Film Genre," *Cinema Journal* 23, no. 3 (Spring 1984), 13; Altman, "Confessions of a Genre Theorist: The Unexpected Truth about the Historical Origins of the Musical, the Western, and the Biopic," Lecture, University of California, Los Angeles, February 1995; Altman, *American Film Musical;* David Neumeyer, "Merging Genres in the 1940s: The Musical and the Dramatic Feature Film," *American Music* 22, no. 1 (Spring 2004), 122–32.

10. By 1946, the peak of film noir production, even John Ford's Western *My Darling Clementine*, included abundant atmospheric low-lit noir visual style in its exquisite cinematography, a sexy ethnic prostitute singing musical numbers in a bar (and would-be femme fatale dying for her sins), and a Tombstone preacher declaring the Bible doesn't forbid dancing, commenting on the moral constraints of Hollywood's Production Code censorship.

11. Biesen, *Blackout*, 1; Schrader, "Notes on Film Noir," 8–10; Schatz, *Boom and Bust*; David Bordwell, "The Bounds of Difference," in David Bordwell, Janet Staiger, and Kristin Thompson, *The Classical Hollywood Cinema: Film Style and Mode of Production to 1960* (New York: Columbia University Press, 1985), 74–75; Naremore, "Film Noir," 14–17.

12. Altman, "A Semantic/Syntactic Approach to Film Genre"; Altman, "Confessions of a Genre Theorist"; Altman, *American Film Musical*.

13. Neumeyer, "Merging Genres"; Schatz, *Boom and Bust*.

14. "Trade Showings: Blues in the Night (Musical Drama)," VAR, October 30, 1941, 3; "'Blues in the Night' In Groove . . . Blanke Prod., Cast and Litvak Solid," HR, October 30, 1941, 3; "'Blues in the Night' Music and Realism," MPH, November 1, 1941, 343; Philip Scheuer, "'Blues in the Night' Tuneful Melodrama," LAT, November 14, 1941, 17; Richard Coe, "Old Mixture in Film," WP, December 26, 1941, 4; Howard Thompson, "Movies: Out of Tune with the World of Jazz," NYT, August 21, 1966, 108; John Gene Hoover, "The Warner Brothers Film Musical, 1927–1980," Ph.D. diss., University of Southern California, July 1985, 259–64; Biesen, *Blackout*; Jewell, *The Golden Age*; Casper, *Postwar Hollywood*; Vincent Brook, *Driven To Darkness* (New Brunswick, NJ: Rutgers University Press, 2009).

15. Hoover, "Warner Brothers Film Musical"; "Casablanca," NYT, November 27, 1942. See also Paul Allen Anderson, "The World Heard: Casablanca and the Music of War," *Critical Inquiry* 32, no. 3 (Spring 2006), 482–515.

16. Casper, *Postwar Hollywood*.

CHAPTER 2: PRELUDES TO THE NOIR MUSICAL

1. With *The Jazz Singer*, Thomas Schatz notes the Hollywood musical developed a "vital relationship with such lowbrow musical forms as jazz and swing." Schatz, *Hollywood Genres* (New York: McGraw-Hill, 1981),187. Vincent Brook links Jewish émigrés to jazz, film noir, the American music/film/theater industry, and the African American experience.

2. Aljean Harmetz, "Lena Horne, Sultry Singer," NYT, May 9, 2010, A1; "Hallelujah!" ads, NYT, USC, Los Angeles, California, April–November 1929. Vidor also directed silent backstage comedy *Show People* in 1928.

3. Mordaunt Hall, "More Gang Fights," NYT, November 19, 1928. *Gang War* was produced by Film Booking Offices of America (FBO Pictures, a low-budget company that merged with RKO). Director Bert Glennon later shot the exquisite shrouded cinematography for John Ford's *Stagecoach*. Another film with the same title, Harry and Leo Popkin's 1940 race movie *Gang War* featured African American gangsters, a nightclub singer and band jammin' hot jazz in a Harlem speakeasy.

4. Universal Collection (UNC), USC, 1929; Richard Barrios, *A Song in the Dark* (New York: Oxford University Press, 1995), 96.

5. UNC; *Broadway*, considered partially "lost," is worthy of restoration.

6. Universal Presents "Broadway" ad, *Photoplay*, UNC, October 1929, 137.

7. The 1929 *Film Spectator* described *Broadway*'s plot about a "hoofer," "his girl," and a

"Broadway racketeer" who "tries to wedge between them." It "unwinds backstage" with "here a little dancing, there a little music" and "a little murder—or two" and "ends by a copper taking the scales of justice into his own hands . . . letting a murderess off because she had loved a rival bootlegger who had been shot." Frank Daugherty, "Broadway," *Film Spectator* 8, no. 2 (June 29, 1929). European director Fejos praised Expressionism, Impressionism, and Cubism. He visited New York speakeasies for "atmosphere" to "see what they look like" and invented a crane for "actual shots" of a "panoramic Broadway," stylized "European trick shots," camera angles, and first-person point-of-view to "bring results even more impressive" than "clever German photographers" with "ultra-modern" futuristic skyscraper pyramids, huge columns, and a "kaleidoscope of color" on a black marble floor. Comparing the film to Dupont's 1925 silent backstage masterpiece *Variety*, critics marveled at its "startling" photography and elaborate design of the nightclub, while complaining about close-ups ("Fejos ought to have forgone his love for big heads") and racy views of girls on dance floors or "in their dressing rooms." Fejos, "not a sound enthusiast; he does not even care for subtitles," said, "I cannot see why a picture cannot be all picture." Hall, "Broadway," NYT, June 2, 1929, X7; NYT, May 19, 1929, X4; NYT, October 14, 1928, X4.

8. "The Burlesque Queen," NYT, October 8, 1929. Critics praised its "striking" photography, "impressive angles," and "exceedingly well recorded" early sound sequences done at Paramount's Astoria studios, but "toward the end the agony is piled on in an extravagant fashion" with only a "glimmer of relief" from depictions of "exploitation," "vulgarity," and the "harshness of life."

9. Schatz, *Genius of the System* (New York: Pantheon, 1988, 1996), 130; Sheri Chinen Biesen, *Blackout: World War II and the Origins of Film Noir* (Baltimore: Johns Hopkins University Press, 2005).

10. "Interview with Stanley Donen," *Movie* (Spring 1977), 28.

11. The film industry's moral blueprint for censorship, the Production Code was written in 1930. In mid-1934, Hollywood's trade association, the Motion Picture Producers and Distributors of America (MPPDA), headed by Will Hays, established the Production Code Administration (PCA), appointing Joseph Breen to enforce industry self-censorship and to negotiate with studios regarding film content that would uphold "compensating moral values" and narrative justice on screen. "Big Five" vertically integrated major studios Paramount, MGM, Twentieth Century-Fox, Warner Bros., and RKO (which owned 77 percent of all first-run theaters) agreed not to exhibit films without a PCA Seal in first-run theaters, and a $25,000 fine was imposed on studios that released unapproved films. Raymond Moley, *The Hays Office* (New York: Bobbs Merrill, 1945), 77–82; Biesen, *Blackout*; Leonard Leff and Jerold Simmons, *The Dame in the Kimono* (New York: Grove, 1990), 57–59; Lea Jacobs, *The Wages of Sin* (Madison: University of Wisconsin, 1991), 25.

12. "Gold Diggers of 1933," program notes, USC, September 15, 1973; Schatz, *Hollywood Genres*, 189–90; Leo Braudy, "The World in a Frame," in Gerald Mast, Marshall Cohen, and Leo Braudy, eds., *Film Theory and Criticism* (New York: Oxford University Press, 1992), 442–43.

13. A.D.S, "An Ambitious Dancer," NYT, February 17, 1934.

14. NYT, January 21, 1939.

15. NYT, September 28, 1940.

16. "John Brahm's impact on the Class B picture is producing one of the strangest

sound effects in recent cinema history. It is that of an unmistakable B buzzing like an A."
NYT, October 27, 1939.

17. H. Mark Glancy, "MGM Film Grosses 1924–1948: The Eddie Mannix Ledger," *Historical Journal of Film, Radio and Television* 12, no. 2 (1992), 134, appendix 1.

18. Schatz, *Boom and Bust*, 204–6, 232–39; see also Biesen, *Blackout*; Robert Sklar, *Movie-Made America* (New York: Random House, 1994), 253.

19. See 11 above. As the war progressed, Washington's Office of Censorship allowed atrocities and violence in propaganda newsreels that violated the industry's PCA limits on criminal violence and political content. Ironically, the Office of War Information (OWI), Bureau of Motion Pictures (BMP), and Office of Censorship regulated screen depictions of combat and home front gangster violence in order to support the war effort, yet they contradicted Hollywood's Production Code censorship. Fred Stanley, "Hollywood Turns to 'Hate' Films: Government Lifts Ban on . . . Brutality," NYT, February 6, 1944; Biesen, *Blackout*; Clayton Koppes and Gregory Black, *Hollywood Goes to War* (New York: The Free Press, 1987), viii, 113, 324–28; Schatz, *Boom and Bust*, 1997; Thomas Doherty, *Projections of War* (New York: Columbia, 1993); Richard B. Jewell, *The Golden Age of Cinema* (Malden, MA: Blackwell, 2007); Moley, *The Hays Office*, 77–82; Leff and Simmons, *The Dame in the Kimono*, 57–59; Jacobs, *The Wages of Sin*, 25.

CHAPTER 3: *BLUES IN THE NIGHT*:
THE NOIR MUSICAL ON THE BRINK OF WORLD WAR II

1. Paul Schrader, "Notes on Film Noir," *Film Comment* 8, no. 1 (1972), 8–10.

2. Richard Coe, "Old Mixture in Film," WP, December 26, 1941, 4. Released a year after low-budget B noir thriller *Stranger on the Third Floor*, *Blues in the Night* included all the elements of film noir. Like other early noir films *Stranger on the Third Floor*, *Citizen Kane*, and *Suspicion*'s finale, *Blues in the Night* was visually darker than famous Warner Bros.' film noir *The Maltese Falcon*. Yet, *Blues in the Night* is not usually considered film noir or discussed in relation to the noir style; rather, it is an unusual hybrid musical. As a musical, it was an anomaly.

3. Kazan had hoped to produce *Hot Nocturne* on Broadway before selling it to Warner Bros. On Christmas 1940 he admitted, "I have made a number of very serious mistakes in connection with *Hot Nocturne*. I must never embark on the production of a play (example, offering it to backers, other theatre workers, etc.) unless I am convinced it is in the best possible shape. . . . You are now doing work on *Hot Nocturne* that you should have done months ago." He came away from the experience disappointed; it was a catalyst propelling Kazan from acting to directing. (Kazan was to receive screen credit with Rossen, but declined.) Elia Kazan, *Kazan on Directing* (New York: Knopf, 2009), 15–16; WBA, USC.

4. John Gene Hoover, "The Warner Brothers Film Musical, 1927–1980," Ph.D. diss., University of Southern California, July 1985, 259–64.

5. Herman Lissauer, WBA, April 8, 1941.

6. "Big Five" vertically integrated major studios Paramount, MGM, Twentieth Century-Fox, Warner Bros., and RKO (which owned 77% of all first-run theaters) agreed not to exhibit films without a PCA Seal in first-run theaters and a $25,000 fine was imposed on studios that released unapproved films. Raymond Moley, *The Hays Office* (New York: Bobbs Merrill, 1945), 77–82; Sheri Chinen Biesen, *Blackout: World War II and the Origins of Film Noir* (Baltimore: Johns Hopkins University Press, 2005); Leonard Leff and Jerold Simmons,

Dame in the Kimono (New York: Grove, 1990), 57–59; Lea Jacobs, *The Wages of Sin* (Madison: University of Wisconsin, 1991), 25; Clayton Koppes and Gregory Black, *Hollywood Goes to War* (New York: The Free Press, 1987), viii, 113, 324–28; Thomas Schatz, *Boom and Bust* (New York: Scribner's, 1997); Thomas Doherty, *Projections of War* (New York: Columbia University Press, 1993).

7. *Blues in the Night*'s relative ease of PCA approval is ironic in light of its many censorable inclusions: psychosis and suicide, illicit affairs, multiple murders, abundant criminal activity, violence and impulsive actions indicative of the noir antihero's battle with external forces of disintegration. His nervous breakdown and near-death hallucinations are conveyed through subjective psychological montages. Specific noir elements include adultery, suicide, drinking, gambling, fighting, murder, and destructive relationships. However, the song "Hang on to your lids, kids, here we go again," was criticized for being a "tag line of a dirty joke." (The Hays Office suggested substituting "Hang on to your shirts, squirts, we are on the go again," which was never implemented.) Walter MacEwen, WBA, June 20–21, 1941.

8. Lloyd Shearer, "Crime Certainly Pays on Screen," NYT, August 8, 1945; Fred Stanley, "Hollywood Turns to 'Hate' Films: Government Lifts Ban on ... Brutality," NYT, February 6, 1944; Stanley, "Hollywood Crime and Romance," NYT, November 19, 1944; Biesen, *Blackout*.

9. Jack Warner, WBA, June 20, 1941.

10. Chuck Hansen, WBA, June 25–July 9, 1941; Henry Blanke, WBA, July 2, 1941.

11. Hal Wallis, WBA, October 2, 1941.

12. Wallis, WBA, June 17, 1941.

13. "Windfall for the Salvagers," NYT, October 26, 1941.

14. *Blues in the Night* cost over $700,000—WSC cites $716,000 and WBA $740,151. WSC, USC, 1941; T. C. Wright to Blanke, WBA, October 11, 1941.

15. WSC, USC, 1941.

16. Robert Rossen, WBA, 1941, 43.

17. Stan Wrightsman dubbed piano for Whorf; Snookie Young and Frankie Zinzer dubbed trumpet solos for Carson; Archie Rosate dubbed clarinet solos for Kazan. Like many wartime noir, *Blues in the Night* was an "in-betweener" or near-A picture. It was more expensive than low-budget B pictures, but less than higher-budget prestige A productions with huge stars such as epic musical spectacles, especially if shot in Technicolor. (*Blues in the Night* was twice as expensive as the tightly budgeted noir *The Maltese Falcon*, but less than *Casablanca* or *Suspicion*, which cost well over a million dollars.) PBC, WSC, USC, 1941.

18. PBC, USC, 1941.

19. PBC, USC, 1941. Warner promoted *Blues in the Night*'s realism in depicting the lives of jazz musicians and hoped its showcase of jazz, blues, and boogie woogie after-hour jam sessions would appeal to swing-lovers, jitterbugs, and hep cats. Promoted as "modern," the seeds of bebop were being sewn. Rooted in the blues, its burgeoning emergence would not be recorded during a wartime musician's strike. Bebop and Latin Afro-Cuban jazz legend Dizzy Gillespie noted, "I'm not what you call a 'blues' player. I mean in the authentic sense of the blues. ... My music is not that deep—not as deep as Hot Lips Page or Charlie Parker, because Yard [Parker] knew the blues." Dizzy Gillespie, *To Be or Not to Bop* (Garden City, NY: Doubleday, 1979), 310. Scott DeVeaux, *Birth of Bebop* (Berkeley: UC Press, 1997), 164.

20. Harold Arlen in John Lahr, "Come Rain or Come Shine," *New Yorker*, September 19, 2005, 92–93.

21. Jack Warner, WBA, 1941; David Hajdu, *Lush Life* (New York: Farrar, Straus and Giroux, 1996).

22. DeVeaux, *Birth of Bebop*, 156–57.

23. DeLeon (Lee) Anthony, WBA, August 29, 1941.

24. Blanke, WBA, August 13, 1941.

25. PBC, USC, 1941.

26. Johnny Mercer in Gene Lees, *Portrait of Johnny* (New York: Hal Leonard, 2006), 246.

27. Rossen, WBA, 1941, 56.

28. PBC, USC, 1941.

29. DeVeaux, *Birth of Bebop*, 156–57.

30. D. Leon Wolffe, "The Blues Are Dead!" *Music and Rhythm* 2, no. 14 (January 1942), 8–50.

31. DeVeaux, *Birth of Bebop*, 156–57.

32. PBC, WBA, USC, 1941.

33. "'Blues in the Night' Music and Realism," MPH, November 1, 1941, 343.

34. "Trade Showings: Blues in the Night (Musical Drama)," VAR, October 30, 1941, 3.

35. "'Blues in the Night' In Groove . . . Blanke Prod., Cast and Litvak Solid," HR, October 30, 1941, 3.

36. Philip Scheuer, "'Blues in the Night' Tuneful Melodrama," LAT, November 14, 1941, 17.

37. Thomas Pryor, "Blues in the Night," NYT, December 12, 1941, 35.

38. *Wall Street Journal*, December 13, 1941, 7.

39. Coe, "Old Mixture in Film," WP, December 26, 1941, 4.

40. Hoover, "Warner Brothers Film Musical."

41. Biesen, *Blackout*, 63.

42. Fred Stanley, "Hollywood Turns to 'Hate' Films: Government Lifts Ban on . . . Brutality," NYT, February 6, 1944; Biesen, *Blackout*; Koppes and Black, *Hollywood Goes to War*; Doherty, *Projections of War*.

43. USC, 1941. Woody Herman's number one hit recording charted eleven weeks, Jimmy Lunceford's number four charted five weeks, Cab Calloway's reached number eight, Artie Shaw's reached number ten, Dinah Shore's was number four for seven weeks, and Rosemary Clooney had a hit years later.

44. Howard Thompson, "Movies: Out of Tune with the World of Jazz," NYT, August 21, 1966, 108.

CHAPTER 4: SMOKY MELODIES: JAZZ NOIR MUSICAL DRAMA

1. Robert Sklar, *Movie-Made America* (New York: Random House, 1994), 253.

2. Fred Stanley, "Hollywood Takes a Hint From Washington," NYT, February 7, 1943; Sheri Chinen Biesen, *Blackout: World War II and the Origins of Film Noir* (Baltimore: Johns Hopkins University Press, 2005); Clayton Koppes and Gregory Black, *Hollywood Goes to War* (New York: The Free Press, 1987); Thomas Schatz, *Boom and Bust: American Cinema in the 1940s* (New York: Scribner's, 1997). Integrated multiethnic screen images were promoted by OWI in wartime contrary to a racially segregated World War II military and American home front. In *Casablanca* Rick and Sam's friendship and camaraderie and Sam

earning a percentage of the club's profits is notable in segregated wartime. *Stormy Weather* included Horne's bluesy version of Arlen's theme song and impressive jazz sequences such as "Jumpin' Jive" with Cab Calloway's orchestra and virtuoso tap dancing by the incomparable Nicholas Brothers.

3. Horne credited her rise and success to the war: "The whole thing that made me a star was the war. Of course the black guys couldn't put Betty Grable's picture in their footlockers. But they could put mine." Horne's jazz numbers were sometimes censored by the PCA. "Ain't It the Truth," for instance, sung in a bubble bath in *Cabin in the Sky*, was deleted as too risqué. (In the segregated South, "ethnic" numbers and sequences were also cut.) Bogart and *Blues in the Night*'s composer and star befriended Horne. "My only friends," she explained, "were the group of New Yorkers who sort of stuck with their own group—like Vincente [Minnelli], Gene Kelly, Yip Harburg, Harold Arlen and Richard Whorf—the sort of hip New Yorkers who allowed Paul Robeson and me in their houses." When Horne, whom critic Frank Nugent called "the nation's top Negro entertainer," spoke out about the treatment of black soldiers, she recalls, "The USO got mad . . . from then on I was labeled a bad little Red girl." After her MGM contract ended in 1950 she was blacklisted from the film industry. Aljean Harmetz, "Lena Horne, Sultry Singer," NYT, May 9, 2010, A1.

4. Ellington noted in his autobiography that he earned a total of $12,500 for composing twenty-eight bars of music for the project. Ellington's *Jump for Joy* was opening at the Mayan theater in Los Angeles. Welles even considered filming Ellington's *Jump for Joy*. Welles later decided to incorporate *The Story of Samba* into a film to be called *It's All True*. Duke Ellington, *Music Is My Mistress* (New York: DaCapo, 1973); Bret Wood, "New Orleans," Kino Video, 2000 DVD.

5. Leonard Feather, "Trumpeter's Jubilee," NYT, October 26, 1941, X6.

6. *Orson Welles Almanac* radio show, 1944.

7. Several independent jazz labels resumed recording in 1943.

8. MHL, AFI, 1941.

9. Richard B. Jewell, "RKO Film Grosses 1929–1951," *Historical Journal of Film, Radio and Television* 14, no. 1 (1994), Appendices 2–3. *Syncopation* was drastically cut, including a scene where a jazz musician is inspired by hobos, suggesting the working-class ethos of *Blues in the Night*.

10. NYT, May 29, 1942.

11. MPH, November 4, 1944.

12. Feather, LAT, March 16, 1973.

13. Mary Beth Haralovich examines how Warner Bros.' pressbook promoted noir *Mildred Pierce* by presenting Joan Crawford as a sexualized femme fatale resembling a wartime pinup in Mary Beth Haralovich, "Selling *Mildred Pierce*: A Case Study in Movie Promotion," in Schatz, *Boom and Bust*, 196–205.

14. The bluesy tenor of musical noir resonated with the many émigré filmmakers and minorities experiencing the isolation and alienation of their circumstances. During the rise of Hitler, many émigré directors and other film workers landed in Hollywood. The Nazis were in a real sense "at war" with their experience, heritage, and even their expressionist cinematic aesthetic. However, most never felt fully at home in their new country and were complicated by the United States being at war with their homeland, which influ-

enced their attitudes and the noir films they made. After the war, as noir and dark musical films projected cultural tensions and xenophobic fears of the Cold War, blacklisted noir filmmakers and African Americans including jazz musicians moved to a more welcoming environment in Paris. Biesen, *Blackout*; Vincent Brook, *Driven To Darkness* (New Brunswick, NJ: Rutgers University Press, 2009).

15. PBC, USC, 1944.

16. Kate Cameron, "'Lady in the Dark' Gorgeous Film," NYDN, February 23, 1944; Archer Winsten, "'Lady in the Dark' Dazzles Its Way into the Paramount," *New York Post*, February 23, 1944; Eileen Creelman, "'Lady in the Dark' Outstanding Picture," *New York Sun*, February 23, 1944; LAE, February 10, 1944. The film earned Academy Award nominations for Best Art Direction, Music, and Cinematography.

17. Alton Cook, NYWT, March 30, 1944; Howard Barnes, NYHT, March 31, 1944; Cameron, NYDN, March 31, 1944.

18. PBC, USC, 1944.

19. Orson Welles letters to Rita Hayworth, Orson Welles Collection, Lilly Library, Indiana University, 1943.

20. USC, WBA, MHL, 1944; technical advisor Louis Comiens had actually served in Martinique with the French army.

21. PBC, USC, WBA, VAR, 1944, 1945.

22. They include working assertive female detectives, love triangles, murdered women, antiheroes betrayed by best friends/partners, men who are builders, Freudian psychoanalysis, psychotic killers. Pierre Renoir in Pièges asks the detective, "Have you read Freud?" Like Maurice Chevalier and Marie Déa in *Pièges*, in *Lured* Ball and Sanders dance and drink champagne as Ethelreda Leopold sings "All for Love" (Chevalier's "Mon Amore") with a big band in his swanky club after meeting at an orchestral concert where they hear Franz Schubert's Symphony No. 8 in B minor (like *Double Indemnity*'s Hollywood Bowl Symphony), rather than in a jazz cellar or backstage alley as in *Phantom Lady*.

23. USC, MHL, 1943–44; Biesen, *Blackout*; Maureen Honey, *Creating Rosie the Riveter* (Amherst: University of Massachusetts Press, 1984), 5–11; Joan Harrison, "Why I Envy Men Producers," HR, October 23, 1944; Lizzie Francke, *Script Girls* (London: BFI, 1994).

24. PBC, Universal Collection (UNC), USC, 1944; Biesen, *Blackout*. *Phantom Lady* also subverts musical stardom. Although Cook's jazz drummer plays in a big band, he is not rich or famous but hangs out in dives picking up "hep kitten" prostitutes. Kansas complains he lives in a dumpy apartment, "Gee, Cliff, with all the money you make . . ."

25. UNC, USC, 1943–44; MHL, February 1943–October 21, 1943.

26. Silvia Stein, USC, MHL, November 20, 1944, August 4, 1945–February 25, 1946.

27. PBC, USC, 1946; for more on sexual violence in wartime noir see Biesen, *Blackout*; Paul Boyer, *By the Bomb's Early Light* (Chapel Hill: University of North Carolina Press, 1984); VAR, March 13, 1946.

28. USC; Francke, *Script Girls*; Biesen, *Blackout*.

29. UNC, PBC, USC, MHL, 1946.

30. PBC, WBA, USC, 1947.

31. VAR, 1947.

32. NYT, January 25, 1947.

33. WSC, USC, 1947.

34. NYT, 9 November 1945, 16.

35. Fred Stanley, "An Old Hollywood Costume," NYT, October 21, 1945; Biesen, *Blackout.*

36. "A Star Is Born," NYT, October 27, 1946. Growing out of wartime documentary newsreels, Hollywood's trend toward realism influenced film noir and musicals and more serious musical dramas, melodramas, and postwar noir musicals. Drawing on conventions of documentary musical shorts featuring jazz bands such as *Jammin' the Blues* and noir musicals such as *Blues in the Night,* a number of dramatic musical biopics such as *Words and Music* (1948), *Moulin Rouge* (1952), *Love Me or Leave Me* (1955), *The Helen Morgan Story* (1957), *The Joker Is Wild* (1957), *St. Louis Blues* (1958), *The Gene Krupa Story* (1959) incorporated serious themes, downbeat endings, conflicted protagonists, and fictional narrative elements. Robert Alda played a very fictionalized Gershwin in *Rhapsody in Blue* (produced in 1943, released in 1945); Cary Grant portrayed Cole Porter in *Night and Day* (1946, transforming his homosexuality into tragic heterosexual affairs); Cornel Wilde interpreted Chopin in an exquisite color noir in *A Song to Remember* (produced 1943–44, released 1945); Robert Walker starred as Jerome Kern in *Till the Clouds Roll By* (1946, directed by *Blues in the Night's* Whorf with Van Heflin, Garland, Sinatra, Shore, and Horne singing "Can't Help Lovin' Dat Man").

37. Nate Chinen, "Charlie Parker, Uptown and Down," NYT, August 24, 2007.

38. PBC, USC, 1946; Biesen, *Blackout;* Brian Taves, "The B Film," in Tino Balio, *Grand Design* (New York: Scribner's, 1993), 313–50; Schatz, *Boom and Bust,* 1997.

39. Nate Chinen, "Charlie Parker"; Sheila Benson, "Taking a Sublime Look at a Jazz Musician's Life," LAT, October 16, 1986; Richard Duffy, "Dexter Gordon," *Jazz Review,* 1–3; USC.

40. PBC, USC, 1947.

41. MPH, May 3, 1947.

42. Herbert Biberman quoted in Philip K. Scheuer, "Elusive Saga of Jazz May Be Found Here: 'New Orleans' Screens Real Story of How American Folk Music Developed," LAT, October 27, 1946.

43. The Nazis even vilified American jazz music and established "youth protection" reeducation camps for rebellious German teens caught listening to jazz. Monica Hesse, "Extent of Nazi Camps Far Greater," WP, June 4, 2009.

44. Scheuer, October 27, 1946.

45. Biberman in Scheuer, "Elusive Saga of Jazz."

46. VAR, April 30, 1947, 10; NYT, June 20, 1947.

47. *Ebony,* December 1947; Jewell, "RKO Film Grosses 1929–1951"; USC, 1947.

48. Michael Sherry, *Gay Artists in Modern American Culture* (Chapel Hill: University of North Carolina Press, 2007), 46–47; Brian Neve, *Film and Politics in America* (New York: Routledge, 1992); David Johnson, *Lavender Scare* (Chicago: University of Chicago Press, 2004); USC, 1947.

49. Marston sued Universal for not promoting *Casbah's* March 1948 release. *Tension* featured a reccuring jazz theme for toxic blonde femme Audrey Totter.

50. PBC, USC, 1948; VAR, September 22, 1948, 8; NYT, November 8, 1948, 24.

51. Howard Thompson, "Movies: Out of Tune With the World of Jazz," NYT, August 21, 1966, 108.

52. After adapting Siodmak's *Pièges* as *Lured,* Sirk directed gothic noir *Sleep, My Love*

(1948) with Claudette Colbert, Robert Cummings, Don Ameche, and femme fatale Hazel Brooks, who featured in Rossen's *Body and Soul* (1947) as a gold-digging nightclub singer performing Carmichael's "Am I Blue" with a jazz band, reprising Bacall in *To Have and Have Not*. By 1948, Hawks adapted *Ball of Fire* (penned by Wilder) as color "history of jazz" musical *A Song Is Born* with an array of jazz greats: Benny Goodman, Tommy Dorsey, Louis Armstrong, Lionel Hampton, and Charlie Barnet.

53. Lloyd Shearer, "Crime Certainly Pays on Screen," NYT, August 8, 1945; Biesen, *Blackout*; Seth Schiesel, "1947 Mystery That Matters," NYT, May 17, 2011, C1.

CHAPTER 5: LE ROUGE ET LE NOIR: FROM *THE RED SHOES* TO *A STAR IS BORN*

1. Stanley Donen in "Coming Apart," *The Century*, ABC, 2000; Drew Casper, *Postwar Hollywood* (Malden, MA: Blackwell, 2007); Tino Balio, ed., *Hollywood in the Age of Television* (Boston: Unwin Hyman, 1990). In 1955 MGM musical *It's Always Fair Weather*, Donen and Gene Kelly explore the disillusionment of war veterans returning to postwar America.

2. During the war, many sought independent deals with 25% capital gains, evading a steep tax on high salaries. Big bands also declined in a postwar era of suburban sprawl as jitterbugs moved away from urban dance halls and nightclubs that were popular in wartime and jazz shifted to vocalists, small combos, television, and festivals. Documentary *Jazz on a Summer's Day* captured an array of jazz luminaries performing music at the 1958 Newport Jazz Festival.

3. Casper, *Postwar Hollywood*; financially unsuccessful musicals declined, notes Peter Lev, *The Fifties* (New York: Scribner's, 2003), 14–15.

4. Thomas Elsaesser, "Tales of Sound and Fury," in *Film Theory and Criticism*, ed. Gerald Mast, Marshall Cohen, and Leo Braudy (New York: Oxford University Press, 1992), 526; Casper, *Postwar Hollywood*.

5. Noir musical melodrama *The Red Shoes* was shot on location in London, Paris, and the south of France. *The Barefoot Contessa* was shot in Italy with an international cast and crew from *The Red Shoes*, *The Bicycle Thief*, and Hollywood. Postwar noir musicals featured tormented antiheroes as in *The Red Shoes*, *Young Man with a Horn*, *The Barefoot Contessa*, and *A Star Is Born*. After playing a talented jazz trumpeter (albeit a deadbeat husband with a roving eye) experiencing hard times with the band in *Blues in the Night*, Jack Carson revealingly portrays a caustic cynical press agent in *A Star Is Born*.

6. The *Miracle* decision reversed the 1915 Mutual vs. Ohio decision (which defined film as a business pure and simple, rather than an art form or communications medium [such as the press], and laid the groundwork for screen censorship). The studio system's collapse and the *Miracle* decision eliminated powerful enforcement mechanisms of Production Code censorship.

7. By 1956 George Stevens' *Giant* challenged PCA interracial marriage restrictions.

8. In this postwar period, gender roles and screen images changed, and international art cinema was influential. Moira Shearer's talented, tormented working noir musical heroine in *The Red Shoes*—willing to give up her dance career for marriage so her composer husband can pursue his art—is indicative of changing gender roles after the war. Strong independent musical noir divas were reformed and took on more redeemer qualities. Lupino's hard-boiled blues singer is willing, like Shearer, to give up her art to nurture her man in *The Man I Love* and *Road House*. While Bacall is a repressed, manipulative spouse in *Young Man with a Horn*, co-star Doris Day (like *Blues in the Night*'s Lane) is a

singing redeemer with a jazz band nurturing a tormented musician antihero. Garland is a jazz singer-star-nurturing wife in *A Star Is Born*. Leslie Caron is a singer-dancer-redeemer in *Glory Alley*. Bacall is "tamed" from being an independent singing diva in *To Have and Have Not* and *The Big Sleep* to a domesticated redeemer in Douglas Sirk's *Written on the Wind*. (Costar Dorothy Malone's wild spoiled nymphomaniac dances to Latin jazz, drives dad to his grave, then settles down to take over his business.)

9. Studios sought a new demographic consumer group: teenagers. Appealing to an emerging youth market, they paired young stars with established ones to also draw older viewers: Doris Day with James Cagney in *Love Me or Leave Me* and Day with Clark Gable in *Teacher's Pet*, Montgomery Clift and John Wayne in *Red River*.

10. Bizarre, childish, out of character, Julian manically buries his face in her breasts like an Oedipal infant: "Do you want to destroy our love?" Lermontov dramatically arrives running interference: "Good evening Mr. Craster. Won't they be missing you at Covent Garden?" Julian projects his resentment, accusing Boris, "You're jealous of her!" Lermontov replies, "Yes—but in a way you'll never understand." He says to Vicky, "Tell him you've left him."

11. Michael Powell, "A Life in Movies," *American Film* (March 1987), 44.

12. Mark Connelly, *The Red Shoes* (London: I. B. Tauris, 2005), 4.

13. *The Red Shoes* was inspired by Hollywood backstage musical drama such as *Dancing Lady*, *Blues in the Night*, 1946 classical music noir *Deception* (produced by *Blues in the Night*'s Henry Blanke), and Gene Kelly's *Cover Girl* mirror-image dance reflecting his subjective "alter ego." Vicky's ballet in *The Red Shoes* simulates the elaborate shrouded style of *The Cabinet of Dr. Caligari* revealing her conflicted point of view as she dances. UFA-trained gay Jewish Austrian émigré Adolf Wohlbrück (Walbrook) played a sadistic homme fatale in 1940 British gothic thriller *Gaslight*, adapted by George Cukor in 1944. Shearer recalled that Walbrook—like Lermontov—wore dark sunglasses and remained aloof on the set. Costar Albert Basserman, *Red Shoes* ballet designer (in the film), died after the arduous filming.

14. *Daily Express*, January 17, 1949; PBC, USC, 1948.

15. *Picture Show*, August 21, 1948; *Picturegoer*, August 28, 1948.

16. *Picturegoer*, August 28, 1948.

17. *Monthly Film Bulletin*, BFI, August 31, 1948.

18. *Picturegoer*, August 28, 1948.

19. *Monthly Film Bulletin*, August 31, 1948.

20. Moira Shearer in Brian McFarlane, *An Autobiography of British Cinema* (London: Methuen/BFI, 1997), 532–35.

21. Michael Powell in Kenneth Turan, LAT, USC, May 17, 2009.

22. Alan Wood, "Inside Story of Mr. Rank," *Everybody's Weekly*, February 23, 1952.

23. Kate Cameron, NYDN, USC, 1948.

24. Alton Cook, NYWT, USC, 1948.

25. PBC, USC, 1951.

26. Michael Powell in Scheuer, LAT, USC, December 19, 1948.

27. Mozelle Britton Dinehart, *Hollywood Nite Life*, USC, 1948.

28. Fred Metchick, research correspondence, 2010.

29. H. Mark Glancy, "MGM Film Grosses 1924–1948," *Historical Journal of Film, Radio and Television* 12, no. 2 (1992), 134; NYT, May 21, 1948.

30. *Dancing Times*, USC, December 1948.

31. Rodgers broke his partnership with Hart in mid-1942 to team with lyricist Oscar Hammerstein II on *Oklahoma!*, then revived *Connecticut Yankee* on Broadway as Hart's health declined. Hart died November 23, 1943, shortly after it opened.

32. Rooney's demise visually evoked the death of washed up gangsters Paul Muni in *Scarface* and James Cagney in *Roaring Twenties*.

33. Glancy, "MGM Film Grosses 1924–1948"; *Dancing Times*, December 1948.

34. Arthur Freed memo to Gene Kelly and Stanley Donen in Hugh Fordin, *That's Entertainment!* (Garden City, NY: Doubleday, 1975), 262; AF, USC, 1949.

35. Vincente Minnelli in Peter Duncan, *In Hollywood Tonight* (London: Werner Laurie, 1952), 34–36.

36. Day told director Martin Scorsese: "That's my life story!" when she saw neo-noir musical *New York, New York*.

37. NYT, April 16, 1949; USC.

38. Beiderbecke had played with Paul Whiteman's band in the 1920s.

39. Unlike a "Rosie the Riveter" career woman or bandsinger Day, Bacall's femme is a nonworking sexual threat who puts on psychological airs and pretends to be educated. In October 1941, as *Blues in the Night* previewed, writer Benjamin Glazer—associate producer of *Four Daughters* and *They Made Me a Criminal*—planned to adapt Baker's novel with Theodore Reed directing. World War II intervened, and Curtiz resumed the project as director after the conflict. *Young Man with a Horn* began filming right after *Sunset Boulevard* in July 1949 through early September 1949 and was released March 11, 1950.

40. Douglas starred in *Champion, Out of the Past, Strange Love of Martha Ivers, Ace in the Hole, The Bad and the Beautiful*, and *The Story of Three Loves*. James was married to Grable. Jimmy Zito dubbed for Hernandez, and Zutty Singleton, Bumps Meyers, Rocky Robinson, Oscar Bradley, and George Washington appeared in the jazz band. The music included bluesy "Moanin' Low," Arlen's "Get Happy" (made famous by Garland), "Sweet Georgia Brown," "Nobody Knows de Trouble I've Seen," Ray Noble's "The Very Thought of You," Mercer's "Too Marvelous for Words," "Chinatown, My Chinatown," Ruskin's "I May Be Wrong but I Think You're Wonderful," and Rodgers and Hart's "With a Song in My Heart."

41. Bacall's femme grabs the antihero's mane in a fiery hair-tugging embrace evocative of the rough sex in noir crime films and Warners color noir *To Have and Have Not* ads. *Young Man with a Horn* capitalized on Bacall's sultry appeal as enticing diva opposite Bogart and Carmichael in musical noirs *To Have and Have Not* and *The Big Sleep*. In the trailer, fatal attraction Bacall warns: "Keep away, Richard," evoking Ilsa and Bogart's Rick in *Casablanca*. Like Lane in *Blues in the Night*, Day pleads: "What are you tryin' to do, Rick? Kill yourself? Because you tried for something that didn't exist? That's what you've done all your life." Like violent noir misogynism, Douglas grabs a black-clad Bacall and throws her across the room: "You cheap! What a dope I was! I thought you were class. Like a real high note you hit once in a lifetime. That's because I couldn't understand what you were saying half the time. Why, you're like those carnival joints I used to work in: big flash on the outside, but on the inside nothing but filth!" PBC, WBA, USC, 1950.

42. VAR, February 8, 1950, 11.

43. NYT, February 10, 1950, 18.

44. USC, WSC, WBA, 1950.

45. Darryl Zanuck, USC, June–December 1950; Rudy Behlmer, *Memo from Darryl F. Zanuck* (New York: Grove, 1993), 174–94; Sheri Chinen Biesen, *Blackout: World War II and the Origins of Film Noir* (Baltimore: Johns Hopkins University Press, 2005).

46. NYT, December 23, 1951, F6; November 2, 1955, 1.

47. Ben Hecht, *A Child of the Century* (New York: Simon & Schuster, 1954); Thomas Schatz, *Boom and Bust* (New York: Scribner's, 1997).

48. Paul Schrader, "Notes on Film Noir," *Film Comment* 8, no. 1 (1972).

49. Murray Schumach, *The Face on the Cutting Room Floor* (New York: Da Capo, 1975), 139; Brian Neve, *Film and Politics in America* (New York: Routledge, 1992). This lighter 'high-key' aesthetic style in noir crime films after the war is sometimes called *film gris*, or "gray film."

50. After *Notorious*, Hitchcock's backstage thriller *Stage Fright* featured murderous star/femme fatale Dietrich singing Cole Porter songs in London; *I Confess* moved from nocturnal shadows to outdoor daylight locations in Quebec; *Dial M For Murder* was shot in WarnerColor 3-D; and Henry Fonda plays a jazz musician arrested for a crime he did not commit in *The Wrong Man* with a lighter 'high-key' documentary location style.

51. PBC, USC, 1951. *The Strip* was produced by MGM's Joseph Pasternak in early January to mid-February 1951, directed by his brother-in-law Laszlo (Leslie) Kardos, and released in August 1951.

52. MGM child stars Rooney and Garland had first gained fame in the late 1930s and early 1940s cheerful Andy Hardy musicals. During the war, Garland achieved success in Minnelli's *Meet Me in St. Louis* while Rooney served in the military overseas. The postwar years brought a different cultural and industrial climate. Garland experienced failure in 1948 with *The Pirate*. Rooney had grown older, beyond youthful Andy Hardy roles. He was so strongly associated with earlier upbeat musicals that when he played serious dramatic parts in downbeat noir-styled films, he encountered a hostile critical response as in *Words and Music*. Rooney sought to break out of musical typecasting in noir roles *Quicksand*, *The Strip*, and *Drive a Crooked Road*.

53. PBC, USC, 1951. New musical stars included Vic Damon and fresh-faced young singing blonde females (Forest resembling Doris Day clad in a skimpy, form-fitting scarlet red leotard).

54. PBC, USC, 1952.

55. NYT, July 30, 1952.

56. Produced by Beckworth Corporation and directed by Curtis Bernhardt, *Miss Sadie Thompson* was shot on location in Hawaii from March through June 1953 and premiered December 23, 1953.

57. Thomas Brady, "Big Color Rush On," NYT, June 17, 1951, X5.

58. Richard Haines, *Technicolor Movies* (Jefferson, NC: McFarlane, 1993), 51–52; "Technicolor Agrees to Let Patents," NYT, February 25, 1950, 11.

59. "Technicolor Alters Practice on Output," NYT, March 13, 1953, 23.

60. 58.4% of 1954 films were color, 41.6% black and white. NYT, March 24, 1955, 39; Thomas Pryor, NYT, April 5, 1955, 33; NYT, April 28, 1956, 10.

61. *Films and Filming* in Charles Hopkins, *Moulin Rouge* program notes, USC, March 1986. Cyd Charisse's noir homage to femme fatales, her "Two-Faced Woman" number—suggesting *Blues In the Night*'s lyric "A Woman's a Two Face"—was cut from *The Band Wagon*, and was instead used in Joan Crawford's *Torch Song*.

62. Zanuck, USC, March 12–May 7, 1953; Rudy Behlmer, *Memo from Darryl F. Zanuck*, 234, 238–39.

63. Thomas Brady, "Uneasy Hollywood," NYT, March 5, 1950, 101.

64. Thomas Doherty, *Hollywood's Censor* (New York: Columbia University Press, 2007), 6.

65. Brady, "Uneasy Hollywood," 1950.

66. Ronald Haver, *A Star is Born: The Making of the 1954 Movie and Its 1983 Restoration* (New York: Knopf, 1988; Applause, 2002), 85.

67. VAR, March 4, 1953, 6; NYT, December 24, 1953, 8.

68. Louis Berg, LAT, August 22, 1954, L10.

69. Shearer in McFarlane, *Autobiography of British Cinema.*

70. Written, produced and directed by Joseph Mankiewicz for his independent company Figaro, financed by United Artists, it was his first color film shot in San Remo, Portofino, Rome and famed Cinecitta studios (with *The Bicycle Thief*'s "Bruno" [Enzo Staiola] in a cameo role).

71. PBC, USC, 1954.

72. Alain Silver and Elizabeth Ward, *Film Noir: An Encyclopedic Reference to the American Style* (Woodstock: Overlook, 1979), 2.

73. Schrader, "Notes on Film Noir," 12.

74. Schrader, "Notes on Film Noir."

75. Shots of the crowd and headlights were actually a Technicolor newsreel of the actual premiere of *The Robe* at Grauman's Chinese Theater intercut with new footage from the Shrine.

76. Cukor cleverly mocks Hollywood's star factory, the musical's makeover aesthetic, and Garland's real-life nightmare makeover (as a blonde, which Cukor "repaired," aesthetically transforming the young Garland into a more suitable, natural-looking Dorothy) for MGM's *The Wizard of Oz.*

77. *The Red Shoes* and *A Star Is Born* inspired Baz Luhrmann's "Red Curtain" trilogy, *Strictly Ballroom, Romeo+Juliet,* and *Moulin Rouge!*

78. WarnerColor was Warner's version of single-strip Kodak Eastmancolor monopack film stock. Haver, *A Star is Born*, 135.

79. Allen in Haver, *A Star is Born.*

80. Haver, *A Star is Born* 125; GCC, USC; Al Harrell, "The Making of *A Star is Born*," *American Cinematographer* (AC) 65, no. 2 (February 1984), 36.

81. Cukor in Haver, *A Star is Born*, 125; GCC, USC; Harrell, "Making of *A Star is Born*," 36.

82. Martin Hart notes "The only problem with Warner's CinemaScope pictures was the fact they continued to use their own WarnerColor lab for several years, sending out the worst looking prints in the history of motion pictures. By the mid-50s, Warner's shut down their lab and went exclusively with Technicolor. The difference in the look of Warner product was obvious, with the studio releasing some of the best looking films to come out of the Hollywood studios during the last decade and a half of dye transfer Technicolor." Martin Hart, "CinemaScope," *American Widescreen Museum*, 1996–2006, 4; GCC, USC, WBA, 1953–1954.

83. Harrell, "Making of *A Star Is Born*," 36.

84. Ibid.

85. Craig Holt, "A Star Is Re-Born," AC (February 1984), 38.

86. Cukor in Haver, *A Star Is Born*, 125; GCC, USC; Harrell, 36.

87. Allen in Harrell, "Making of *A Star Is Born*," 37.

88. Moss Hart, GCC, USC, 1953-54; Haver, *A Star Is Born*, 124.

89. Cukor, GCC, USC, February 1954; Jack Warner, WBA, JWC, USC, February 25, 1954; Haver, *A Star Is Born*, 177.

90. VAR, August-September 1953; GCC, WBA, USC, AFI, 1953-1954; Haver, *A Star Is Born*; Lev, *Fifties*.

91. *A Star Is Born* included several sequences shot on location at the Shrine Auditorium, the Central Police Station in Los Angeles, Westside Drive-In, Holmby Hills, Malibu, Beverly Hills, and the Church of the Good Shepherd in Santa Monica. Trouble began even before filming commenced. In September 1953 *Daily Variety* reported that Garland's longtime musical arranger/vocal coach Hugh "Skip" Martin had an argument with the star regarding vocal style (while recording "Lose That Long Face"), walked off the set, and left the picture. Ibid.

92. In October 1953 Fox expert Milton Krasner made test shots of Garland's "The Man That Got Away" in CinemaScope and helped transition formats, then photographer Sam Leavitt (who shot documentary-styled noir *The Thief*, worked with Harry Stradling to film Berry's noir *Tension*, Minnelli's *The Pirate*, and was familiar with the new Eastman "monopack" color process) replaced three-strip Technicolor cameraman Winton Hoch (who replaced *A Star Is Born*'s original photographer Stradling after production delays caused a scheduling conflict with another picture.) Ibid.

93. Roger Edens, an instrumental mentor of Garland at MGM, "moonlighted" uncredited on the picture and helped conceive several numbers, including "Someone at Last," "Born in a Trunk" and "Lose That Long Face" to capitalize on Garland's popular homage to vaudeville in her live stage performances. "Born in a Trunk" was the final sequence shot. Ray Heindorf was musical director; Martin is credited with orchestrations. Ibid.

94. NYT, October 12, 1954, 23.

95. WSC, PBC, WBA, USC, 1954.

96. "A Star Is Born," VAR, September 29, 1954, 6.

97. Bosley Crowther, NYT, October 12, 1954, 23.

98. Grace Kelly won for *The Country Girl*. WBA, USC, AFI, MHL, 1954.

CHAPTER 6: DARK MUSICAL MELODRAMA:
FROM *YOUNG AT HEART* TO *WEST SIDE STORY*

1. Douglas directed noir crime films *San Quentin, Walk a Crooked Mile, Kiss Tomorrow Goodbye*, and *I Was a Communist for the FBI*. Assistant director Al Alleborn worked on *Four Daughters, The Maltese Falcon, Casablanca, My Dream Is Yours*, and *I Was a Communist for the FBI*. The film was scripted by *Casablanca/Four Daughters'* Julius Epstein.

2. The scene is a color noir variation on Ilsa's famous entrance in Rick's gin joint as he drinks away his sorrow in *Casablanca*, and of Keyes overhearing Neff's murder confession in *Double Indemnity* as well as a clear reference to *A Star Is Born*. The unglamorous, expressionistic "low-key" mise-en-scène evokes film noir, *The Cabinet of Dr. Caligari* and *Citizen Kane*.

3. Like *The Red Shoes* when Vicky leaves tormented antihero Lermontov for mild-mannered composer Julian, her husband becomes an antihero once they're married. De-

spite Maine's destructive ways in *A Star Is Born*, he kills himself rather than forcing his wife to give up her performing career.

4. PBC, WBA, USC, 1954; VAR, December 15, 1954, 6; NYT, January 20, 1955, 35.

5. Even Cukor's 1940 *Philadelphia Story* comedy was remade as a color musical *High Society* with Sinatra and Armstrong in 1956.

6. Popular song titles were used for film titles that promoted the music in *Blues in the Night, Stormy Weather, Rhapsody in Blue, Night and Day, Body and Soul, The Man I Love, Love Me or Leave Me,* and *Pete Kelly's Blues*. Heindorf also worked on Berkeley *Gold Diggers* musicals, *42nd Street, Footlight Parade, Four Daughters, The Roaring Twenties, Brother Orchid, The Hard Way, Rhapsody in Blue, Night and Day, My Dream is Yours, Flamingo Road, She's Back on Broadway, Calamity Jane, Sincerely Yours, Serenade,* and *The Helen Morgan Story*.

7. Melcher wanted to shoot a new ending and re-release *Young at Heart* with a new title.

8. WSC, WBA, USC, AFI, 1954; MPH, December 18, 1954, 249–50.

9. *A Star Is Born*'s George Cukor was at one point considered to direct. The film boasted nostalgic 1920s songs that the real Etting sang: "Love Me or Leave Me," "I'll Never Stop Loving You," "Never Look Back," "You Made Me Love You," "Mean to Me," "Everybody Loves My Baby," "Stay on the Right Side of the Road," "It All Depends on You," "At Sundown," "Shaking the Blues Away," and "Ten Cents a Dance."

10. A. E. Hotchner, *Doris Day: Her Own Story* (New York: William Morrow, 1975).

11. Ava Gardner, *Ava: My Story* (New York: Bantam, 1992).

12. MGM, USC, 1955; Eddie Mannix Ledger, MHL, 1955; PCA correspondence in MPAA/PCA File, MHL, 1954–55; AFI; VAR, October 6, 1954. By 1955, Gene Kelly returned to MGM from Europe to play a returning veteran reuniting with his buddies, but disheartened by postwar society in *It's Always Fair Weather* (codirected with Stanley Donen), revealing a dark underside to MGM musicals *Singin' in the Rain* and *On the Town* with joyous sailors on shore leave celebrating romance in "New York, New York—a wonderful town."

13. PBC, MGM, USC, 1955.

14. NYT, May 27, 1955, 14.

15. VAR, May 25, 1955, 6.

16. VAR, May 25, 1955, 6; NYT, May 27, 1955, 14.

17. MGM, USC, AFI; VAR, March 13, 1957.

18. *Dragnet*'s famous theme music "dun da dun dun, dun da dun dun" was originally scored uncredited by *Double Indemnity* composer Miklós Rózsa as "Danger Ahead" for Siodmak's 1946 noir *The Killers*. Webb loved jazz and cops; his first wife was blues nightclub singer Julie London. WSC, WBA, USC, 1955.

19. PBC, USC, WBA, 1955.

20. VAR, August 3, 1955, 6; NYT, August 19, 1955.

21. WSC, WBA, USC, 1955.

22. *Sweet Smell of Success* followed *Marty* (1955) and *Trapeze* (1956).

23. They played scantily clad acrobats in *Trapeze*. Lancaster made his film debut playing a boxer turned hoodlum who is entranced by jazz singer Ava Gardner in Siodmak's *The Killers*. He was a tormented vet in noir *Kiss the Blood off My Hands*. His torrid tumbling in crashing surf in a wet bathing suit with Deborah Kerr in Fred Zinnemann's 1953 Best Picture *From Here to Eternity* was acclaimed. Curtis was known for his comedy—even playing in tragic backstage drama *Houdini* and swashbucklers.

24. A. H. Weiler, "Sweet Smell of Success," NYT, June 28, 1957; AFI.

25. Like playboy Tone jealously whisking Crawford away from Gable and show people in *Dancing Lady*.

26. Filmed at the 21 Club, in the Broadway theater district, Times Square, and Tin Pan Alley's Brill Building. Eventually Lehman left and went on to write the scripts for *North by Northwest* and *West Side Story*. Ernest Lehman Collection (ELC), USC, MHL, 1955–57; AFI; HR, August 10, 1955; *Vanity Fair*, April 2000, 415–32; LAT, December 25, 2000.

27. PBC, USC, 1957.

28. USC, MHL, AFI, 1957–59; NYHT, January 6, 1958; NYT, May 24, 1959.

29. John Wilson, "What Makes 'Pop' Music Popular," NYT, December 8, 1957, SM13.

30. Thomas Pryor, "New 'Role' Ahead," NYT, March 6, 1956, 27.

31. In real life, costar Judy Tyler, a Broadway actress who graced the cover of *Life* and performed in *Bop Girl Goes Calypso*, tragically died in an auto accident at 24, just before the film *Jailhouse Rock*'s premiere that could have made her a star.

32. Davis played with Kenny Clark, Pierre Michelot, Barney Wilen, and Rene Urtreger. Miles Davis with Quincy Troupe, *Miles* (New York: Touchstone, 1989), 217–18; *Elevator to the Gallows* publicity, Criterion, 2005; Gene Moskowitz, "Films Along the Seine," NYT, April 20, 1958, X7. *Elevator to the Gallows'* juvenile delinquent *Romeo and Juliet*-style couple also resembled *West Side Story*, which was already onstage in New York. Famed cabaret *Salón México* was also influential to Leonard Bernstein and inspired Aaron Copeland's *El Salón México*. Charles Ramirez Berg, *Cinema of Solitude* (Austin: University of Texas Press, 1992).

33. Honda's dark color atomic sci-fi film was a follow-up to low-budget cult hit *Godzilla*. VAR, HR, 1959; USC; Paul Boyer, *By the Bomb's Early Light* (Chapel Hill: University of North Carolina Press, 1984).

34. "We'll Meet Again," which also concludes Dennis Potter's dark musical *The Singing Detective*. Walsh's *White Heat* famously ends with Cagney's psychotic gangster Cody Jarrett yelling "Top of the world, Ma!" as he perishes in an explosive blaze. Fiery burns suggested atomic trauma and nuclear fears in *The Big Heat*: Ford's wife is killed in a car bomb, and moll Gloria Graham is scalded and scarred, recalling atomic weapons like *Gilda*. Hitchcock suggested homosexuality in Cold War suspense thriller *North by Northwest* (1959) as color displaced black and white for noir stories.

35. In 1955, as Laurents and Bernstein considered Robbins' *Romeo and Juliet* project in Los Angeles, Bernstein noticed a topical *Los Angeles Times* headline, "Gang Riots on Oliveira St." Arthur Gelb, NYT, June 13, 1955, 18; Lewis Funke, NYT, June 19, 1955, X1; Arthur Laurents, *Original Story* (New York: Applause, 2000), 334, 346; Humphrey Burton, *Leonard Bernstein* (New York: Anchor Books-Doubleday, 1994), 270; Sheri Chinen Biesen, *Blackout: World War II and the Origins of Film Noir* (Baltimore: Johns Hopkins University Press, 2005); Roy Hoopes, *Cain* (New York: Holt, Rinehart and Winston, 1982), 467.

36. In 1948, the year before *West Side Story*'s 1949 inception, Robert Warshow published his essay "The Gangster as Tragic Hero," in which he articulated the futility of the American dream as seen in Hollywood gangster films in which "one is punished for success." He expounded on the ominous duality of the American dream, a mythic cultural construct comprising not only a romantic utopian ideal (as in escapist musicals), but also a turbulent underside—to ultimately suggest its potential transformation into a violent nightmare (as in film noir, gangster pictures and darker incarnations of musicals) where an antihero's fame and success leads to failure and death. Warshow observed the doomed

fate of individuals in an urban crowd, inverting the American dream's rugged individualism and upward mobility. Robert Warshow, "The Gangster as Tragic Hero," *Partisan Review* (New Brunswick, NJ, 1948) repr. in *The Immediate Experience* (Garden City, NY: Doubleday, 1970).

37. Drew Casper, research correspondence, 1996.

38. They had dropped Robbins' original *Romeo and Juliet* story but, in 1955, decided to make a similar type of Broadway musical out of Cain's *Serenade*, which led to a rethinking of Robbins' original *Romeo and Juliet* idea and resulted in dropping *Serenade* and focusing on the new project, now to be centered on ethnic gang rivalries. New Yorkers all, they set their story in New York City rather than Los Angeles. Laurents, *Original Story*, 334, 346.

39. Leonard Bernstein in Craig Zadan, *Sondheim and Co.* (New York: DaCapo, 1994), 17.

40. Robert Ray, *A Certain Tendency of the Hollywood Cinema, 1930–1980* (Princeton: Princeton University Press, 1985), 134–37.

41. Bernstein, who had scored the riveting soundtrack for Kazan's social realist crime film *On the Waterfront*, was initially *West Side Story*'s lyricist as well as composer, but he was juggling projects such as *Candide*. Bernstein was harassed by HUAC while composing the score and sought help from his friend, Senator John F. Kennedy. The musical's premiere was attended by Jackie Kennedy. Burton, *Leonard Bernstein*; Laurents, *Original Story*.

42. Bernstein in Howard Taubman, "A Foot in Each Camp," NYT, October 13, 1957, 129.

43. Harold Prince in Zadan, *Sondheim and Co.*, 28–29; Taubman, "A Foot in Each Camp."

44. Harold Mirisch, USC, September 12, 1960.

45. It was produced for Robert Wise's Beta Productions and B & P Enterprises, Mirisch, and Seven Arts.

46. Wise estimated the final cost at $7.5 million, Mirisch at $6.75 million, VAR at $6 million. Robert Wise interviewed by Biesen (RW), 1998; Mirisch, *I Thought We Were Making Movies Not History* (Madison: University of Wisconsin Press, 2008), 127; VAR, USC, 1961.

47. *West Side Story* shatters utopian innocence as well as classical musical mythology at a time when the studio system, classical musicals, film noir, and gangster films were in decline. In this early postclassical era, *West Side Story*'s unlikely convergence of escapist musical style and subversive cynicism inspired by social realist film noir and gangster crime films foreshadowed the inbred dialectical violence that escalated in America in the 1960s.

48. 70-mm formats (shot in 65 mm, projected in 70 mm) like Todd-AO (used for musical *Oklahoma!*) in 1955, Panavision (Panavision-designed MGM Camera 65) in 1956, and Super Panavision 70 introduced in 1959 and used in *West Side Story* (creating a 2.20:1 aspect ratio with spherical lenses, differing from anamorphic systems such as Ultra Panavision 70 or CinemaScope's earlier 35mm anamorphic system used for noir musicals like *A Star Is Born*). See also Tino Balio, ed., *Hollywood in the Age of Television* (Boston: Unwin Hyman, 1990); Drew Casper, *Postwar Hollywood* (Malden, MA: Blackwell, 2007); David Cook, *A History of Narrative Film* (New York: W. W. Norton, 1996, 2004); Peter Lev, *The Fifties* (New York: Scribner's, 2003).

49. Gene Arneel, "Pix' Big and Bold Bid for Gold," VAR, August 8, 1956, 3.

50. Thomas Doherty, *Teenagers and Teenpics* (Boston: Unwin Hyman, 1988), 231.

51. Fred Stanley, "All is Confusion," NYT, October 17, 1943. Hollywood's teenage gang-

ster cycle in the postwar era was influenced by noir, social realism, wartime documentary, Italian neorealism, TV anthology dramas, and the New York stage, including method acting.

52. Murray Schumach, "Violence in Films Seen On Decrease: Juvenile Delinquency Scripts Drop as a Result of Drive," NYT, July 17, 1961; MHL.

53. Stephen Sondheim, Lehman, ELC, USC, HRC, University of Texas at Austin, 1960, 55.

54. Laurents, *Original Story*; Michael Sherry, *Gay Artists in Modern American Culture* (Chapel Hill: University of North Carolina Press, 2007); David Johnson, *Lavender Scare* (Chicago: University of Chicago Press, 2004).

55. A euphemism for drugs.

56. Lehman, ELC, USC, HRC, June 17, 1960; RW.

57. Wise in Jerry Kutner, "Interview, Robert Wise," *Bright Lights* 10–11 (1993), 33; RW; Eugene Archer, "Wise 'Story' Direction," NYT, October 15, 1961.

58. Kutner, "Interview, Robert Wise"; Wise, "West Side Story: Problems of Style," RWC, USC, January 21, 1960, 1–2; RW. To achieve a stylized Technicolor dissolve between the dress shop and the dance at the gym using color-separated figures.

59. Wise in Kutner, "Life at the Top," 33; RWC USC.

60. Wise and art director Boris Leven articulated the film's production design: "We open on a series of highly stylized 'abstract-real' shots" with a "direct overhead aerial view of the lower two-thirds of Manhattan . . . laying horizontally across the screen and covering it . . . spilling out of the frame showing the small pattern that the streets and buildings form at that distance. . . . We pan in and down . . . until the entire screen is filled with the building and street pattern." Black-and-white still photos were taken in New York to simulate gritty realism in stylized artwork, sketches, and storyboards by Leven to expressively articulate the film's dark visuals. "*West Side Story*: A Visual Interpretation," Boris Leven Collection, USC, undated, 1–8.

61. He noted that "dances and song numbers done in completely realistic settings and given straight realistic treatment" in previous musicals "have a very unreal feeling. In the case of *West Side Story*: First, it is a musical drama, not a musical comedy, so many of the accepted musical conventions will not work for us. Second, its story is based on a most contemporary and serious problem, which has to be treated with as much honesty as possible within the frame of the musical picture. Third, the biggest impact made by the stage version was the highly stylized dance numbers and lyrical quality of the love story with its highly theatrical treatment." To "make *West Side Story* even more distinctive than it was on the stage," Wise shot (and Leven designed) "all exteriors" as "real locations or completely realistic sets" with a "distinctly styled photographic and cinematic treatment" with dance numbers and songs given a "strong theatrical treatment" but "smoothly worked in and out of the basic style so there is no jar . . . to have a quality that is based on reality but which achieves a sense of being larger than life, of a not-quite-real world." Wise, RWC, ELC, USC, HRC; RW.

62. "Musical Advance: 'West Side Story' Expands on Screen," NYT, October 22, 1961, Section 2, 1.

63. James Powers, HR, September 22, 1961, 3; *Saturday Review*, October 14, 1961, 40; VAR, September 27, 1961, 3.

64. Joel Finler, *The Hollywood Story* (Crown, 1988, 2003), 277.

65. David Cook, *A History of Narrative Film*, 487; VAR, March 1962, May 1966; Finler, *The Hollywood Story*, 277.

CHAPTER 7: THE LEGACY OF THE NOIR MUSICAL

1. Joel Finler, *The Hollywood Story* (Crown, 1988, 2003), 277. Thomas Schatz cites rentals of $79.9 million in "The New Hollywood," in *Film Theory Goes to the Movies*, ed. Jim Collins, Hillary Radner, and Ava Preacher Collins (New York: Routledge, 1993), 289; David A. Cook cites grosses of $135 million in *A History of Narrative Film* (New York: W. W. Norton, 1996, 2004), 860.

2. Mark Harris, *Pictures at a Revolution* (New York: Penguin, 2008), 101, 422.

3. Howard Thompson, "Movies: Out of Tune With the World of Jazz," NYT, August 21, 1966, 108.

4. Other musical films that explored racial themes included Basil Dearden's *All Night Long* (UK, 1962 jazz version of Shakespeare's *Othello* with Charles Mingus, Dave Brubeck, Patrick McGoohan, Richard Attenborough, Betsy Blair, cowritten by blacklisted Paul Jarrico); Paul Henreid's *Ballad in Blue/Blues for Lovers* (UK, 1964, with Ray Charles); and Leo Penn's *A Man Called Adam* (1966).

5. Father of actor Sean Penn.

6. Thompson, "Movies: Out of Tune With the World of Jazz," 108; USC.

7. Finler, *The Hollywood Story*, 277; Schatz, "The New Hollywood," 292. In *Rosemary's Baby*, John Cassavetes sells his soul, wife (Mia Farrow), and baby to the devil for a shot at fame.

8. John Cawelti, "Chinatown and Generic Transformation" in *Film Theory and Criticism*, ed., Mast, Cohen, and Braudy (New York: Oxford University Press, 1992), 511. Assassinations of President Kennedy, Robert Kennedy, Martin Luther King Jr., and Malcolm X shattered a spirit of optimism and idealism, marking the end of Kennedy's "Camelot" in a cynical Vietnam era.

9. Liza Minnelli was a second-generation *A Star Is Born* star, following her mother Judy Garland.

10. Roger Greenspun, NYT, February 14, 1972; VAR, February 16, 1972, 18; WP, AFI, 1972.

11. *Box Office*, April 10, 1972; AFI; USC; VAR, February–March 1972.

12. VAR, December 12, 1979, 22; Vincent Canby, NYT, December 20, 1979; USC.

13. Robert Firsching, NYT, *All Movie Guide*.

14. Kevin Thomas, "Manipulation in the Music Biz," LAT, October 16, 1975; *Box Office*, 1975, PBC, USC. Experimental postclassical revisionist pictures show how "musical" films and music were changing, evolving in a variety of diverging directions. Jazz/blues was being displaced, overtaken by rock 'n' roll, rhythm-and-blues, soul, funk, reggae, and fusion. Anticipating music videos, films cross-promoted popular songs/albums as ancillary merchandise publicizing a presold commodity as recorded hits replaced jazz scores by Arlen, Gershwin, Ellington, and Bernstein. In Perry Henzell's *The Harder They Come*, Jimmy Cliff plays a musician-outlaw who jams reggae tunes—entangled with drugs, sex, a crooked minister, and corrupt record producer—gunned down in an unvarnished Jamaican "indie" crime film.

15. Martin Scorsese, BBC interview, 1995; *New York, New York* commentary, 2005.

16. Scorsese in, *Martin Scorsese*, Mary Pat Kelly (New York: Thunder's Mouth, 1991), 102; Vincent LoBrutto, *Martin Scorsese* (Westport, CT: Praeger, 2008), 204.

17. Filming began without a completed screenplay. Scorsese in Jonathan Kaplan, "Taxi Dancer," *Film Comment* 13, no. 4 (1977), 41–43.

18. Scorsese, Liza Minnelli, and Kelly in *Martin Scorsese*, Kelly, 99–110; LoBrutto, *Martin Scorsese*, 204; VAR, June 22, 1977; Scorsese in *Scorsese on Scorsese*, David Thomson and Ian Christie (London: Faber & Faber 1989), 69; Scorsese in "Taxi Dancer," Kaplan, 41–43; *Dialogue*, 1984 in *Martin Scorsese*, Les Keyser (New York: Twayne, 1992), 88–89.

19. Andrew Sarris, "The Big Apple is Polished in Hollywood," *Village Voice*, July 4, 1977, 37–38, 40; David Dugas, 1977, 11, in, *Films of Martin Scorsese*, Leighton Grist (New York: St. Martin's, 2000), 158; David Thomson, *Biographical Dictionary of Film* (London: André Deutsch, 1994); Kaplan, "Taxi Dancer," 41–43.

20. Richard Glatzer, *Magill's* (Englewood Cliffs, NJ: Salem Press, 1984), 567–69; Keyser, *Martin Scorsese*, 85–89; USC, October 1978. Tom Milne, *Monthly Film Bulletin* 44, no. 524, September 1977, 194–95; VAR, June 22, 1977; HR, June 20, 1977.

21. *New York, New York*'s estimated cost was $9.7 million, $2.5 million over budget (some cite $14 million). *Star Wars* grossed over $500 million worldwide, earning another estimated $1.5 billion a year in merchandising. David Cook, *A History of Narrative Film*, 858–60; Scorsese in *Scorsese on Scorsese*, Thompson and Christie, 69, 72; USC, 1977; Kaplan, "Taxi Dancer"; Scorsese in *Martin Scorsese*, Kelly, 99–110; J. Hoberman, "Ten Years that Shook the World," *American Film* (June 1985), 34–59; Schatz cites $177 million rentals for *Star Wars* in 1977 (with another $38 million as a reissue in 1978) and $102.5 million rentals for *Jaws* in 1975 in "The New Hollywood," 294–98; Peter Biskind, *Easy Riders, Raging Bulls* (New York: Simon & Schuster, 1999), 344; Keyser, *Martin Scorsese*; Harris, *Pictures at a Revolution*.

22. DeNiro's character drew on his volatile persona as Vietnam veteran Travis Bickle in *Taxi Driver*. Released two years after the end of the Vietnam War, *New York, New York* color noir publicity in black, white, and red featured a nostalgic Minnelli and a cleaned-up DeNiro wearing a jazzy Hawaiian shirt blowing a sax, with taglines that heralded: "The war was over and the world was falling in love again. A love story is like a song. It's beautiful while it lasts." *Rolling Stone* promoted it as "Scorsese's Back-Lot Sounds" where DeNiro "Trades his .44 for a New Axe." PBC, USC, 1977; Keyser, *Martin Scorsese*; Chris Haderfield, *Rolling Stone*, June 16, 1977, 36–37; Mark Goodman, "Tripping With Martin Scorsese," *Penthouse* 8, no. 9, May 1977.

23. Vincent Canby, NYT, June 23, 1977; VAR, June 22, 1977; HR, June 20, 1977.

24. Hoberman, "Ten Years"; Schatz, "The New Hollywood"; Biskind, *Easy Riders*; David Cook, *A History*; Keyser, *Martin Scorsese*; Harris, *Pictures at a Revolution*.

25. Liza's big production number, "Happy Endings," evocative of Garland in *A Star is Born*, had been previously cut for *New York, New York*'s original release. Harrell, "The Making of *A Star is Born*," 36; LAE, August 16, 1981, E5; Glatzer, *Magill's*; USC.

26. During the 1978–86 period spanning *Pennies from Heaven* and *The Singing Detective*'s production, Britain's media industry transformed from a duopoly to an increasingly competitive multichannel commercial model by the late 1980s. Peter Lennon, "A Man with a Lash," *The Listener*, 116, no. 2987 (November 20, 1986), 14; Sean Day-Lewis, "Potter

Switches Screens," *Daily Telegraph*, October 20, 1980, 10; John Cook, *Dennis Potter* (Manchester: Manchester University Press, 1995), 62, 162, 192–93.

27. Potter's dark musicals thematically convey personal transformation inspired by illness. The increased energy and optimism permeating *Pennies from Heaven* (in the aspirations of its characters) was in many ways motivated by Potter's treatment of razoxane (a miracle drug temporarily "curing" his debilitating psoriatic anthropathy illness) in clinical trials at Guys Hospital in February 1977—spurring a flurry of writing with Potter suddenly liberated from his illness. (The drug produced carcinogenic side-effects leading to Potter's death.) Lennon, "A Man with a Lash,"; Sean Day-Lewis, "Potter Switches Screens"; John Cook, *Dennis Potter.*

28. In his final 1994 televised interview before his death, Potter argues multinational conglomerate takeover of the industry shifted emphasis away from aesthetic style/genre creativity to consolidate and interlace corporate-political power, ownership, and control of media so "a commercial value is placed on everything," and the audience is no longer "citizens" but "consumers." Dennis Potter in Melvyn Bragg, Channel 4, *Seeing The Blossom* (London: Faber & Faber, 1994), 14–8; Lennon, "A Man with a Lash."

29. Gordon spent fifteen years in Paris and had recorded with Powell there; Young died shortly after returning to the U.S. from France. Gordon explained on the set of *Round Midnight*, "I would love to see Duke Ellington's dream come true. . . . You know why it's so demanding for me to do this film? Because I have to carry with me the image of people like Charlie Parker and Lester Young, who never had the chance to express what I'm doing now. I have to bring their images to the screen." As Tavernier recalled, "He had a big photo of Duke and a big photo of Lester hanging in his trailer. He said, 'I want to look at them before shooting, every day.'" Gordon's father took him to see Ellington perform live. Ellington, Young, Parker, and Jacquet inspired Gordon. Tavernier noted, "It's hard to believe Duke Ellington only did two film scores in his life. He was one of the greatest musicians of the century and nobody called upon his talents in that area." Bertrand Tavernier, PBC, USC, 1986.

30. Carter noted: "It took a damn Frenchman to finally make a serious movie about us!" Tavernier recalled studio reluctance to do a "story about jazz" or "an old black guy." *Round Midnight* starred blacklisted director John Berry as Blue Note's bartender. Tavernier noted the affinity blacklisted filmmakers had with American jazz musicians in exile in Paris. Winkler noted: "When I did *New York, New York* with Scorsese, we had a hard time finding the proper ending for the film. . . . One of the endings we discussed was DeNiro's character going to Paris to play because his music was never appreciated in America." Tavernier, Winkler, PBC, USC, 1986; Jean-Pierre Coursodon, "Round Midnight: An Interview with Bertrand Tavernier," *Cineaste* 15, no. 2 (1986), 18–23; Richard Phillips, "An Interview with Bertrand Tavernier," Sydney Film Festival, July 10, 1999.

31. Tavernier, PBC, USC, 1986. Dale quips: "They're always paying all the wrong people in this world. . . . Well, this establishment has never been known for its . . . conviviality."

32. Tavernier in Michael Dempsey, "All the Colors," *Film Quarterly* 40, no. 3 (1987), 2–5. Like a self-destructive noir antihero, Tavernier described Dale and Paudras' friendship with Powell "in and out of hospitals, taking care of him" and his return to New York in a "comeback that actually was to kill him."

33. Tavernier in Dempsey, "All the Colors."

34. Tavernier in Coursodon, "Round Midnight"; PBC, USC, 1986.

35. PBC, USC, 1986; Phillips, "An Interview with Bertrand Tavernier"; Coursodon, "Round Midnight"; Dempsey, "All the Colors."

36. Coursodon, "Round Midnight"; PBC, USC, 1986; Dempsey, "All the Colors"; Phillips, "An Interview with Bertrand Tavernier."

37. Gordon died four years after his celebrated performance. Phillips "An Interview with Bertrand Tavernier"; PBC, USC, 1986; Janet Maslin, NYT, September 30, 1986; VAR, April 16, 1986; Sheila Benson, LAT, October 16, 1986.

38. Janet Maslin, NYT, September 26, 1988.

39. It was considerably over budget, although Eastwood cited the film's cost at $9.1 million. PBC, USC, 1988.

40. David Heuring, "The Fabulous Baker Boys: Lounge Lizards in Love," AC, November 1989, 50.

41. Roger Ebert, *Chicago Sun-Times*, October 13, 1989.

42. Pauline Kael, *New Yorker*, October 16, 1989; Rita Kempley, WP, October 13, 1989; Janet Maslin, NYT, October 13, 1989.

43. Michael Ballhaus in "The Fabulous Baker Boys," David Heuring.

44. *American Film*, June 1990, 50.

45. Elvis Mitchell, "Sibling Ivories," *LA Weekly*, October 27–November 2, 1989, 55.

46. PBC, USC, 1989.

47. Kinney became Warner Communications in 1972. Matsushita bought MCA-Universal in 1990, acquired by Canada's Seagram in 1995 then France's Vivendi in 2000, sold to General Electric (GE) forming NBC Universal in 2004 merging with Comcast in 2011.

48. On July 1, 2013, News Corp split and created 21st Century Fox which includes 20th Century Fox studio. "In terms of filmmaking," Schatz suggests, "conglomeration has intensified the studios' blockbuster mentality while fostering the strategic expansion of established movie 'brands' into worldwide entertainment franchises." Schatz, "Film Industry Studies and Hollywood History" in *Media Industries*, ed. Jennifer Holt and Alisa Perren (Malden, MA: Wiley-Blackwell, 2009), 45.

49. Former wife of blockbuster star Tom Cruise.

50. Baz Luhrmann in "Baz Luhrmann Talks Awards and *Moulin Rouge*," Rebecca Murray, *Hollywood Movies*, PBC, USC, September 2, 2003.

51. Elvis Mitchell, "An Eyeful, an Earful," NYT, May 18, 2001. Martin created shots of Paris by designing a collage of Montmartre streets in miniature (at one-fifth or one-sixth scale) using photographs and film with real people digitally added. Like Ferrer in Huston's color noir biopic, Leguizamo used painful cumbersome forty-pound prostheses (with movable ankles and feet) to simulate Lautrec's short stature. (His feet and lower legs were digitally erased using computer special effects.) Kidman suffered broken ribs.

52. VAR, May 9, 2001; Elvis Mitchell, "An Eyeful, an Earful"; David Cook, 2004; AFI; PBC, USC, 2001.

53. Elvis Mitchell, "'Chicago,' Bare Legs and All, Makes It to Film," NYT, December 17, 2002; *Entertainment Weekly* (EW), January 17, 2003; PBC, USC, 2002. The play was adapted as 1942 nonmusical film *Roxie Hart* starring musical star Ginger Rogers.

54. David Rooney, "Chicago," VAR, December 10, 2002; PBC, USC, 2002.

55. David Rooney, "Chicago"; Elvis Mitchell, "'Chicago,' Bare Legs and All," 2002; EW, 2003; PBC, USC, 2002.

56. Elaborate stories mock high-concept genre formula, yet engage in visceral heightening of "sensation" visually reliant on special effects that provide a mass-mediated postmodern musical spectacle thrill-ride. They are produced abroad in a runaway era of global coproduction. These "sensational" dark musicals used women and misogynistic sexual violence as an allegory to critique the blockbuster era.

Index

Page numbers in *italics* indicate illustrations.

Scott, Adrian, 70–71, 96
Scott, Lizbeth, 46, 47, 98
Second Chorus, 18
Selznick, David O., 16, 96
Serenade, 134, 135
Seven Brides for Seven Brothers, 105
sex in noir musicals, 47–48, 53, 55, 58–62
Shanghai Express, 13, 52
The Shanghai Gesture, 18
Shearer, Moira, 80, 84, 85, 86, 104
Sheridan, Ann, 17
Sherman, Lowell, 14
Sherman, Vincent, 100
She's Back on Broadway, 37, 121
Shore, Sig, 152
Show Boat, 10, 16
Shurlock, Geoffrey, 129
Sinatra, Frank, 118–19, 120, 122
The Singing Detective, 37, 158–60
The Singing Fool, 10
Singin' in the Rain, 14, 102
Siodmak, Robert, 17, 55, 56, 74, 96
Sirk, Douglas, 55, 186–88
Snow White and the Seven Dwarfs, 16
social realist films, 71, 132, 135, 175, 186n36.
    See also *On the Waterfront*; *West Side Story*
Sondheim, Stephen, 137, 140
The Sound of Music, 145, 148
A Star Is Born (1937), 11, 16, 116
A Star Is Born (1954), 105–17; *Black Angel* and,
    62; *Blues in the Night* and, 26; categorization
    of, 1, 2; color noir style in, 105–8, 163; design
    of, 108–10; Garland and, 76, 105, 110, 111,
    111, 114, 117, 175; influence of, 174, 175;
    "The Man That Got Away" number in,
    111–14; musical noir style in, 110; *New York,
    New York* and, 154; *Pete Kelly's Blues* and, 126;
    plot of, 105, 113–14; premier, promotion,
    and reception of, *111*, *113*, 115–17; pro-
    duction of, 114–15; restoration of, 157; scene
    from, 1; theme of, 9; *Young at Heart* and, 119,
    120–21
Sternberg, Joseph von, 10, 13, 18
Stewart, James "Jimmy," 18, 103
Stormy Weather, 40, 184n2
The Story of Jazz, 41, 42, 43
The Story of Three Loves, 104

The Stranger, 67
Strayhorn, Billy, 119
The Strip, 98
studios: Big Five, 180n11; conglomeration of,
    167–68, 200n48; decline of, 4, 76–78, 110,
    121. See also Warner Bros.
style and production: of *Blues in the Night*,
    23–25; of *The Red Shoes*, 84–85; of *Round
    Midnight*, 163–64; of *A Star Is Born*, 105–8,
    110, 114–15; during wartime, 39; of *West Side
    Story*, 137–39, 141–43
Suddenly, Last Summer, 135
Sunset Boulevard, 95
Superfly, 152
Super Panavision 70, 138
Suspicion, 19, 35
Swanson, Gloria, 11
Sweet Smell of Success, 128–30, 132, 148
Swing High, Swing Low, 16
swing music, 28, 30, 33–34
Symphony in Black, 44
Syncopation, 43, 69, 70

Tavernier, Bertrand, 160–64
Technicolor, 101, 108–9, 138, 142
technologies, new: 70mm, 195n48; techno-
    philia, 78–79. See also widescreen
television: competition with, 138, 139;
    conversion to color, 145; impact on
    Hollywood, 77–79, 97, 101
Tension, 72
Thank Your Lucky Stars, 37
That's the Way of the World, 152–53
themes: camaraderie, 22, 36; captivity, 107;
    Cold War fears, 133–35; fame, 131–32, 151,
    154, 165; family life in suburbia, 119;
    fatalism, 23, 106; of film noir, 5–6; impact
    of television on, 79; of noir musicals, 9,
    40, 73–75, 173–74; of postclassical dark
    musicals, 146; of postwar film noir, 73, 76,
    80; of *The Red Shoes*, 82, 83–84; of *Round
    Midnight*, 160–62; of *The Singing Detective*,
    159; of *A Star Is Born* (1954), 110. See also
    antiheroes
There's No Business Like Show Business, 105
They Made Me a Criminal, 16, 19
The Third Man, 80, 96

This Gun for Hire, 8, 9, 19, 39, 46–47
Tierney, Gene, 18, 67–68
To Have and Have Not: categorization of, 2, 19;
    Gilda and, 59, 60, 62; iconic gesture in, 13;
    music in, 8, 9, 46; noir elements of, 52–53;
    overseas setting of, 48; publicity still, 54;
    WWII and, 39
Top Hat, 16
Touch of Evil, 4, 134
Trapeze, 128
Turner, Lana, 17, 18
Turney, Catherine, 46, 64

Underworld, 10

Van Upp, Virginia, 46, 50, 58–62, 100
Vidor, Charles, 39, 50, 58, 123
Vidor, King, 10
Vietnam War, 148–49
violence: misogynistic, 48, 60, 61–62, 75; in
    New York, New York, 154, 156; in noir crime
    films, 23; in *West Side Story*, 140–41; WWII,
    19
visual conventions of film noir, 4–5, 6, 76,
    107–8, 141, 176. *See also* lighting
visual style in 1950s, 98
Vorkapich, Slavko, 11, 14

Walbrook, Anton, 80, *81, 83,* 140
Wallis, Hal, 20, 25
Walsh, Raoul, 11, 64, 98, 134
Warner Bros.: art department of, 5–6; Busby
    Berkeley backstage musicals, 14–15; crime
    films of, 25; Fox Movietone News and, 30;
    halt in production at, 103; mobilization for
    WWII, 36; noir musicals and, 8, 22; recycling
    of sets by, 25; *A Star Is Born* and, 114–15

Webb, Jack, 98, 126
Weill, Kurt, 49
Welles, Orson: Hayworth and, 52, 58, 62; jazz
    and, 41–42; *The Stranger* and, 67; in *The
    Third Man*, 96; *Touch of Evil*, 4, 134
Wellman, William, 11, 16
Westerns, 79, 179n10
West Side Story: Bernstein and, 135; cultural
    context of, 136; musical style in, 141–43;
    origins of, 135–36; production of, 137–39;
    reception of, 143–44; on stage, 137; *Sweet
    Smell of Success* and, 129; youth market and,
    139–41
Whale, James, 16
What Price Hollywood?, 11, 13–14
Whitaker, Forest, 165
White Christmas, 78
White Heat, 134
Whorf, Richard, 57, *57,* 175
widescreen, 77–78, 97–98, 101, 115
Wiene, Robert, 12
Wilder, Billy, 37, 55, 58, 71, 95, 97
Wise, Robert, 134, 138, 141–43, 145
The Wizard of Oz, 17, 28, 40, 101
women: color noir and, 91; expanded roles for,
    46. *See also* female characters
Words and Music, 89, 89–90, 101–2
World War II, 35–36, 38, 39

You and Me, 16, 50
Young, Lester, 44, *45*
Young at Heart, 2, 118–22, *120*
Young Man with a Horn, 2, 9, 37, 92–95, *94,* 146
youth market, 130–31, 139–41, 188n9

Zanuck, Darryl, 95–97, 102
Ziegfeld Girl, 17–18, 50